A Collection of Canadian Plays
Volume 2

Bastet Books. Toronto. 1973

In the comparatively short time since Volume I of this series was released, significant changes have taken place on the Canadian theatre scene. When we laid the groundwork for this publishing venture, "A Collection of Canadian Plays" — to become, as the years go by, an anthology — very few works by Canadian authors were being presented. Long gone were the days of 1967 and Centennial Year, and the days of an all-Canadian Dominion Drama Festival.

It would be wrong to indulge in self-congratulatory enthusiasm and say that the ultimate goals have been achieved; but there are few theatrical organizations in Canada today which have not presented at least one original Canadian play — and this besides the outstanding efforts of some of the groups which devote their entire programs to the now acceptable Canadian playwright. These plays are frequently shown before capacity audiences, in fairly extended runs. This of course means box-office as well as artistic success, and one wonders how long it will be before the few remaining much-assisted — by public money — larger stages in Canada admit that their excuse for not using Canadian talent for box-office reasons is no longer valid.

An equally interesting development is the number of Canadian publishing houses now printing Canadian plays. This fact is only truly appreciated by those who are aware, firstly of the incredible communication difficulties in a country of Canada's size, and secondly of the lamentable lack of printed dramatic material available to English and drama teachers who up until quite recently depended largely on non-Canadian material. Correspondence received from educational institutions interested in integrating Canadian plays as curricula texts has been very gratifying indeed. It indicates that in a few years' time, some Canadian playwrights' names will be household words amongst our young people — the future generation of theatre-goers.

In our current choice of plays, we have again attempted to introduce five entirely different writing styles and approaches.

The cover drawing is the tragic heroine of our first selection, "Wedding in White".

R.K.

Bastet Books are published and distributed by Simon & Pierre, Publishers, P.O. Box 280, Adelaide Street Postal Station, Toronto 1, Ontario.

Publishing Editor	Rolf Kalman
Assistant to the Publishing Editor	Marian M. Wilson
Associate Editor	Mark Dwor
Staff Writer	Jean Stewart Hannant
Designed by	Design Workshop
Cover Artist	Lena Wilson Endicott

Printed and bound in Canada by T. H. Best Printing Company Limited

ISBN 0-9690455-0-6

98379

Wedding in White

William Fruet

William Fruet was born in Lethbridge, Alberta, and was originally known principally as an actor, and a good one. He won scholarships from the University of Alberta and the Royal Academy of Dramatic Art, but chose to receive his training at the Canadian Theatre School in Toronto. After a leading role in the National Film Board's feature film "The Drylanders", Mr. Fruet's career took him to Hollywood for four years, and it was there that his long-cherished desire to write finally caught up with him. He returned to Canada to write for the CBC.

His first major break as a writer, however, came four years later with the release of his film "Goin' Down the Road", which was listed as one of the year's ten best by American critic Judith Crist and which won the Canadian Film Award for Best Screenplay in 1969. This was followed by his original screenplay for "Rip-Off".

Then came "Wedding in White".

"Wedding in White" properly was begun in 1943, when William Fruet was ten years old. In his own words, " . . . this young girl was wheeling a baby buggy down the street, and this very old man was with her. I knew it was not her father or grandfather. I knew it was her husband just by the way he walked with her, and I knew there was a tremendous imbalance. Years later I brought it up to my mother and she revealed the whole story to me." The story, in fact, was that the girl had been raped by a soldier and forced, for the sake of her family's reputation, into a marriage with a "respectable" substitute — an old and sloppy grotesque.

Thus "Wedding in White" was conceived, though the actual writing of the play was not begun until 1965, in California. It was first produced as a stage play at the Poor Alex Theatre in Toronto, with a stellar Canadian cast that included Paul Bradley and Doug McGrath of "Goin' Down the Road" fame, and was in fact directed by Doug McGrath. The play opened to both critical and popular acclaim; it played to packed houses during its eight-week run, and aroused a passionate response in its audiences. Producer John Vidette of Dermet Productions in Toronto saw its film possibilities, and developed it as a motion picture with author William Fruet himself as director. On this occasion, the cast included the distinguished British actor Donald Pleasence and an eighteen-year-old American actress, Carol Kane, in the leading roles. The film won three Canadian Film Awards — for Best Picture of the Year, Best Supporting Actress for Doris Petrie's flawless portrayal of the hapless mother, and Best Art Direction for Karen Bromley.

The special quality of William Fruet's work, and of "Wedding in White" in particular, was most accurately summed up by critic John Hofsess, who wrote:

"He has a damning knowledge about mankind, but he doesn't choose to deplore or condemn . . . The sympathy that he asks of an audience for his characters is hard won . . . he doesn't invent 'charming' incidents. He doesn't conceal their flaws. You come away from 'Wedding in White' with a good feeling . . . you know you haven't been lied to, browbeaten, or shoddily entertained."

The photographs used to illustrate "Wedding in White" are from the motion picture version.

All rights, including performing rights, to "Wedding in White" are reserved by Dermet Productions. For information and enquiry, write: Dermet Productions, 579 Church Street, Toronto, Ontario M4Y 2E4.

The single softcover edition of "Wedding in White" is not available from Simon & Pierre Publishers. All enquiries should be directed to Dermet Productions, 579 Church Street, Toronto, Ontario M4Y 2E4.

Cast of Characters

Jim, a middle-aged army veteran
Mary, his wife
Jeanie, their daughter
Jimmie, their son
Billy, Jimmie's friend
Dollie, Jeanie's friend
Sandy, old army friend of Jim's
Sarah, old friend of Mary's
Barnie, an old wino
Hattie, his wife
Jock, a soldier
Assorted soldiers in club;
Sundry wedding guests

Scene one

The play takes place somewhere in Western Canada, in a small town, near the end of the second World War.

The master set consists of a large living room, stage left, and a small dining room, stage right. The front door to the house and a stairway indicating an upper floor, are on the extreme left of the living room. Beneath the stairway another door opens to the cellar. This same corner of the room has become Jim's personal little sanctuary consisting of a large black leather chair, an old gramaphone, a small whisky cabinet, a display of shell casings and other war souvenirs. Several army group photos hang beside pictures of King George V and Queen Mary. A union jack is draped as a background. The remainder of the living room is a clutter of odd pieces of old worn out furniture: a faded and sagging chesterfield, covered in doilies and needlework, scatter rugs and cheap bric-a-brac everywhere. An old dresser sits strangely alone and out of place in this setting.

The dining room is separated by a small archway. In the centre of the room sits a large circular table with an old tarnished brass chandelier hanging directly above. One naked bulb lights the room in a dim yellow pallor. A china cabinet sits along one wall and french doors open to a partial kitchen set seen in the back.

Throughout the house, gaping cracks in the plaster and a lack of general upkeep over the years, will indicate the kind of people and conditions lived under here. An atmosphere of mustiness and slow decay.

(The house lights slowly dim. Fade in the distant sound of drums and bagpipes, playing a stirring march tune of war.)
(The music builds as the theatre grows darker, giving the illusion of coming closer. When the theatre has reached complete darkness, the music will be a deafening pitch with the clapping bam of the bass drum and the wheezing whine of the pipes everywhere.)

(The music suddenly stops abruptly and we hear only the crisp noise of hobnailed boots marching in unison . . .)

(The curtain rises on the stage in darkness.)

(Cut sound.)

(Silence . . . four beats.)

(The setting is plunged into light.)

The front door opens and three men in army uniforms enter with a lot of noise and laughter. The two younger men are of the regular army and carry duffel bags, while old Jim wears the uniform of the Veteran's Guard, and carries a large case of beer under his arm. He is a puffy cheeked Scot in his early sixties, whose dialect is a combination of British and Scots slang, carried over from the days of the first World War. When he speaks, it is in a wheezing raspy voice, from years of tobacco smoking. Usually a sober and self-centered man, he is presently experiencing a rare moment of joy, having just met his son Jimmie and friend Billy, who have come for a weekend leave. Jimmie is about thirty-five but looks much older because of his missing top teeth and sunken cheeks. He is a loud-mouthed, illiterate and obnoxious extrovert, with an answer for everything delivered at the top of his voice. To old Jim however he is a model son, who can do no wrong; a hard-drinking, whoring soldier. Billy, his friend, is a contrast to Jimmie: a sly quiet introvert, until he has drunk his fill . . . then the shyness leaves him and an ugly meanness takes over. He speaks in a broken harsh Newfoundland accent.

Jim: *(Calling)* Hi there we're home! Tip, he's home!

Jimmie: *(With a loud "whoop")* YAAAAA-AAAA-HOOOOOOOOO! Where the hell are ya Mom?

Mary: *(Off)* Is it youse, Jim?

Jimmie: There's my girl!

Mary: *(Crying out.)* Och Jimmie, my boyyyy!

(Jimmie gives her a swat on the behind and picking her up, swings her off her feet.)

Jimmie: WHEEEEEEE!

Mary: Oh Jimmie, be careful!

Jimmie: Ha Ha just look at her willya! Still got an eye for the good lookers eh?

Jim: *(Slapping him on the back.)* Well dammit man, look who you take after, heyyy!

(Loud guffaws of laughter.)

Jimmie: Yes sir! Ya know, you're still the only woman I'm gonna marry Mom! That's what I used to tell her, Billy!

Mary: *(Holding him at arm's length.)* Let me look at you, let me look at you. Oh, tch, I think you've lost weight!

Jimmie: You're gettin' skinny as hell yourself!

(Laughter)

Mary: Oh, you!

Jimmie: *(Pulling Billy over.)* Billy boy I want you to meet the finest little woman in this damn town — my Mom! Mom, this here's my mate Billy. He didn't have nowheres to go to on his leave, so I brought him home with me!

Billy: *(Nods with a forced smile.)*

Mary: Pleased to meet you, I'm sure.

Jimmie: Bloke didn't want to come! So I says look here boy, any pal of mine is always welcome in my folk's home!

Jim: *(Patting Jimmie on the back again.)* The lad's right! I've always told him that.

Mary: Oh yes, any friend of Jimmie's is always welcome here. Come in, Billy.

Jim: *(Closing the front door.)* Why don't we all come in? What the devil are we standing here for?

Jimmie: *(Spotting Jeanie.)* Well I'll be gone to hell!

(Entering, they are now able to see Jeanie standing at the top of the stairs watching. She is a sloppy unkempt girl of sixteen; a late child left with the mark of feeble-mindedness. She is

indifferent towards her mother, but regards her father with respect heavily blended with fear.)

Jim: *(Gruffly)* Hey you, don't you see who's here?

Jimmie: She's all growed up! That's the kid sister, Billy. I told you about her sure! Well you come on down here and let us have a look at you Jeanie!

Jim: Come on, come on, your brother wants to see you!

Mary: *(To Billy.)* Cat's got her tongue. She's shy that one.

Jeanie: *(Slowly coming down.)* . . . Hi Jimmie.

(Jimmie goes to meet her at the foot of the stairs, lifting her off.)

Jimmie: Hi yourself! Come on, give your brother a big hug! *(He gives her a quick embrace, taking her over to the group.)* Say hello to Billy, my buddy!

Jeanie: Hello . . .

Billy: How are ya kid.

Jimmie: Ho ho, she's no kid anymore! Even got a couple of plums growing under that sweater!

Mary: Jimmie!

(Old Jim breaks into loud guffaws of laughter, hanging on every word his son says, ready to laugh, to please, to impress.)

Jim: *(To Billy.)* Ain't he a devil, this one!

Jimmie: *(Giving Jeanie a squeeze.)* Ah hell Ma, she knows I'm only kidding her! *(He goes to his duffel bag.)* Hey, I think there's something in here for you!

Jeanie: *(Her eyes lighting up.)* . . . me?

Jimmie: Yep. Don't know any other Jeanies, and that's what this says on it — "To Jeanie".

Jeanie: Gee, what is it?

Jimmie: Open it up and see! Heyyy, I smell something cooking! *(They all follow Jimmie into the living room leaving Jeanie forgotten.)* Billy you just sit yourself down! This here's home for a couple of days, and you act like it was, see!

Jim: *(Echoing Jimmie.)* Aye you do like the lad says Bill, make yourself at home.

Mary: I been holding supper for youse. Was the bus late or something?

Jim: Good God, woman, can't I buy my boy a beer, after not seeing him for a year?

Jimmie: Me and Billy worked us up one hell of a thirst on that bus, eh boy?

Billy: You said it!

Jimmie: Actually we did get hung up. Where was it, Calgary? Yeah, that's right. This driver guy says fifteen minutes stop, see? So me and Billy beats it over to the beer parlour and this SOB took off without us. I was sayin to Billy here, what if we'd been shippin overseas or something? Where the hell would we have been then? Now that ain't no way to run no bus company!

Jim: You're absolutely right son. They got no right doing that. You paid for your ticket and it's their job to see that you get there!

Jimmie: Oh those buggers ain't heard the last of me yet, I'll tell you Dad, no sir! We had to wait a whole stinkin hour for the next one! Christ, I mean they don't even stop that thing long enough to let you have a leak!

Billy: I'm still splittin. Where's the head?

Jimmie: *(Making a complete production of it.)* Well ya see those stairs? Straight up and the door on the right, and she's starin you in the face. *(Billy stares up.)* An don't fall in mate!

Jim: *(Chuckles)* I'll take the bags up to the room.

Jimmie: Here let me give you a hand.

Jim: No no, just sit yourself down and take the weight off your feet.

Mary: Aye, you must be weary after that long ride, and hungry too I'll bet.

Jimmie: Starving, Mom, starving!

Mary: Well it's only going to take me a minute to put it on the table.

(She scurries off to the kitchen. Jimmie goes over to where old Jim struggles with the bags and the case of beer.)

Jimmie: Here mate.

Jim: I can manage.

Jimmie: Come on now don't argue with me or I'll take you over my knee! *(Sweeps up one of the bags and the case of beer.)*

Jim: *(Chuckling)* Alright alright. By God, I bet you could too! You're gettin bigger every time I see you!

Jimmie: 'Sides you didn't think I was going to trust you all alone with this do you? *(Holds up case of beer.)*

Jim: *(Eyes lighting.)* Hah! Aye, we'll have us a fast one before supper, eh?

(They have now reached the top of the landing and Jimmie gives the bathroom door a kick as he passes.)

Jimmie: That's a hell of a waste of good beer! *(Jim bursts into laughter.)* . . . and don't shake it more than twice or you're playing with it!

(We hear an inaudible comment from Billy. The old man pats his son affectionately on the back as they enter one of the bedroom doors.)

Jim: Still the same kidder, aren't ya! You an Bill can have your old room an Mother an me will take Jeanie's. She can sleep on the chesterfield downstairs.

(The stage is empty except for Jeanie, who still clutching her gift goes quickly into the living room and begins to unwrap it, being careful not to wrinkle the tissue paper in order to save it. She takes out a small brooch of the Maple Leaf, framed in rhinestones. It is a cheap and gaudy piece of jewellery but she is pleased with it. Billy comes out of the bathroom still zipping his fly. He sees her and stops, just standing and watching her for a brief time; he surveys the setting, noticing the absence of the others, then starts slowly down the stairs.)

Billy: Like it? Pretty nice, huh?

Jeanie: Yeah. Wait'll I show Dollie this!

Billy: Who?

Jeanie: Dollie, she's my best friend. She's got lots of nice things like this.

Billy: Your friend, huh? Same age as you?

Jeanie: Two years older, but that don't matter. Do you think it does?

Billy: I dunno . . .

(Jeanie gets up and going to the dresser to see, pins it close to one shoulder. Billy watches her every move.)

Billy: If you want, I can send you a couple more things like that . . . ?

Jeanie: *(Taken)* . . . for me?

Billy: Sure . . . guy I know, s'got lots of 'em . . .

Jeanie: Gee, yeah! *(Swinging back to the mirror.)* Boy will that brown her off!

Billy: Whozat?

Jeanie: Dollie. She's just like that, that's all. She's my friend, but boy does she think she's smart. Doesn't like anybody having things she hasn't got. I only got one other brooch that Mom gave me, but you should see all the things she's got. Earrings and even a pearl necklace. It ain't real but it looks pretty nice.

Billy: Why don't you bring her around? I wouldn't mind meeting her . . .

A9

(He gives a silly laugh, but Jeanie misses the implication.)

Jeanie: You will. She's going to call on me later . . . *(Forced sigh.)* She'll probably start putting on the dog for Jimmie. She saw an old picture of him and she thinks he's real cute. I got it in my wallet. Want to see it?

Billy: *(Shrugs)* Yeah, sure.

Jeanie: I don't have very many . . . you should see all she's got. All the kids at school have.

Billy: You an her still go to school?

Jeanie: Naw, she works. I'm gonna quit after this summer. I hate it.

Billy: Never did me no good. *(Hands her back the wallet.)*

Jeanie: I could get a job as a waitress tomorrow, and you make pretty good money too. I mean, what good's going to school if you don't want to be something special?

Billy: Where ya's goin later?

Jeanie: *(Shrugs)* Just fool around, I guess . . .

Billy: Maybe we can all get together an do something.

Jeanie: What . . . ?

Billy: I don't know. Ain't you got any shows around here? Or scoff a few beers maybe.

Jeanie: *(Wide eyed)* In a beer parlour?

Billy: Don't matter to me. Beer's — beer . . .

Jeanie: My dad would crown me.

Billy: Well good beer never hurt anybody.

Jeanie: Yeah but he treats me like I'm still a child. He don't like me going out nowhere.

Billy: You look pretty grown up to me . . .

(Jeanie blushes. Billy comes closer, keeping an eye out for the others.)

Billy: You know, you shouldn't wear that thing there . . . here let me show you.

(He removes it and leaning closer to her, pins it over one of her breasts. Jeanie is taken by this small show of attention, unaware of any ulterior motive on his part.)

Billy: There . . . that's how you should wear it.

(We hear a burst of laughter from upstairs, causing Billy to step back quickly. Jeanie crosses to the mirror to admire herself.)

Jeanie: Let me see . . .

(As she admires herself, Billy smirks to himself behind her back, confident and sure of himself with this girl. Mary appears in the dining room carrying a dish of steaming potatoes.)

Mary: You'll wear that mirror out, the way you're always in front of it. I could use a little help, ya know . . . *(Seeing Billy she changes to complete sweetness.)* Oh . . . I didn't mean to interrupt, Mr. Billy.

Billy: We was just talking.

Mary: *(Sweetly)* Come on then Jeanie and give me a hand dear. *(To Billy)* Would you mind calling Jimmie and Dad then? I don't want it to get cold. I spect they're in one of the bedrooms upstairs.
(Jeanie gives a weary sigh and goes into the dining room while Billy goes upstairs.)

Jeanie: *(Anxious)* Do you like Jimmie's friend?

Mary: *(Absently)* Aye, he seems nice. Very quiet.

Jeanie: He promised to send me some things.

Mary: What sort of things?

Jeanie: Some more nice things like this that Jimmie brought.

Mary: You no asked him I hope?

Jeanie: No! *(Catching her mother's intent stare.)* What's wrong?

Mary: *(Scornfully)* Have you no decency? What do you mean by putting that brooch there? If your father sees that . . .

(Loud burst of laughter from upstairs.)

. . . now put it on properly, or don't wear it at all! *(Shaking her head.)* I don't know what's to become of you . . .

(Mary angrily exits to the kitchen. Jeanie sighs and goes to the mirror.)

Billy: *(Off)* Aye, well drink up then, drink up!

(The bedroom door opens and the three come out of the room.)

Jimmie: *(Suddenly)* Hey hey, show the old man some of those pictures ya got Billy! Wait'll you see these Dad!

(They stop on the stairway landing as Billy reaches into his tunic and produces some postcard photos. Billy and Jimmy watch the old man's reactions with sheepish grins. None of them notice Jeanie below in the living room.)

Jim: *(His eyes lighting up.)* Ho ho, the old sixty-niner eh! *(Goes to the next.)* My God, where did you get these? !

(Jimmie and Billy burst into snorts of laughter.)

Billy: Guy I know s'got lots of 'em . . .

(They start down the stairs chuckling.)

Curtain

Dinner finished and the three men sit about the dining room table engaged in conversation. Old Jim rambles on about conditions at the POW camp, but it is Dollie sitting in the living room who holds the attention of Jimmie and Billy. She is well developed physically and covered in an array of cheap jewellery. Excessive makeup covers her pouty face, and while she is attractive, she has an unwashed grimy look about her. Throughout the scene she is aware of the admiring eyes upon her, and goes through a series of exaggerated sighs and gestures as she waits for Jeanie. *(Throughout the play she chews gum feverishly.)*

Jim: . . . that's what's wrong. They're too easy on 'em. Spect we should treat 'em like bloody royalty, they do!

Dollie: *(Calling)* Hurry up Duke!

Jeanie: *(Off)* Relax, eh?

Dollie: *(For the benefit of Jimmie and Billy.)* Some people! . . .
(Jimmie and Billy give her acknowledging smiles, and each other knowing looks.)

Jim: . . . no, as far as I'm concerned prisoners of war got no privileges. They're nothing but bastards what gave up!

Jimmie: *(Making conversation, his eyes still on Dollie.)* Dad's one of the guards at this POW camp they got outside town.

Jim: *(Eager to impress.)* Four thousand men in that camp! Mind you it's not like being in the regular service. Don't I wish I was young enough, but someone's got to watch 'em. And I do my job well if I do say so myself.

Billy: Don't make no sense to me. Looking after a bunch of bastards you're supposed to kill.

Jim: My very sentiments. But they're clever beggars though. Here, I'll show you something, I'll wager you never seen before . . .

(He gets up, and passes through archway past Dollie, to his private corner, where he keeps a

shrine of souvenirs. Once more there is an interplay of looks between Dollie and the other two.)

Billy: *(Hushed whisper.)* What do you say mate?

Jimmie: . . . a week's pay says she's handled more meat than a barracks butcher!
(Dollie flips through a magazine aware they are discussing her, but unable to hear their comments.)

Jim: Here it is, I knew it was somewhere . . . *(He returns carrying a whiskey bottle with a model ship built inside)* . . . ever see anything like that?

Jimmie: *(Taking it.)* Well I'll be gone to hell! How about that Billy? !

Billy: Jeeeze, how'd that ship get in there?
(They are putting the old man on, while he oblivious to this, babbles on, coloring his story.)

Jim: Ho ho, there's a story behind that, let me tell you. Went into the compound one day an there's this kraut hiding something behind his back. "Hand it over", I says. He shakes his head. So I says to the S.O.B., I says, "You step out of line with me you bastard, and I'll crack your bloody skull open with the butt of this gun . . ." *(He takes a dramatic pause, the other two nodding mockingly.)* . . . well he backs off see.

Jimmie: *(helping him along.)* Shit pouring out of his pants I'll bet.

Jim: *(Laughing)* Aye aye! "Give it over", I says. He drops it right there and is gone like a shot out of hell!
(He slaps himself on the knee, breaking into loud laughter. The other two laugh at him.)

Jimmie: Should have put the boots to him dad!

Jim: *(Quickly)* I woulda I woulda, if I could have caught him! Aye, I'd of taught him a lesson for once an all, I'll tell ya!

Billy: *(Handing it back.)* Pretty sharp Pop . . .

Jim: It's a very complicated business. Ya see they build it a little bit at a time. Got all kinds of strings and things they do it with. Clever buggers alright . . .
(He is interrupted as Mary bustles through from the kitchen wearing a faded old hat and putting on a shabby coat.)

Mary: Well I'm on my way. I hope the supper was good Billy?

Billy: Just fine just fine . . .
(Jimmie gives a belch of approval.)

Mary: It wasn't much I'm afraid, but it's so hard to get things these days with a war on an all.

Jimmie: *(Suddenly aware of her.)* Where you going Ma? Ain't you comin' over to the Legion with us?

Mary: No no I've got to go out for a few hours . . . I'll see you when you get home, son.
(She glides through the living room, stopping at the foot of the stairs.)

Mary: Jeanie you clear up for me now hear? . . . Well, bye by again — I'll have some nice hot rolls and tea waiting for you when you get home.

Jimmie: So long kid . . .
(Jim gives an acknowledging grunt and Billy a slight wave as the old woman disappears out the front door.)

Jimmie: *(No real concern)* Where's she goin anyways?

Jim: *(Brushing it off.)* Oh she's got to help out for a few hours . . . anyway, like I was sayin'. . .
(We hear the barking and whimpering of a dog coming from the cellar.)

. . .Oh God, didn't anybody feed me dog yet? !

Jimmie: You got a dog now?

Jim: *(Rising and scraping some scraps together.)* Aye. Figured it might be safer for mother, with me away so much. We've had a couple of escapes from that camp. Trouble is no one feeds the poor bugger. Ain't going to have a dog long that way I always say.

(Jimmie winks to Billy and follows the old man through the living-room to the cellar stairs.)

Jimmie: *(To Dollie as he passes.)* How you doing kid . . . ?
(She shrugs giving him a smile. When he is behind her back, Jimmie makes a goose gesture with his finger to Billy, and they exchange broad grins.)

Jim: *(Entering the cellar.)* Hi Rex, come on boy! Ain't had him long . . . still got to be trained a bit . . .

Jimmie: *(Entering cellar.)* S'long as he knows who's master!
(Billy rises and casually saunters into the living-room. Dollie pretends to be engrossed in her magazine. Billy slowly eyes her up and down before he speaks.)

Billy: How's she goin . . . ?

Dollie: *(Shrugs)* Okay I guess . . .

Billy: Yeah, Jeanie was sayin ya might come over tonight . . . I'm Billy.

Dollie: Hi . . . *(Yelling out.)* Jeeze Dougal how much longer ya going to be? ?

Jeanie: *(Off)* A minute . . .

Jim's Voice: *(Off)* No ya don't . . . get down damn it! . . . Alright now — heel! Come on come on, ya don't get a bloody thing til ya do like I said — HEEL!
(We hear loud laughter from Jimmie, then a burst of barking.)

Jim's Voice: *(Off)* Son-of-a-bitch! !

(Loud yelping from the dog.)

Aye you know that don't you! That's my foot! Let's try it again . . . up now . . .

(Jeanie bounds down the stairs and noticing the absence of her father, makes a "s-h-h-h" gesture with her finger and motions for Dollie to follow her sneak out.)

Billy: Hey where ya's goin?

Dollie: *(Teasing)* Could be anywhere . . .

Jeanie: *(Urging)* Come on quick.

Billy: *(Quickly)* I mean, maybe we could meet-cha's later huh?

Dollie: *(As they disappear out the door.)* Maybe . . . So long.

Billy: *(Following to the open door.)* Okay then don't forget . . . later huh!

(Jimmie comes stumbling through the cellar door, snorting with laughter. Billy curses himself at having let the thing slip out of his hands.)

Jimmie: *(Still laughing.)* Keeey-Rist, you should see him down there, beating the shit out of that poor thing!

Jim's Voice: *(Off)* . . . now play dead . . . *(Whine from the dog.)*

Jimmie: *(A new burst of laughter.)* Hear him hear him! !

Billy: *(Angry)* Hey look how long we gonna hang around? I don't want to go no friggin Legion tonight!

Jimmie: Awww, now I can't just walk out on the old man yet . . . It'll be okay . . . We'll find some poon tang boy . . . *(He playfully puts his arm around Billy in a hug.)*

Billy: *(Trying to shove him off.)* Fuck off Jimmie!

Jimmie: *(Still hanging on to him.)* That little piece really got your stones hard eh! *(Grabbing at him.)* Hey let's have a feel!

Billy: Bastard! *(He manages to free himself and he and Jimmie giggling like kids jockey for position each trying to grab the other's crotch.)*

Jim's Voice: *(Off)* . . . Now sic em! Sic emmm! ! ! !

(Loud frustrated barks from dog.)

Curtain

A15

Scene three   Legion Club

(Two flats mask off the master set. The setting now is a servicemen's Legion club, where dart boards, beer tables, flags and shields are situated about the room. In the background we hear the clink of glasses and the steady drone of conversation and laughter. Old time music is provided by an off stage accordion and saxaphone.

At a table centre stage, completely filled with glasses of draught beer, sit Jimmie and Billy with Sandy and his lady friend Sarah, two old friends of Jim's. Sandy is also a wheezing old Scots in his early sixties, who loves drink, song and army life. Froth coats his mouth, and his face wears a permanent flush, from the many years of such a life. Sarah is round, middle aged and also Scots. She has been widowed from the first world war and is still bitter for her fate; that of having had to be a cleaning woman, to scrape together a living and raise her children. Sandy has escorted her for years, and the relationship has grown to be the same as that of an old married couple. While she tends to nag him, she knows her place; submissive respect, predominant among these women toward their men. An ugly hump protrudes from her back.

Seated at a table next to them is Hattie, a vinegar faced and dirty old hag and her husband Barnie, a seedy looking heap, in paint splattered overalls. They have one glass of beer before them and hungrily eye Jimmie's table. They are the kind who frequent a place like this, conning all the free beer they can get. Throughout the scene they hang on every word at Jimmie's table, throwing in comments, laughing at all times with the group . . . and always working closer in an attempt to integrate.

Jimmie, Billy and Sandy have had a good deal to drink, so voices are loud, and spirits brave.)

Sandy: *(Wagging a finger in Billy's face.)* Yes sir, I've known Jimmie . . . well me and his father's been friends since . . . since I can remember! So . . . I've known Jimmie since he was a wee boy . . . A baby! Isn't that right Jimmie?

Jimmie: *(Giving him a teasing punch.)* Ah hell Sandy, it must of been before that!

A16

(A cackle from Hattie and Barnie.)

Sandy: *(Puff of laughter.)* Ah he's a kidder this boy . . . always been a kidder, yes sir. *(Laughs)*

Jimmie: *(Amused)* Drink up Sandy drink up, we're gettin way ahead of you!

Sandy: Hell I been here all day! You . . . you could never catch up to me! *(Burst of silly giggling.)* Nobody can drink Sandy under the table!

Sarah: Aye, an ain't you the proud one.

Sandy: *(Moaning)* Awww, God almighty . . .

Sarah: Well where's the fun in just sittin drinking all the time?

Jimmie: The little woman wants to dance Sandy!

Billy: *(Mischievously)* How bout me Mam, how bout me? !

Sarah: *(Standing)* Aye, why not. Come on then son.
(Billy grabs her and clumsily begins to whirl her about, causing her to cry out good naturedly.)

Sandy: Aww, he's a good bloke!

Jimmie: But no friggin dancer I'll tell ya!

Hattie: You should see my old man here, dance. Eh Honey? ! *(Barnie's head bobs in agreement.)* *(As Jimmie and Sandy laugh at the antics of Billy, Jim appears leading another old Vet by the arm.)*

Jim: *(Bursting with pride.)* Here he is! Aye Scotty, this here's wee Jimmie! Home on leave he is. You remember Scotty don't you Jim? !

Hattie: *(Trying to get Jim's attention.)* Hey Mister . . . ? *(But no one pays her any attention.)*

Jimmie: *(Standing and offering an unsteady but vigorous handshake.)* How are ya mate. Sure sure, you . . . now don't tell me. It was at the post office with dad here!

Scotty: *(Pleased)* Aye, that's right. Worked together with your dad for years.

Jimmie: Sure, I never forget a face! Names . . . now that's a different matter. But I never forget a face!

Jim: That's one thing I'll say for the boy; never forgets a face.

Hattie: An that's a fine looking boy you got there too!

Jimmie: Never forget a good screw either.

(Round of smutty laughter. Hattie and Barnie scream at this.)

(On the far end of the room Billy begins to get playful, patting Sarah on the buttocks. She ignores it, but when he persists, she makes him release her and waddles indignantly back to the table.)

Scotty: Have you been over yet Jimmie?

(Jimmie interprets this as a pointed question, and his gay clownish mood switches to sober hostility.)

Jimmie: That's a very interesting story . . .

Jim: *(Cutting in.)* He's asked for active duty a hundred times now. Haven't you son? They won't let him off.

Jimmie: You know what that prick of a sarge tells me? "Dougal, you're the only guy who knows where the hell anything is in this place . . ." Sure!

Jim: *(Adding)* See, he's head of the stores, there at the base where he is.

(Billy and Sarah have taken their seats . . . She looks appealing to Sandy who hasn't noticed any of the carrying on. Billy just sits with a pious smirk on his face.)

Jimmie: *(His anger growing, he bangs the table.)* That's what he said! Remember Billy, me telling you? !

Billy: Jim's the boy. Don't matter what you want! Want a new duffel bag or a stinkin pair of shoe laces . . . Jimmie's the only guy who can get it for you!

Hattie: You tell em soldier! *(Billy grins back.)*

Jimmie: *(The martyr.)* That's what I get for doing my job so well . . .

Scotty: *(Offering consolation.)* Every job counts. They'll give you your chance in time . . .

Jimmie: *(Waving him off.)* Ohhhh no, that's not what you were gettin at . . . *(A hush falls over the group.)* Listen commere . . . *(His hostility growing.)* Commere commere! *(Pointing him out.)* You don't think it's important what I do, the crap I got to put up with huh? !

Jim: Scotty didn't mean anything like that Jimmie . . .

Jimmie: *(Waving him off.)* No no let him speak for himself dad! . . .
(Hattie has now gotten up and stands right at their table, eager for the action.)

You're so smart you tell me something then, you tell me; somebody needs a rifle and I don't give him one, what happens then, huh? What happens eh? !

Scotty: *(Lost)* I don't know . . . ?

Jimmie: He's S.O.L. — that's what! !
(Billy bursts into snorts of laughter.)

Jimmie: Am I right Billy, am I right? ! You damn right I am! !

Hattie: *(Cackling)* Jeeze that's a good one! This boy's got a head on his shoulders. *(To Billy)* What's your name Honey?

(Barnie quickly moves over.)

Jimmie: *(Eager to pick a fight with anyone.)* Field-Marshal Montgomery . . .

Hattie: *(Realizing she isn't going to make it with Jimmie.)* Hah, you ain't no Field-Marshal Montgomery . . . anyway I was talkin to him.

Jim: *(To Hattie and Barnie.)* Come on come on you two . . .

Billy: *(Grinning)* He was just pulling your leg. I'm Billy.

Hattie: 'At's a nice name. Very nice. Mine's Mrs. Smith, but my friends call me Hattie. That's Barnie, my old man . . . *(Barnie reaches across to shake hands and reaches for a glass of beer with the other)* . . . Betcha can't guess what he does for a living?

Jimmie: *(Scoffing)* Nothing!

Hattie: Who asked you?

Jimmie: Piss off!

Jim: *(Intervening)* Listen, you two, what is it you want here?

Barnie: Jiss trynna be friendly that's all.

Jimmie: *(Losing his temper.)* Horse shit! You get your arse and your old lady's out of here!

Barnie: It's a free country!

Jimmie: *(Giving Barnie a shove.)* We ain't feedin no pikers beer. Get the hell out of here!

Jim: You heard the boy, shove off!

(Hattie and Barnie off stage cussing between themselves.)

Sandy: Ah those two are always sponging. I don't know why the hell they let them in here. This is supposed to be a club for service men only!

Jim: Aye.

Billy: *(Amused by the episode.)* I think they're goofy as hell. *(Giggles)*

Barnie's Voice Off: That's the one there!

(Barnie and Hattie return with a very husky young soldier. A small group follows behind and forms about the table.)

A18

Barnie: *(To soldier.)* You know what he said? He called me a piker!

Soldier: *(To Jim.)* You say that?

Billy: He didn't say nothing.

Soldier: You shut up, I ain't talking to you!

Jim: *(Not backing off.)* Go on get out of here, we don't want no trouble!

Hattie: He said it Jock! I was right here!

Barnie: Called me a piker! *(Thrusting his hand into his pocket and producing a few bills.)* I got money . . . see see! Yes sir, ain't nobody can call Barnie a piker!

Soldier: *(Thumping Jim on the chest.)* You better watch who you're calling names old man!

Jim: *(Pointing to Jimmie.)* Listen, you want me to put the boy on you? !

(Jimmie goes white. The crowd begins to intervene.)

Voice One: Here Here!

Voice Two: Take your fight outside!

Another Voice: We don't want it in here!

(A chorus joins in.)

Soldier: *(Challenging Jimmie.)* Come on outside then! I'll take you anytime!

(A hush falls and all eyes are on Jimmie, waiting to see if he will meet the challenge . . . he sits frozen in fear.)

Soldier: Ahhh, you chicken livered! *(He takes a wild swipe at Jimmie from across the table, sending several glasses crashing to the floor.)*

(The crowd quickly steps in, repeating "No fighting in here": "Break it up", etc. Jock is led off as some sort of hero with a chorus of comments such as "That a boy Jock" "Guy must be yellow" "Good boy Jock", etc.)

(Jim is unable to hide his shame and disappointment as he just looks to Jimmie. Jimmie trying to cover, attempts to pick up a glass of beer but is trembling so much he can't.)

Jimmie: *(His lips quivering.)* The bastard . . . let's get the hell out of here!

Curtain

Scene four   **The house, later that night.**

The living and dining room are dark. A beam of light spills across the set, from the kitchen where we hear the muffled conversation of the men. Mary comes from the kitchen, in her robe and slippers.

Mary: *(Weary)* Good night then . . .
(Jimmie appears from the kitchen carrying a bottle of beer. He is very drunk now, and can hardly steady himself. He feigns a false cheerfulness.)

Jimmie: Going to bed Ma?

Mary: Aye, I'm a bit weary . . .
(He puts his arm around her, walking her to the stairway.)

Jimmie: How hell are ya Ma? How's going kid?

Mary: Seem to be having a lot of back aches lately Jimmie . . .

Jimmie: Ahh, you're the hardest little worker in the world, ya know that.

Mary: I guess me age is catching up with me though.

Jimmie: *(Patting her on the back.)* You never looked better . . . take it from me.

Mary: Ohh, you always was a flatterer.

Jimmie: You got good ole Jimmie's word. An if I say it, then it's God's truth . . . *(His head bobbing in agreement with himself.)* . . . yes sir.

Mary: Don't be drinkin too much tonight eh son . . . ?

Jimmie: *(Tilting up the bottle.)* Last one — right here.

Mary: Alright then. I'll see you in the morning. I won't wake you early; let you sleep in good and late. *(Kisses him on the cheek.)*

Jimmie: *(With a wave.)* Keep smiling . . . keep smiling kid.

(Mary disappears into the darkness of the stairs and into one of the rooms. Jimmie, unable to stand anymore, flops down on the chesterfield, and sits alone in the darkness, feeling sorry for himself. He mutters inaudibly. Jim and Sandy wander in from the kitchen.)

Jim: What you sitting in here all alone for lad?

(Sandy switches on a light, and Billy staggers in plopping a case of beer in the centre of the floor.)

Billy: Ahhh, forget it Jim! *(He plops down in a chair. Jimmie glares at him.)*

Sandy: *(Trying to cheer Jimmie.)* Suuuuure. I've always said it, and I'll say it again, "Ain't nothing worth gettin in a fight over."

Jimmie: *(Growling)* Then shut your God damn mouth.

Sandy: Now hold on Jimmie, hold on. It's old Sandy your friend. I didn't mean nothing by it.

Jim: Aye son, that's no way to talk.

Jimmie: Awww, the stupid ole bugger's been going on about it all night!

(Jimmie struggles to stand up. It is not a vicious or loud threat, but merely a drunken threat.)

Jimmie: *(To Sandy.)* You wanna fight me? You wanna fight me huh?! Come on then, come on . . . *(Puts his fists up.)*

Sandy: *(Wounded)* Jimmie boy . . .

Jimmie: Put up or shut up! Just shut up hear?! *(Kicking the case of beer.)* Go-waan, take your bloody beer with you!

(Jim takes hold of Jimmie before he falls down.)

Jim: Now come on son, come on, sit down!

(Jimmie attempting to wave his father off, keels over onto the chesterfield.)

Jimmie: I'm alright, I'm alright . . . Listen listen . . . you wanna know something? You wanna

A20

know why I didn't kick the crap out of that guy dad? Ca . . . cause that's all it would mean . . . that's all! Woulda been the end of it! I come home on leave . . . to see you an mom . . . an they throw me in the jug. That what you want? Huh? !

Jim: I know I know son. *(Taking him by the arm.)* Come on, you better go up to bed. You've had too much to drink. Give me a hand Billy.

Jimmie: *(Whimpering with self pity.)* I'm okay . . . I'm okay . . . *(He struggles to his feet.)* I'm sorry . . . *(Backing off and up the stairs.)* . . . soooorry . .
(Jimmie stumbles off up the stairs. Sandy slowly rises, a hurt man.)

Jim: *(Following Sandy to the door.)* Sandy you're no leavin . . . Listen I know that boy. He's just had too much to drink. He'd never say those kind of things if he was sober . . .
(But Sandy is the wounded man and drunkenly fumbles for the door-knob.)

Sandy: *(Wagging his head.)* I know I know . . . Jim you and me's always been friends — right?

Jim: . . . Right.

Sandy: Friends?

Jim: Friends . . .

(They shake hands vigorously.)

Sandy: Best friend I ever had!

(He weaves out the door and into the darkness. Jim closes the door, and drifts back into the room — a sorry man.)

Jim: *(Half to himself.)* Never seen the boy act like that before. He's a good boy. You're his friend Billy . . . you never seen him act like that before did you?

Billy: Good head Jimmie . . . good head.

Jim: *(Reassured)* Sure. God I ought to know, he's my own son! . . . Ah, I think I've had enough myself. I'd better go up and make sure he's okay . . .

(Jim heads for the stairs slowly. Billy stays in his chair facing the front doorway. He gives the old man a wave.)

Billy: Okay, night Pop. Don't worry bout him . . . Jimmie's a hundred per cent . . . hundred per cent.

(Jim nods with gratitude, starts up the stairs. Billy gives a big yawn, looks at his watch, and settles himself more comfortably in the chair. His eyes fix on the front door . . . waiting.)

Black out:

(Lights come up on Billy still in the chair, his shoes and jacket now off and tie loosened. He is on the verge of dozing, when the laughter of Jeanie and Dollie can be heard outside. He comes to, quickly.)

(The door opens and they enter, flopping about in fits of laughter. Jeanie suddenly realizes where they are, waves Dollie to kill it. They continue in muffled giggles . . .)

(A silly smile comes over Billy's face, as he watches their antics. They come in and flop down beside his chair, and between fits of hysterical laughter, relate their story of the evening, as though they were sharing it with an old friend.)

Dollie: Ohhhh, you should have seen these two goons that followed us home! Eh Duke? !

Jeanie: Yeah!

Dollie: Boy did they like you!

Jeanie: *(Shrieking)* Me? ? ! You ya mean! !

(They nearly collapse laughing. Billy half joins them, but doesn't follow the conversation at all.)

Dollie: If you could have seen their faces!

Jeanie: Real jerks!

Dollie: Ever see Mutt and Jeff in person? !

(More laughter.)

Billy: This a couple of guys you met?

Dollie: Met! We did everything we could not to meet them! They wouldn't leave us alone. Everywhere we went . . . they were sure to go . . . wagging their tails behind them!

Jeanie: (*Snorts of laughter.*)

Dollie: An herrrrr, "please ta meetcha!". Honestly Duke!

Jeanie: Well they paid for our coffee and stuff didn't they! Sides I can't be like you. You should see her Billy. She tells the guy to . . . well I can't say, but boyyyyy!

Billy: (*Eager*) What'd she say?

Dollie: (*Daring her*) Go ahead . . . tell him.

Jeanie: Oh no, not me!

Dollie: What'd I tell you about starting things you can't finish? (*Teasing Billy.*) Anyway I told him . . .

(*She stops, she and Jeanie bursting into another fit of giggling, Billy scowls, becoming impatient with them.*)

Billy: Well common. What'd ya say?

Dollie: (*Playing with him.*) You shouldn't be so curious . . . it killed the cat . . .

(*Billy waits with a blank look on his face.*)

Dollie: . . . You know what I mean?

Billy: (*Annoyed*) Well what's so funny about that?

Dollie: Oooooo-kay then . . . (*She takes a long teasing pause and speaks in suggestive tones.*) . . . What's something . . . you got . . . that I haven't?

Billy: (*A silly grin lighting his face.*) Well let's see . . . that's an open question . . .

Dollie: (*Before he can give an answer.*) Bad breath!

Billy: (*Feeling foolish.*) Hah! Real funny.

(*The girls go through another session of giggling.*)

Dollie: Awww, it's just a joke you play on fellows. Don't be a sore head.

Billy: (*No humour.*) Ummm. You want a beer?

Dollie: (*Making a face.*) Beer — yuk!

Billy: (*To Jeanie.*) How about you?

Jeanie: (*Wishing she could please him.*) Gee I . . . I can't.

(*It is Dollie who interests Billy, by being coy and putting him down. Jeanie is unable to compete, not having Dollie's looks or drive. She is soon a forgotten party as Billy and Dollie engage in their childish game.*)

Dollie: (*Challenging*) I used to know a guy who could take a bottle down without stopping . . .

Billy: Hell that's easy! Watch this.

(*He tilts the bottle and drains it. While it has not gone down too easy, he manages to conceal his discomfort and smirks back at her defiantly.*)

Dollie: (*Poking him playfully in the stomach.*) He was an idiot too! (*Laughter*) Boy if I hit you in the gut now — bam, beer all over the place! . . . (*She gives a teasing laugh.*)

Billy: . . . go ahead.

Dollie: Are you kidding?

Billy: Gwan, hit it . . .

Dollie: (*Drawing back her fist, teasing.*) . . . Ooo-kay . . . (*She holds.*)

Billy: (*Tensing*) Come on . . .

(*She suddenly unleashes, hitting him hard in the stomach. He flushes having obviously felt pain, but forces a leering grin back.*)

Billy: See, you can't hurt me.

Dollie: *(Wringing her hand.)* Jeeeze, I hurt my knuckle on one of those buttons!

Billy: Hurt yourself instead huh?! Hell you'll be okay. *(Fumbles with her hand awkwardly, then lets go.)*

Dollie: I've got to put some cold water on it . . .

(She moves off into the dark kitchen, dragging Jeanie with her. Billy quickly rises, checking for any sounds from upstairs. We hear the running of the tap and a muffled argument between the girls.)

Dollie: *(Off)* Go-wan, I said.

Jeanie: Boyyyy . . .

(Jeanie comes out, stands looking at him embarrassed.)

Jeanie: *(Shrugs)* . . . She wants you to go in there.

(Billy gets up and quickly goes in. There is a long silence, then giggling and muffled sounds from the kitchen. Jeanie lost for something to do, sighs to herself and begins to make up the chesterfield into a bed.)

Jeanie: *(Giving a feeble warning.)* I'm still here you know Dollie . . . (No answer.) An I'm sleeping down here tonight . . . soooo.

(Silence is her only answer. She shrugs, plops the pillow down on the sloppily made bed, and goes up the stairs and into the bathroom. There is a long silence with occasional sounds of heavy breathing . . . then . . .)

Dollie's Voice: *(Off)* Okay okay sonny.

Billy's Voice: *(Off)* What's wrong . . . ?

Dollie's Voice: *(Off)* I-said-quit-it!

(Sounds of a struggle.)

Billy's Voice: *(Off)* Shit!!

(Dollie suddenly plunges out of the darkness of the kitchen, her hair all tossed.)

Dollie: *(Grabbing her coat.)* I'm getting out of here, you're nuts!

Billy: *(Following)* God damn cock teaser!

Dollie: Get you!

(Billy starts to cross, now enraged.)

Dollie: *(Stopping him cold.)* I'll yell so loud, this whole house'll be awake in one second! *(She scurries out the front door.)*

(Billy stands there cursing under his breath, wanting to go after her, afraid the commotion may have already awakened those upstairs.)
(Jeanie comes out of the bathroom, in a nightie and an old robe thrown about her. She stops surprised when she sees him standing there alone, then continues down the stairs. She tosses her bundle of clothes on one of the chairs saying nothing as Billy watches her every move.)

Billy: *(Feeling he must say something.)* . . . Your friend went home.

Jeanie: *(Shrugs)* I didn't know whether you wanted to go in there or not. She made me ask you. She has to always get her way . . .

Billy: *(Lamely)* Nothing happened you know . . . hell just kidding around a bit. *(Notices the chesterfield made into a bed.)* You sleeping down here?

Jeanie: Mom and dad got my room. You an Jimmie are sleeping in theirs.
(Billy's eyes go to the quietness upstairs, then back to her. Awkwardly he begins to fumble with little pieces of business, stalling for time.)

Billy: Yeah . . . it's gettin late. Guess everybody's asleep up there . . . huh?

Jeanie: *(Not sensing anything.)* Guess so . . . Hey don't tell em what time I came home eh?

Billy: Naw . . .

(As Billy moves about, he comes to her heap of clothing on the chair. His eyes fall upon her exposed undergarments; the brassiere, panties. He studies her.)

Billy: That . . . that Dollie, ah, she ain't much you know. Hell you're prettier than . . . she is even.

Jeanie: Are you kidding? All the fellows go after her.

Billy: You . . . you got great long red hair . . . (Awkwardly moves closer to her.) . . . all ya gotta do, is fix it different. I mean more grown up.

(His eyes keep darting to the rooms upstairs, then back to her. She just stands listening.)

Billy: You know? Curl it up like women do.

(He gives a final heavy sigh, then awkwardly gives her a quick rough kiss. It has caught her completely by surprise, and she doesn't respond in any way.)

Billy: (Releasing her.) Well, you . . . go to bed then an I'll turn off the lights on my way up . . .

(He stands there watching as she obeys, taking off her robe and slipping into bed. He tip-toes across to the light switch and the lights go out. There is a short silence and we hear only his heavy breathing.)

Billy's Voice: Well . . . goodnight then.

Jeanie's Voice: Night Billy . . .

(We see his silhouette cross back to the foot of the chesterfield.)

Billy: (Clearing his throat.) You don't really want me to go up, do you?

Jeanie's Voice: What do you mean . . . ?

Billy's Voice: . . . You know.

(No answer. We see his form go to the chesterfield and sit on the edge.)

Billy's Voice: . . . Huh?

(We see his form disappear into the darkness of the chesterfield and hear a startled noise from Jeanie.)

Jeanie's Voice: What . . . what are you doing?

Billy's Voice: (Angry) Don't play dumb now you!

(We hear the sounds of someone getting up from one of the beds upstairs. Quietness.)

Jeanie's Voice: Please don't Billy . . .

(From the darkness upstairs, we hear Jimmie puking in his room.)

Jeanie's Voice: (Whimpering) No please don't do that . . .

Billy's Voice: (Snarling) You make one more god damn sound, and I'll smash your head to a pulp!!

End of Act One Curtain

A25

A26

Act two   three months later . . .

(It is the evening of a cold November day. When the curtain rises Jim wanders about the living room in a state of confusion.)

Jim: Tip? . . . Tip what time is it?

Mary: *(Off)* You've plenty of time. It's only six thirty Jim.

Jim: Fussin' with a lot of fancy duds that's all. Well it's not for me I'll tell ya!

(Mary enters from the kitchen carrying a freshly pressed pair of men's trousers. She hurries along to the stairs.)

Mary: I know, I know. There's your pants. Mind not to get 'em creased now.

Jim: Alright, woman, alright!

(Jim goes upstairs as Jeanie enters, shivering and bundled in a heavy winter coat.)

Mary: *(Coming down the stairs.)* Do you have any idea of the time, girl?

Jeanie: *(Shrugs)* Around six ain't it?

Mary: I mean your supper. I bin keepin it warm three quarters of an hour now!

Jeanie: I can't help it, there were no buses. I ain't hungry anyway.

Mary: Nonsense, a body can't live without food. Everything's on the stove. I haven't much time.

Jim: *(Off)* Tip! Where the devil are my medals? ?

Mary: *(Sighing)* Your father's fit to be tied tonight.

Jim: You didn't leave 'em on the blazer when you sent it for cleaning, did you?

Mary: They're in where they should be! With your cuff links in the top drawer!

(Pause)

Jim: So they are, so they are . . . confound it, they could get marked up just lying about like this you know!

Mary: (*Exasperated*) Listen to him. Did you ever hear so much complaining from one man? Been a bundle of nerves all afternoon. Pretends not to be the least bit interested in the presentation. To hear him tell it, he's doing them a big favour just by showing up tonight.

Jeanie: (*Distant*) What presentation?

Mary: Now I told you about it. Sometimes I don't think you hear a word I say! The Legion get-together tonight. Your Dad's going to be honoured by his squad.

Jeanie: . . . Oh that . . .

Mary: What do you mean, "oh that"? It's a real fine thing that they're doin! (*To herself.*) I hope it cheers him some. He's been so with the moods since Jimmie was here in the summer . . . (*Afterthought*) . . . so strange, them just up and leavin like that the next mornin . . . not even a goodbye . . . it's all the drinking they do . . . (*Seeing Jeanie staring off.*) . . . what's wrong with you?

Jeanie: (*Over-reaction.*) Nothing . . .

(*Jim has started down the stairs. He moves with a certain care, as though he may soil the fresh blazer he wears.*)

Jim: Well . . . how do I look?

Mary: Very becoming Jim.

Jim: Aye they must have shrunk me blazer a bit at the cleaners . . . tight fit. Darn thing's always catching lint too.

Mary: Did you prepare a thank you speech Jim?

Jim: I said it before, I'll not be making any fancy speeches. I'll say thank you an that's all.

Mary: Jim you must say something.

Jim: Aw now look here, did I ask 'em to give me any blinkin award? Did I now?

Mary: I hope not.

Jim: It wouldn't be me if I said anything else! My boys know me as a man of simple tastes and one who expresses himself the same way.

Mary: It seems a shame.

Jim: Aye, well that's the way it's gonna be. Did you get the job girl?

Jeanie: (*Quietly*) . . . No.

Mary: You didn't? But I'm sure Grace said they needed help bad. You didn't tell them about your last job, did you?

Jeanie: They talked with me, then said there were no positions open.

Mary: What a pity. You might've been able to get a little extra sugar too. Grace always does . . . Maybe you could get on doing the offices with me.

Jeanie: I'm not doing cleaning!

Mary: I'd rather you had a nice job in a shop too, but . . .

Jeanie: I won't do it!

Jim: You'll bloody well do what your mother tells you! Going to that blinking high school for two years taking up typing and everything an what the hell good did it do you? Got the sack first week you had a job. And that was a good job in an office an everything!

Jeanie: Yes sir.

Mary: I'll talk to Mr. Rogers an see if I can get you on a couple nights a week with me, till you can find a good job, eh! (*Knock on door.*) . . . That must be Sarah. Come in.
(*Sarah enters laden down with pastry tins and packaged food.*)

Sarah: Just me it is!

Mary: Here, let me give you a hand dear. Oh my goodness, what have you got in all these things?

Sarah: I made up three dozen cookies this aft and the rest is mostly sandwiches for the darts tournament. Hullo Jim, Jeanie!

Jeanie: Mrs. McIver.

Jim: Well I dare say it looks like we'll have us quite a feed tonight. I'm just going up to get my coat, Sandy should be here any minute.

(He exits upstairs.)

Mary: Isn't that a new coat you're wearing Sarah? I don't think I've seen it before.

Sarah: Aye, got it the Eagle's rummage sale last week, so it isn't really new.

Mary: Near new though. Oh that was lucky, finding something that nice.

Sarah: Found me three nice dresses too.

Mary: Tch! Oh I do wish I'd been able to peek in. Isn't it lovely Jeanie?

Jeanie: Uh huh.

Mary: I'd love to see the dresses! I'll just fetch me salad and cake and we'll be off then.
(Exits to kitchen.)

Sarah: How have you been Jeanie?

Jeanie: Okay I guess.

Sarah: And how's school?

Jeanie: *(Making a noise with pursed lips.)* Quit!

Sarah: Oh I didn't know that.

Jeanie: Dad says "what do I need an education for anyways . . . girls only end up getting married and then it's all a waste". I didn't like it anyway . . .

Sarah: Oh learnins a good thing. Though I think it's most important a girl should learn the makin of a good home . . .

(Sound of car horn off. Sarah goes to the front door window.)

. . . that must be Sandy now! Aye it's him. He's here – Jim, Mary!

(She quickly gathers her belongings as Jim comes down the stairs with his heavy army winter coat and hat.)

Jim: Here, is he? Tip . . . !

Sarah: *(Starting out the front door.)* Well, bye bye Jeanie.

Jim: An no running around now, hear? I don't want you hanging around that dance hall on 13th street! Come on, Tip!

Mary: *(Rushing through)* I'll be but a second! *(She fumbles about putting on her heavy coat, powdering her nose and a last look in the dresser mirror.)*

Jim: *(Off)* She can't go nowhere without a tea and a pee . . . Tip! ! !

Mary: Alright alright. Bye bye Jeanie. Mind what your father said and clean up for me now. An see if you can find some scraps for the dog.

(She exits on the run. Jeanie pushes her food aside and begins wandering aimlessly about the house, lost in thought. She cranks the gramaphone and puts on a record, The White Cliffs of Dover by Gracie Fields. Going past the mirror, she hesitates to study herself. Slowly she runs her hand across her abdomen. The front door flies open, causing her to jump with a start. Dollie enters.)

Dollie: God what a time I had getting out tonight! You'd think I was some little kid! Nobody home is there?

Jeanie: *(Still nervous)* Th . . . they just left.

Dollie: *(Flopping down on the sofa.)* "Stay away from the goddam soldiers" he says. The only guy I know who isn't a soldier is him! Oh, I just love that song . . . My mother nearly cries every time she hears it. *(Suddenly up and wandering into the dining room.)* Hey, got anything to eat? I'm starving! *(Picks at Jeanie's plate.)* If my mother serves potatoes again tomorrow, I'll vomit! Get the job?

Jeanie: Naww, they wanted someone older.

Dollie: No loss. I wouldn't want a job like that. "Yes Mam", "No Mam", "What's it gonna be today Mam? ", "Oh thank you Mam" *(Making a face.)* Ouuuuck! And you'd have to dress up all the time.

Jeanie: I know. I didn't want the darn thing anyway. I don't like addin' up money and everything . . . just don't like doin it, that's all. *(Dollie produces a package of cigarettes and offers one to Jeanie. Throughout the rest of the scene they go through a series of smoking gymnastics.)*

Dollie: My father says if I don't get a job soon, he's kicking me out — yuk yuk! 'Sides he hasn't got any room to talk. Every time I see the old fart, he's just sitting there with a gut full of beer! Aw, I'll go back to the cannery in the spring. Have to get some money somewhere if I want to go to the coast to see my sister.

(She wanders about.)

Jeanie: *(Enviously)* You really going to Vancouver Dollie?

Dollie: *(From kitchen)* Maybe. I don't know. If I can get some money somewhere. Bus is about eighty bucks return. Won't cost me nothing to stay there though. My brother-in-law told me to come and see them anytime. Jeeze you ought to see him too Jeanie! Is he ever cute! And got a real terrific job in one of the defence plants. He treats me real swell, which bugs my sister.

Jeanie: Is he the one who . . .?

Dollie: . . . Yeah.

Jeanie: You shouldn't go there then Dollie.

Dollie: *(Mocking)* Oh jeeze Dougal, when you gonna learn that all guys want that! You just gotta make up your mind who you're givin and who you're not. *(Snickers)* Anyway he gave me ten dollars not to tell my sister. *(Challenging)* Why don't you try it some time? It won't kill ya.

Jeanie: No thanks.

Dollie: *(Exasperated)* Ohhh! That's your trouble, ya never try nothin! After the first time — pfffftttt! . . . But you'll never know 'cause you're gutless!

Jeanie: I am not!

Dollie: Oh yes you are! You got a yellow streak right up the middle of your back!

Jeanie: Well if you're so smart, I could tell you something too!

Dollie: *(Sarcastic)* What? !

(Jeanie is sorry she said anything . . . remains silent.)

Dollie: *(Badgering her.)* What — come on — what? I'm waiting!

(Jeanie's lip begins to quiver.)

Dollie: What, I said? What? What? What? See, you're yellow!

(Jeanie bursts into tears and runs up the stairs into her room. Dollie gives an exasperated sigh, calling up after her.)

Dollie: Oh come on Dougal I was only kidding! *(Waits)* What a creep! *(Realizes Jeanie is not coming back.)* Aww come on Dougal, I got a whole pack of cigarettes tonight an everything . . . *(Angry)* Well I'm going then! *(She starts from the door.)* You coming? ? *(Waits)* I'm leaving! *(Exiting)* Creep!

Curtain

Scene two *The Dougal home later that night. Jeanie sits in a faded housecoat, curling her hair at the dining-room table. The sounds of approaching voices and laughter grows louder with the singing of "I've got Sixpence". The front door opens and Mary and Sarah enter, followed by Jim and Sandy, who, very intoxicated, struggle to support one another. Sandy is in the same age group as Jim with the same red face from too much drinking during his life and a heavy wheeze at all times. The two of them take a stance in the doorway and put the finishing touches to the last chorus.*

Jim and Sandy:
I've got no pence . . .
Jolly Jolly no pence . . .
I've got no pence . . . to send home to my wife!
I've got no pence to spendddd . . .
And no pence to lendddddd . . .
And no pence to send home to my wife!
Pooooor wife!
(Sandy and Jim applaud themselves with laughter, while Mary and Sarah pretend to be annoyed but are delighted by every second of it.)

Mary: Come in now and close the door, before we all freeze to death! *(To Jeanie)* Did you ever hear the likes of it? All the way home they've been carrying on like that!

Sarah: *(To Jim and Sandy)* A pair of fools; that's all ya are.

Mary: I thought for sure we'd be arrested.

Jim: *(Very drunk)* Hah! Ne . . . Need more an the bloomin police force to take a couple of infantry men . . . Eh Sandy? !

Sandy: At's for sure — I'll tell you!

Sarah: Sandy ya no have to shout like that!

Sandy: *(Wagging his finger.)* I mean if a man can't sing a bit . . . when he's happy, what is there? Nothing — that's what! Nothing! !

Sarah: You're disgustin.

Jim: *(His head bobbing in agreement.)* Ayeeeee. An if it weren't fer a few chaps like us . . . there wouldn't be no Canada! Right? ?

Sandy: Right! You said it Jim boy. You said it.

Mary: (To Jeanie.) Tonight they won the whole war an are gonna make short work of this one.

Jim: (Drunken anger.) Listen here, lookin after them bloody Jerries in a camp, is just as important as any other job in this war — Hear!

Mary: (Trying to calm him.) I no meant anything by it Jim . . .

Jim: (Raving on) An you show me anyone what says different an I'll show you a son-of-a-bitchin liar! Aye an just show me one of em blinkin police what could do the job we do! It's something for them to keep an eye on just a couple of prisoners! Sandy and me is been trained to guard a whole camp with thousands in it. Every one of em a hundred times dangerouser an somebody who broke into a shop or somethin!

Sandy: Aye, an people ought to be more aware of it!

Jim: It's us what looks out fer the bloody police an every one else in this country, when it comes down to it!

Sandy: (Clapping) I could no said it better myself! (Sees Jeanie for the first time.) Ahhhhh, there she is. By golly if she doesn't get prettier everytime I see her! Have ya got a kiss for ole Sandy lass?

Sarah: Sandy you behave yourself.

(Jim joins Sandy's loud laughter at Jeanie's embarrassment.)

Sandy: Ahh, I guess I'm not the handsome beggar I use to be! If I was a few years younger I could give some lad a run for his money, eh Jim!

Jim: (Knowing laugh.) Aye . . . that you could, that you could! Mother you got a few ales in the fridge for me an Sandy?

(Jim starts off in the direction of the kitchen. Mary on his heels.)

Mary: Oh Jim, now I don't think you should be having any more . . . Have some tea instead, why not . . . ?

(Sandy holds his gaze on Jeanie, a silly smile on his face. While she is frightened a little, she is enjoying his attention.)

Sandy: You know it's true Jeanie. I was a real terror in France . . . (Laughing) Aye, old Sandy here, if you'll believe it!

Jeanie: Were you?

Sandy: Them French women just wouldn't leave me alone! An them women are really something let me tell you!

Sarah: Tch, Sandy . . .

Sandy: You just ask your Dad, he'll tell you! (Begins to move closer to Jeanie.) Yes Sir . . . ole sad eyes Sandy they use to call me . . . cause that's what the women use to like — my sad eyes!
(Sandy begins to sing in a very shaky voice.)

Sandy: I — I — I dream of Jeanie with the light brown hairrrr . . . La da da da — daaaa Da da da daaaa . . .

(He gives her a little pat on the shoulder, then lets his arm rest there. Sarah comes over.)

Sandy: You don't mind ole Sandy singing a wee bit do you?

Jeanie: (Awkwardly) No . . .

Sarah: You'll not be winning any awards for singing Sandy. Now sit down.

(Sarah gently takes Sandy's arm trying to guide him away, but he does not budge.)

Sandy: It's not awards I'd be wanting if I had a daughter lovely as Jeanie here . . .

Sarah: Don't be making a fool of yourself.

Sandy: (Maudlin) Aye, that's what I am an I know it. A fool I never married and had a family of my own. A little girl . . .

Sarah: . . . good grief.

Sandy: *(To Jeanie)* You don't know how lonely it can be by yourself all the time. When you're young you manage, but who cares about me now eh? No one . . . Aye when you're old . . . *(His arm falls about her waist now.)* Ahhh, do you no remember when you were a little one lass, and you use to sit on my lap and cuddle up to ole Sandy? Eh? You were always giving me kisses then . . . *(Whispering)* Just a wee one eh . . . ?

Sarah: *(Embarrassed)* Sandy, leave Jeanie be!

(Sarah pulls at him. Sandy suddenly reels about on her snarling.)

Sandy: Who the hell you think you're pushin?! Keep your bloody hands to yourself!

(Jim enters from kitchen, his arms filled with bottles of open beer.)

Jim: Hi Sandy, the ship'll not run dry tonight!

Sandy: Glory be! Here let me give you a hand, man!

(He goes quickly to Jim and they divide the load, laughing and nearly falling over one another.)

Sarah: You're not going to be drinking more are you?

Mary: Jim please . . . I wish you wouldn't.

Jim: Listen, since when the hell can't I have a few quiet drinks with a friend in my own home?!

Sandy: Sh-h-h-h Jim. Don't be yelling in front of wee Jeanie. She's just a young lass.

Mary: You'll have regrets tomorrow.

Jim: Come on boy, we'll go down the cellar, so's we don't disturb certain folks.

(They exit through the doorway beneath the stairs, going to the cellar.)

Sandy: Ahhh, you're a lucky man Jimmie Dougal; your own house, fine wife and a lovely beautiful daughter . . .

Sarah: *(With a sigh)* Ah, it always ends up with too much drinking. I like a pint or two myself, now or then but . . .

Mary: It's men's ways Sarah. I just made us a pot of tea and we can sit down and have a nice chat of our own without them. It'll just take me a minute to get it. Jeanie, will you put some cups love. I've scads of things to tell *(Going into kitchen)* you Sarah! You'll not guess who's getting married? Joe and Mollie's girl, and that little bit of nothing no more than nineteen!

Sarah: Aye they seem to grow up a lot faster these days. I guess the war's got to do with it . . . *(Sarah's eyes follow Jeanie as she sets some places at the table. The old woman feels a certain resentment because of Sandy's flirtation with the girl. We hear a burst of laughter from Sandy and Jim in the cellar as they break into song in the background.)*

Jeanie: *(Giggles)* Gee they're funny when they drink. Specially Sandy and everything he said. Listen to them!

Sarah: Aye they can never seem to hold their tongues when they've got the drink in 'em. You mustn't pay him too much attention when he gets like that. Old men like flattering young girls with a lot of sweet talk, but it don't mean anything with 'em.

Jeanie: Mom always tells Dad the same thing — and she's never wrong. Tomorrow he'll wish he hadn't.

Mary: Here we are. Oh you should have seen it all Jeanie, it was so nice. I dare say I was so touched by it, I nearly came to tears two or three times. All the clapping and cheers — well I knew your Dad was liked, but I nay knew that much. Did you see the lovely plaque they gave him?

Jeanie: Oouu, that's nice! Is it gold?

Mary: Well the plate part with the writing on is, I guess. Wouldn't it Sarah?

Sarah: Oh yes they always make them out of gold.

Mary: An when he got up and made his thank you speech, he made 'em laugh, didn't he Sarah?

Sarah: Aye.

Mary: I don't mind saying Isabel Mckay looked a bit green with it all.

Sarah: Oh she was that all right. Seen her and the Sergeant Major going home early, saying she had her bad headache.

Mary: Aye, well she'd best not try her bossiness with me anymore. And your Dad and Sandy won the doubles too! Although the Calgary group tallied more points for the evening. Your Dad says it was luck, that's all.

Jeanie: Did they give anything away?

Mary: Aye, Elsie won the door prize. It was a nice lamp too. *(Sitting heavily)* Ohhh that feels good. Nothing like a wee cup of tea when you want relaxation. I thought sure my poor legs were going to give out on me tonight.

Sarah: I'm a bit weary myself, Mary.

Mary: It's the veins. I should go to the doctor, but I know he'll want me to go into the hospital . . . and it would cost so much money.

(A loud burst of laughter from the cellar.)

Sarah: It's not right you know . . .

Mary: Oh Sarah, let them be. I suppose they've got good reasons for celebrating tonight.

Sarah: If Harry were alive he'd not be down there. He was a gentleman, Mary, that he was . . . a gentleman. God bless him.

Mary: He was a fine man. It's been hard for you living alone these years, eh Sarah?

(Sarah is almost on the verge of tears as she goes on in choking tones.)

Sarah: It was no' as bad when my daughter Betty was with me. But she has her own family now. Aye there've been times when it's been so lonely . . . *(Blows her nose)* . . . A body has to go on and manage the best it can though.

Mary: Have you no ever thought . . . Jeanie not so much cake, you'll be a mess of pimples in the morning. You know that! *(Back to Sarah)* Have you no ever thought of wedding again Sarah?

Sarah: *(Laughing)* Ach, and who'd want the likes of me? A few years ago when I was younger, I thought about it, but I couldn't find eyes for any other man. And I was busier then, doing more things . . . If you were meaning him downstairs there — not on your life. The only thing that man wants, is someone looking and cleaning up after him. Aye a housekeeper!

Mary: I spect he is a bit difficult.

Sarah: Oh he can be sweet enough when he wants inviting to dinner or something. Aye it will have to be a patient woman who'll put up with Sandy Travers.

Mary: Let me fill you again . . .

Sarah: No thank ye Mary. I best get on my way if I'm going to catch the last bus.

Mary: You're not going home on the bus are you? Get Sandy to drive you.

Sarah: He'll not be in any condition for driving a car. Besides, once he's started drinking and singing, he's settled in for the night. I don't feel like waiting about for hours. *(Rising)* I'll just get my purse an coat.

Mary: Sarah, it's a bitter night. If you won't call him, I will. *(Going to doorway to basement.)* Sandy! Sarah's leaving now!

(Continued laughter and song is their answer.)

Sandy and Jim:
I don't care — what the hell ya say!
I don't give a damn — in any any — way!

(She closes the door, muffling their song to the background again.)

Mary: Take yourself another sweater then. Jeanie fetch it.

Sarah: No no Mary I'm fine. Don't go fussin.

Mary: You'll catch your death of cold standing there on the corner waiting for that bus. You bundle up!

Sarah: My coat's fine . . .

Mary: (*Helping her on with clothes.*) It's damp out tonight. Just slip it on now. Don't be telling me. I ride them buses enough to know the heating's no good in em!

Sarah: It's not too bad if you get a seat away from the doors. Bye bye Jeanie, take care of yourself.

Mary: I'll be calling you Sarah . . .

Sarah: Aye. Will you be going to the church for Bingo on Wednesday?

Mary: Aye.

Sarah: Bye bye then.

(*Mary goes out on the veranda with Sarah. We hear them call their "goodbyes". The laughter and singing of Jim and Sandy rises, then fades off again. Mary comes back shivering, and closing the door peers out into the darkness, through the window.*)

Mary: It's turned even colder. I do hope she'll not have a long wait . . .

Jeanie: Why does Mrs. McIver walk all bent over like that?

Mary: (*Distant*) Ah, she had a bad fall when she was young . . . Her husband was very drunk . . . and beat her up. She no remembers it though . . . (*Aware*)

And those aren't things for your ears young lady. Ahh me, I'll just clear the dishes and turn in. You sure aren't much help to your old mother. Didn't I ask you to clear up for me when I was leaving . . . ? Turn out the parlor lights and get yourself to bed now.

(*Mary moves tiredly through her task of clearing the table and taking the dishes into the kitchen. Always in the background the sudden bursts of laughter and song; then quiet again. Jeanie starts to turn out the lamps, when she catches her form in the dresser mirror. She studies herself for a long time, then gently brings her hand to her abdomen and touches it. The kitchen light goes out and Mary comes through the darkness of the dining-room and upon Jeanie. She watches the girl's ritual.*)

Mary: What are you doing? . . .

(*Jeanie startled, swings about. There is a long pause; the girl's eyes cast to the floor.*)

Mary: Jeanie . . . ?

Jeanie: (*Mumbling*) . . . nothing.

Mary: Why were you looking at yourself like that?

(*Jeanie does not look at her, just shakes her head.*)

Mary: Is something . . . wrong?

Jeanie: (*Afraid*) You won't tell Dad?

Mary: (*Frightened*) Tell him what?

Jeanie: I think I'm in trouble . . .

Mary: (*Afraid to ask*) How?

Jeanie: (*A whisper*) . . . a . . . a baby.

(*Mary gives a reflex gasp, bringing her hand to her mouth to muffle it. There is a long stunned silence as she stares horrified at Jeanie.*)

Mary: . . . you've been with a man.

(*Jeanie nods*)

Mary: (*Broken*) . . . God in heaven.

Jeanie: . . . Just once.

Mary: (*In agony*) Shhhhhhh! (*Sotto voce*) Go upstairs.

(Jeanie begins to whimper, quickly vanishes up the stairs. The old woman moves with a numbness about the room, turning off the lights. Slowly she walks through the semi-darkness to the stairs. Unable to bear the strain any longer, she sinks to a sitting position on the stairs, and dropping her head on her knees, begins to quietly weep.)

Mary: . . . oh God . . . God no . . .

(A bright edge of light spills through from the partly open cellar door. There is a round of laughter from Jim and Sandy as they break into an old army song.)

Jim and Sandy:
Roll me oooooover . . .
In the clooooover
Roooll me over — lay me down — an do it
againnnnn . . .

Blackout

Scene three   *It is early next morning in the Dougal home. The stage is empty except for Sandy asleep on the chesterfield. He cuddles a small scatter rug, thrown over him and snores gently. Mary, in robe and slippers, enters dining room from the kitchen. She sits at the table, sipping on a cup of tea, lost and heavy in thought. Her thoughts are suddenly interrupted by the retching of Jim clearing his throat upstairs. She moves quickly across to the stairs, watching for any sign of him.*

Jim: *(Off)* Oh my God . . . my God . . . *(Moans)*

His bedroom door is heard opening, and he stumbles across and into the bathroom, flushing the toilet and running the taps as he clears his throat. Another groan.

Mary: *(Calling)* Is it you Jim?

Jim: *(Off)* Ayee . . .

Mary: *(Hopefully)* It's early. You've only been to bed a few hours. Why don't you try an get more sleep.

Jim: *(Off)* Ayee.

Jim comes out of the bathroom, crosses to his bedroom. Mary goes quickly up the stairs and enters Jeanie's bedroom.

Mary: *(Off)* Jeanie . . . get up now.

Jeanie: *(Sleepy sounds)* What for? It's so early.

Mary: Do as I say. Get up.

Mary comes silently down the stairs. She feels the chill in the air and goes to one of the heating vents in the living room, feeling for heat. She goes down the cellar. The dog starts barking. Jeanie crosses into the bathroom.

Mary: *(Off)* Shhhh Rex! It's only mother . . .

From the cellar come the sounds of coal being shovelled. Upstairs Jim begins to retch again. His door is heard opening and he crosses, trying the bathroom door.

Jim: Are ya in there Jeanie?

Jeanie: I'll be out in a second.

Jim: Well hurry it up. Your old dad's in a bad way.

Sandy stirs, shivers, bringing the rug closer about himself.

Jim: *(Insistent)* Jeanie? !

Toilet flushes. Door opens and Jeanie comes out.

Jeanie: I just only went in there . . .

Jim enters, slamming the door behind him. Inside more coughing and retching. Jeanie comes down the stairs, shivering from the cold. She enters the living room, stops and stares briefly at the form of Sandy, then crosses to the heating vent and tries warming herself. Sandy's head slowly comes up and he watches her. Not noticing him she turns her backside toward the vent and lifts her nighty and robe higher about her so the heat will go up and inside her clothing. Sandy's head slowly looks about to see if they are alone.

(He sinks back into sleep again. Mary comes up from the cellar.)

Mary: What are you doing, standing there displaying yourself like that? Get in there and have your breakfast.

Jeanie: It's too cold.

Mary: I've put coal in the furnace. The house'll be warm soon.

(Jeanie crosses and sits shivering at the dining room table.)

Mary: I've not slept a wink all night. *(A hushed last hope.)* Are you sure Jeanie?

Jeanie: *(Lazily)* Well nothing's happened for three months.

Mary: Don't be smug! Do you realize the trouble you're in?

Jeanie: Yes.

Mary: *(Wrathfully)* Who was he?

Jeanie: . . . just a soldier.

Mary: Why do you want to protect this man?

Jeanie: I don't want to protect nobody.

Mary: Then tell me who he is!

Jeanie: *(After a long pause.)* . . . it was that Billy.

Mary: *(Stung)* . . . Jimmie's friend?

(Jeanie nods)

Mary: But how? Where?

Jeanie: He did it to me while you were all sleeping.

Mary: . . . You let him?

Jeanie: He made me! I didn't want to, but he made me.

Mary: *(Enraged)* What's wrong with your tongue? Why didn't you yell so someone would hear you? ? ?

Jeanie: *(Whimpering)* He had his hand over my face . . . I could hardly breathe . . . an I was scared. It was so fast . . . he was on top of me . . . I started crying. Then it was over an he said everything would be okay if I didn't tell nobody . . .

Mary: *(To herself)* . . . and your brother brought him here . . .

Jeanie: The next morning he came down by himself, just before they left. An he told me I'd better not tell anybody ever, or he'd come back . . . and get me for it . . .

Mary: It's filth! Do you understand that — filth!
(Jeanie nods. Jim is heard coughing and moving about upstairs.)

Jim: *(Off)* Tip, I can't sleep no more. You can start my breakfast.

Mary: I knew he'd not last long.

(*Jim's bedroom door is heard opening upstairs. Mary quickly goes about setting the breakfast table. Jim starts down the stairs. He stops when he gets to Sandy in the living room.*)

Jim: Has Sandy no moved about yet Tip?

Mary: Shhh, you'd best not wake him Jim.

Jim: (*Loud laugh*) That ole bugger'll have one big head this morning I'll wager. (*Enters dining room*) I'll say one thing for that man. He can be flat on the floor from drink, but he'll no pass out. Never in all the time I've known him! No sir! (*To Jeanie*) Well don't you say good morning anymore?

Jeanie: Morning sir.

Mary: I'll have it for you in a second Jim. (*Scurries off into the kitchen.*)

Jim: (*Holding his head*) Ohhh, God almighty, you'd think a man could have a wee bit of pleasure without paying such a price.

Mary: (*Off*) Bit under are ya?

Jim: Aye.

Mary: (*Entering with cereal.*) You should know when to stop.

Jim: (*Growling*) I know. I know.

Mary: Here's your porridge. Eat it while it's hot. I'll start your eggs. (*Goes off*)

Jim: Turn em over. I don't want em looking at me this morning.

Mary: (*Off*) What time are you on duty?

Jim: Not till noon. (*Groans*) It was a good night wasn't it Tip? I mean I think it went over don't you? Everyone seemed to be having a good time.

Mary: Aye it was lovely.

Jim: Aye it was a good evening if I do say so

myself. Did my thank you speech go off all right?

Mary: You were fine Jim.

Jim: (*A grunt of agreement*) Aye, well that's the part I don't care for. Don't mind when it's just my boys. But when there's strangers about, and ladies . . . Never was much for that stuff you know.

Mary: Here's your toast dear.

Jim: So if they ask me again, I'll make that part clear right at the beginning. No speech makin! . . . what's this? No butter?

Mary: Jeanie wasn't able to get any yesterday.

Jim: Well hell's bells I can't eat my toast without butter woman!

Mary: I can't help it Jim.

Jim: (*Standing and banging fist.*) It don't matter a damn anyway! Just try and get a little butter in this town, just try! I'd like to know where in hell it's going, that's what I'd like to know! I know there's plenty of butter in that camp there, for them Gerries! It's a fine mess when you're feedin it for them and not ourselves isn't it! (*He sits again, now calmer.*) I'll see if I can wangle some from Nelson in stores.

Mary: Aye why don't you.

Jim: Hate toast without butter. (*To Jeanie*) Pour your dad some coffee. I hope the hell there's sugar in the house.

Mary: Aye, there is, there is. (*Exits to the kitchen.*)

(*Jeanie pours the coffee. She begins to exit.*)

Jim: Where you going?

Jeanie: Get dressed . . .

(*He gives a grunt signifying permission to leave. Jeanie goes upstairs. Mary returns from the kitchen with the eggs.*)

Mary: (Calling) You can lay out your dad's uniform Jeanie.

Jim: You not eatin Tip?

Mary: Aye. Been up for some time. (Waiting) I could no sleep last night.

Jim: Oh, the leg actin up on ya again is it?

Mary: A bit . . . along with other things . . .

(There is a long pause as Mary searches for words. Jim dunks his toast and noisily slurps at the hot coffee, not concerned.)

Mary: (Hushed) I'm afraid something's happened, and I can no find the words to tell you Jim.

Jim: (Grunts) . . .

Mary: It's to do with Jeanie.

Jim: What about her? (Long empty pause. Jim continues to eat.) Come on, come on, what is it Tip?

Mary: (Whispers) She's in trouble . . .

Jim: Aye, you already said that.

Mary: Woman trouble.

Jim stops eating, now aware of the subject matter and tries to comprehend it. There is a pause.

Mary: . . . she's pregnant . . .

He sits staring at her, his mouth tight, his eyes cold.

Jim: My Jeanie?

Mary: Now Jim please before . . .

(He leaps to attention almost upsetting the table.)

Jim: Where is she? !

Mary: Jim listen first.

Jim: (Starting towards the stairs.) Jeanie? ! (He reaches the stairs and stands at the foot of them waiting.) . . . Jeanie! ! !

Mary: Please Jim what are you going to do?

Jim: I want to hear it from her.

Mary: (Hovering about him.) It wasn't her fault. You didn't let me finish.

Jim: (Sharp) Let her tell it!

They both stand waiting. Jeanie's head slowly peeks from the doorway of her bedroom.

Mary: (Meekly) Come down dear.

Slowly Jeanie makes her way down until she is standing in front of her father. There is a long silence.

Jim: . . . what is it your mother says?

Jeanie: I'm sorry.

Jim stands there trembling. Suddenly he lashes out, sending Jeanie sprawling to the middle of the living room floor.

Jim: You little bitch! !

Mary: (Grabbing onto him.) Jim Jim stop it! !

Jim: (Standing over her and striking her several times as he screams.) You're disgusting do you hear! ! A slut! ! ! A good for nothing — bloody slut! ! !

Mary stands screaming trying to pull him off while Jeanie has crouched into a ball to protect herself from the rain of blows.

Mary: Jim in the name of God!

Jim: I'll show you what I think of you slut! Where's my belt? ! !

He lunges off toward the kitchen, Mary following, pleading for him to stop. She rushes back and sees Sandy half sitting, awake and bewildered from all the noise and commotion. Jeanie lies crumpled on the floor sobbing.

A43

Mary: Sandy! Oh God Sandy come quick! !

Sandy: *(Getting to his feet.)* What is it? ? What's wrong? ? !

Mary: *(Pointing to the kitchen.)* He'll kill her he'll kill her! Stop him, you've got to stop him – please! ! !

Sandy: *(Moving quickly to the kitchen.)* Jim come to your senses man!

Mary: *(Gathering Jeanie up by the arms and helping her toward the stairs.)* Oh jeanie Jeanie Jeanie. My Jeanie.

Mary guides the sobbing girl quickly up the stairs and into Jeanie's bedroom. The door is locked after them. Over this action we hear the arguing of Jim and Sandy from the kitchen.

Sandy: Hey Jim, are you daft man?!

Jim: Get out of my way damn it! !

Sandy: Take it easy man. Give me the belt! . . . Jim! !

(Jim comes through from the kitchen wielding a large strap. Sandy, having a hard time, clings to him.)

Jim: Leave go, I'll teach her! ! !

Sandy: Jim! Come on now Jim!

Jim: *(Screaming)* Dammit do you understand what I said! ! !

Sandy: You'll no hit her or I'll call the police, so help me!

(Jim stands there trembling.)

Jim: You don't understand do you? ! I've got a whore for a daughter! I'm a disgraced man Sandy!

Quick blackout Curtain

(Evening, one week later. Jeanie sits at the dining room table cutting pictures from a magazine. There are sounds of footsteps on the veranda outside and she hurries upstairs. The front door opens and Mary enters. The old woman moves with weariness as she removes her coat, etc. She shuffles towards the kitchen as Jeanie slips halfway down the stairs, calling to her.)

Jeanie: *(Loud whisper)* Is Dad with you?

Mary: *(With a start)* Oh Jeanie you startled me.

Jeanie: Is he?

Mary: No it's alright, come down. He'll not be off till eight. Did you prepare the vegetables like I asked?

Jeanie: *(Eager)* Uhhuh! And I cleaned the bathroom and made the beds.

Mary: *(Sitting with a sigh.)* Oh, I'm a bit weary. Got to catch my breath. I just dread these Wednesdays and doing that big office.

Jeanie: I'll put the kettle on for some tea for you Mom.

Mary: Thank ye Jeanie. It's just too big an office for one person. I was chatting with the manager tonight. He even knows me by name. Always telling me how nice and clean I get the place for them. He was saying tonight that they can't remember ever having anyone who did as good a job as I do . . . What's this you been doing? Cutting out? Oh, this here's a nice one Jeanie. What are you going to do with them?

Jeanie: Hang them up in my room with the others I guess.

Mary: How about this one with all the food in it?

Jeanie: *(Shrugs)* I don't know. I just like it so I cut it out too. *(Pause)* Has Dad said anything about me . . . ?

Mary: *(Quietly)* Aye. He says you're to go away.

Jeanie: (Shocked) Go away? Where?

Mary: I don't know Jeanie. It's only what he said.

Jeanie: (Frightened) But I don't want to go away. I want to stay with you.

Mary: We'll just have to wait and see . . .

Jeanie: (Starting to whimper) I'd . . . I'd be afraid all alone . . .

(She bursts into sobs and falls at her mother's knee, clinging to her.)

Mary: I know I know . . . don't cry now. (She rocks Jeanie gently in her arms as she would a child.)

Jeanie: I don't ever want to go away . . .

Mary: Some day you'll have to. You'll be getting married and having a family of your . . . (She stops suddenly aware of what she is saying.) . . . aye. I've planned so long how some day, you'd have a fine wedding . . . all lovely at the church and everything . . . and I could start saving a little now and then . . . so we could maybe have the reception at the King George Hotel . . .

Jeanie: (Faintly) It's so fancy there . . .

Mary: Aye. I've worked some of the big banquets that have been there. Not out front, but I could see all the fine trays and things going in and out. When I'd tell dad about it he'd say "don't make the food taste any better". . . (Pause) . . . Imagine, inviting all our friends there. And my Jeanie in a long white dress . . . (Heavy sigh) . . . it'll no be now I guess.

Jeanie: Last year at school a girl got rid of one with a knitting needle . . .

Mary: God forgive you!

Jeanie: I didn't mean anything.

Mary: Don't even think such thoughts, or He'll strike you down where you stand! To give birth is a sacred thing.

Jeanie: But I don't want no baby.

Mary: (Fatalistic) It's His will, and punishment for tempting the lust of a man.

Jeanie: I didn't mean to tempt nobody.

Mary: No woman does. It's something . . . a cross our good Lord gave us to bear.

(Sounds of someone tramping snow from their feet are heard outside on the veranda. Jeanie becomes alert and scrambles upstairs. Jim enters the front door.)

Jim: Damn cold wind out there tonight, I'll tell ya . . .

Mary: (Quickly on her feet getting dinner.) Soon's you get your things off, come sit down and get some warm supper in ya.

Jim: . . . Aye.

Mary: (From the kitchen.) Bit early aren't ya?

Jim: Gerries inside tonight. Don't need all of us freezing our asses off in them towers in this kind of weather. Smitty can handle things.

(Jim sits, trying to rub the circulation back into his hands. Mary casually goes through the motion of making up a tray, watching him closely to determine his mood.)

Mary: I'd better take Jeanie up something. You know, she prepared most of the dinner for me tonight . . . (No answer) . . . Cleaned the house up real nice too, don't you think? (Still no answer) She's a big help to me when she wants to be . . . Could I call her down to eat with us Jim?

Jim: I no want to see the likes of her . . .

Mary: You must . . . still love her some Jim? No matter what happened . . .

Jim: She can come down when I've finished.

Mary: Have you nothing in your heart? (No answer) You no really want her to go away I hope?

A46

Jim: I'm a man of my word.

Mary: But where?

Jim: At's her bloody worry not mine!

Mary: Ah but she's only sixteen. She's never been away from us. Where could she possibly go?

Jim: Aye she's been about more than we imagined. A regular little woman of the world.

Mary: That's not so. She never had so much as a boyfriend all through school.

Jim: Mary I've travelled half the world and I know the kind of women that take up with men the way she did. It's in em and there's nothing you can do about it! Loose women eager for the pleasures of the flesh. In the army we call them sluts.

Mary: Jeanie's not that kind of girl! I brought her up best I know how — to believe in God and what's good.

Jim: It's in em! Oh I've had my eye on that one for a while now. I could see the makins of a tramp. Struttin about in them high heel shoes, her tits stickin out. Plastering all that red shit on her face!

Mary: What about the man? Does he get no blame?

Jim: Bah! What woman don't know! When they're off in the dark with a man and he's feeling them all over! I knew she weren't the brightest, but I no thought her to be a bloody fool!

Mary: (Sadly) Aye, but she's good and could love and make a fine home for some man.

Jim: (Sarcastic) Oh God, love is it now! Ayee like in the movie pictures ehhh? With all the fine music and all. No man would want her now.

A long pause.

Mary: (Quietly) Wasn't much different with you and me Jim . . .

Jim: . . . what do you mean?

Mary: You took me before we were wed.

Jim: It was a hell of a lot different, I'll tell ya.

Mary: I was but sixteen . . . just taken my first job then with the Kerr family, remember? They'd all gone out that night . . . and you came over. They were shipping you overseas and you'd come to tell me. Just the two of us in that big house. I knew you wanted me that way . . . but I was so afraid and I knew it wasn't right. We were in my room, on the bed . . . I tried, but I couldn't stop you.

Jim: (Defensive) I don't remember that.

Mary: I understood and I wanted to be good to you . . . I just didn't want it to be there like that. Women dream there really will be fine music like in the pictures. And everything will be wonderful. How I cried afterwards, remember? And I prayed to God a thousand times to forgive me . . .

Jim: That was all a long time ago Tip. Anyway you know I wanted to marry you.

Mary: It was a long wait those years, wondering if you'd come back. If you'd still want me. I asked you to marry me before you went, but you wouldn't.

Jim: There was a war on. I might have been killed.

Mary: Aye . . .

Jim: (Flustered) Why do you twist things like this, trying to make me look no better than he is?

Mary: Jim, if you'd no come back, I'd been no better off than Jeanie. I would have been a terrible disappointment to some other man on his wedding night.

Jim: (Growing angry) Listen, there's plenty of difference! We don't even know who the son of a bitch is! He could be a bloody chink or a wog for all I know! And I no left you pregnant, woman . . .

A48

Mary: You took me though didn't you?

Jim: *(Losing his temper.)* Yes dammit I took you! What of it?

Mary: I'll not let you send Jeanie away Jim.

Jim: *(Astounded)* **You'll** not let me . . . ? and what is it **you** will do?

Mary: I want her to stay here with us . . . and have her baby.

Jim: *(Not believing his ears.)* What? !

Mary: *(Urgent plea.)* Oh look Jim, I've thought about it. After she's had the baby, she could find herself a job, and I could watch it through the day, while she was away working.

Jim: Are you daft?

Mary: It would be something for me. You've got the service and Jeanie's young with her whole life yet. I'd look after and care for the baby real well.

Jim: Aye . . . you could wheel it down the street and say, "Good morning, Mrs. Brown. How do you like our wee bastard today? "

Mary: It will still be Jeanie's . . . a warm little baby. I want it.

Jim: To hell with it! Have I no been shamed enough already? God knows how many times and **who** she spread her legs for! And now you ask me to keep the offspring of this filth! She's to leave and not set foot back here again, do you hear? I never want to be reminded of the shame she brought in this house!

Mary: It was that Billy who brought it!

Jim: *(Crashing his fist to the table.)* That's a bloody lie and you know it! He's Jimmies friend! He's a soldier! A man of honour!

(Mary rises, drained of any further fight. It is probably the first time the old woman has stood up to Jim in all the years of their marriage, and she has lost. Slowly she climbs the stairs . . .)

Mary: I no understand, I guess. A wee baby . . . honour . . .

(Jim waits until she has disappeared, then moves to the living room. He goes to his corner and cranks the phonograph. From the cabinet he takes a full whisky bottle. He places the needle on the record, and sitting in his large leather chair, pours a drink. The whine of the bagpipes playing a stirring march tune fills the room . . .)

Blackout

A49

Scene two   *The scene is several hours later as the lights come up on Jim sprawled asleep in the large armchair. The clock chimes four . . . then silence. Jim snores quietly. There is a knock on the front door and then scratching on the window pane. The door opens and Sandy totters in, very drunk. His hat sits crooked and a silly smile is glued to his face.*

Sandy: *(Singing)* Just a wee doch an doris . . . just a week doch eh loveeee . . . Hey Jimmie — ho ho! Come on, wake up Jim boy. *(Sees bottle)* Well now what ya got here? How now brown cow!

Jim: *(Slowly waking)* Aye . . . ? Sandy is it?

Sandy: Aye it's your ole buddy Sandy at's who!

Jim: Huh! Must have dozed off, that's what I did.

Sandy: That's what you did alright. I bet that's what ya did. I seen the light still on. I says, "Is that my friend Jim's house? " "Yep" I says. "Well what's he doin up at this hour? " I asked. "Well I don't know" I says. "Might be something wrong so I better go in an see" says I. An there you were — just like that when I came in. *(He eyes the bottle.)*

Jim: No no, just dozed off that's all. Well go on man, have some. *(Holds out his glass.)* Pour me a wee drop too.

Sandy: Well I don't mind if I do — aye!

Jim: At the club were you?

Sandy: *(Wagging his head.)* Noooooo . . .

Jim: Not on duty?

Sandy: Nope.

Jim: Well come on!

Sandy: *(Giggling)* Was looking after Sarah tonight, I was.

Jim: Ah, Sarah!

Sandy: Felt it was my duty after the dreadful way I behaved last Saturday night. Staying here and drinking an all! (Bursts out giggling)

Jim: She's a good woman.

Sandy: (Sober) My very words Jimmie, my very words. Made up a real fine dinner too she did. A meal fit for a king!

Jim: Tell me . . . is she any good in bed?

Sandy: (Feigning innocence) Ehhh?

Jim: Come on you ole bugger.

Sandy: How could you think it of me Jimmie? ?

Jim: She's been without a husband a good many years. I fancy she'd be alright?

Sandy: Like it was her last! (Gleeful laughter) Aye Jimmie, we'll say she's appreciative as hell! Let's put it that way eh!

Jim: Ach, you could fall in a shit house an come up covered in diamonds! I'll be damned if I know where you get your strength!

Sandy: I'm just a young boy at heart, that's what! It's what's in the heart.

Jim: (Scoffing) It's what's in the balls ya mean! Travers you're luckier than a dog with two cocks! Still screwin at your age.

Sandy: (Swaggering pride) Right! An listen Jimmie, I can give em women anythin those green laddies can — an a hell of a lot longer too! Nawww, they're not the men we was in our day. You show me one who could stand up to me even now! Go on show me one!

Jim: Aye, I believe ya.

Sandy: Can't be done I'll tell ya! An they're not men of principle anymore, like we was Jimmie. Now you take the rat's ass who did wee Jeanie in. An then up an deserts her! A fine soft young girl like her . . . You can no call that a man! (Seeing Jim) Ahhh, I should have no mentioned it. I'm sorry.

Jim: My shame is that you were here to see such happenings that morning. (Woeful shake of his head.) I don't know where I might a gone wrong. Always I did my best to be a good husband and father.

Sandy: (Patting Jim's shoulder.) You've done well.

Jim: No I've not. I've failed.

Sandy: Listen there ain't a better man anywhere what I know. An anybody what says different, will have to account to me!

Jim: (Depths of self pity) Aye, thank ye Sandy.

Sandy: And you must never think any of it your fault. The shames that it could ever happen in the house of such a fine honorable man.

Jim: Here let me fill ya . . . (Pours Sandy a drink)

Sandy: Aye, just a wee one. Thank ye. Yes, there should be some kind of laws or something. Snot right . . . (Wags his head.)

Jim: The law's for the rich, not the likes of you and I. Not the men who have known hard work all their lives.

Sandy: Aye, but we're the ones they call Johnnie on the spot when they go an get a war on their hands! Chaps like you an me. Yet anyone who pleases can come and cast shame on your home and name, and they don't give a damn 'bout that!

Jim: Aye.
The two sit quietly considering these thoughts and sipping their drinks.

Sandy: Maybe you can find her a husband somewhere . . . aye that's what you gotta do Jimmie.

Jim: Bahhh! Who the hell would want her now?

Sandy: If I was younger I sure as hell would! She's a fine looking girl. (Snaps his finger) I'd marry her like that!

A52

Loud raptures of laughter from Jim.

Sandy: I would, I would! A wee wife and little ones, something I've always wanted. But it's never been found to happen that way for me.

Jim: *(Being serious)* Aye man but you'd no take one who'd fallen?

Sandy: Ahh, that's where you're wrong Jim. There's no finer girl. Cause she was taken advantage of, don't change the fact that she's bred from good stock. Don't I know it! An that's what counts. She strayed, ayeee. But I could straighten her out fast!

Jim: *(Studying him.)* Oh it's with kindness you speak now . . .

Sandy: Jeanie's a lovely . . . any man would be honoured — I've said. But the lass has a mind of her own. She'd never want the likes of an old man like me. She's young . . . aye young and soft . . . *(His voice trails away as he dwells on this image.)* . . .
(Jim stands and paces in thought for a while. He keeps stopping as though studying Sandy, who continues contentedly on his drink. A smile comes to Jim's face and he chuckles to himself, having reached a decision. He fills the glasses once more.)

Jim: *(Toasting)* . . . to our friendship.

Sandy: Aye. Thank ye Jimmie.

(Jim walks over to the stairs.)

Jim: Jeanie!

Sandy: *(Quickly)* Oh Jim Jim, shhh. Don't be waking the Mrs. an all.

Jim: Drink up my friend! Put on the victrola and give us some music.

(Mary appears from her bedroom pulling her robe about her. She comes quickly down the stairs. Sandy struggles over to the phonograph humming and ready for the start of a good party.)

Mary: *(Frightened)* What is it Jim?

Jim: Wake the girl and bring her down.

Mary: But why Jim?

Jim: Do as I say Tip. An tell her to brush her hair a bit.

(Mary frightened obeys and goes up to Jeanie's bedroom. Jim goes back to where Sandy stands, teetering, attempting to read the label of the record. Jim begins to chuckle loudly.)

Sandy: What's so funny Jimmie?

Jim: *(Putting on the record.)* I was only thinking. If you **were** to marry Jeanie, you'd be my son-in-law! *(Loud laughter.)*

Sandy: *(A big grin.)* Aye, that's right! *(Pause)* An, an you'd be my father-in-law! ! !

(They lapse into raptures of laughter, each considering the other in their respective roles. The record begins to play but the machine has run down and we get the whining wheeze of the bagpipes in slow time, setting a mocking background to their laughter.)

Blackout

A53

Scene three   *(Week later. Lights come up on Jeanie alone in the living room, slumped across a sofa chair. She chomps on an apple and leafs through a comic book. Her whole attitude is once again relaxed and lazy.)*

Mary: *(Off from kitchen)* Jeanie? Are you comin in here to help me or not?

Jeanie: *(Not moving)* . . . uh huh . . .

(Brief silence.)

Mary: *(Off)* You know it's for you that all this is being done?

Jeanie: I know . . .

Mary: *(Off)* Well, then, you might lend a hand!

Jeanie: *(Impatient sigh)* What do you want me to do?

Mary: *(Off)* Oh honestly! You know right well there's a million things you could be helpin me with. There's sandwiches to be made. The whole house'll have to be gone over. Or did you think these things just get done by themselves before a wedding? *(Peeking in)* Look at you just lolling about! Pity we don't all have us such leisure time. It'll be different after ya married ya know. *(Pointed)* I'll not be picking up around here after the two of you.

Jeanie: I'm not feeling so good . . .

Mary: The baby?

(Jeanie rises, goes over to the full length mirror.)

Jeanie: I guess so . . . *(She studies her now slightly protruding tummy showing beneath the tight jeans. She gently rubs herself in a circular motion.)* . . . there it goes again!

Mary: *(Coming over)* What is it?

Jeanie: Something inside.

Mary: *(Brightly)* Aye. It's the baby kicking.

Jeanie: *(With distaste)* Is it alive already?

A54

Mary: It's early for movement but that's a good sign.

Jeanie: *(Viewing her stomach)* Goooood!

Mary: Let me. *(Places her hand on Jeanie's abdomen.)*

Jeanie: Feel anything?

Mary: No . . .

Jeanie: How can it move when it hardly even shows?

Mary: Ahh, it's wee but it's alive.

Jeanie: I'm not going to like this.

Mary: *(Bringing her hand away.)* It's been a long time, but once you've had the feeling you never forget it. You were a restless one. Started kicking right at three months and didn't let up till you were born.

Jeanie: What are they kicking for?

Mary: They're just movin about.

Jeanie: *(Hopefully)* Maybe I shouldn't do anything. Can't tell, I could strain something.

Mary: Aye, you best sit for a spell. Keep comfy. *(Weary)* The good Lord should have given me another pair of hands. I don't know how I can get it all done in time.

Jeanie: Why aren't we having the reception at the Legion instead of here?

Mary: Cause it cost too much and there won't be very many. Just a few friends of Dad's and Sandy's.

Jeanie: Huh. That isn't going to be much of a wedding.

Mary: Dad says it's best that way. I wanted so much just to have your Aunt Lil, but he says no. I spect it would take a lot of explaining.

Jeanie: There won't be anyone here that I know. I want Dollie to come.

Mary: That rascal. I don't know that I want her about here.

Jeanie: *(Pouting)* She's my best friend. I want somebody.

Mary: If your Dad says . . . *(There is a knock at the door.)* Oh tch . . . who can that be? I've so much to do . . .

(She bustles to the door and opens it.)

Mary: *(Surprised)* Sarah . . . Well fancy, come in, come in . . .

Sarah: *(Entering)* Hello, Mary . . .

(Mary, not prepared for this visit, behaves in a strained and nervous manner. Sarah's eyes keep constantly going to Jeanie, who has edged off to a distant corner.)

Mary: *(Exaggerated)* I was just sayin to myself in the kitchen "I must call Sarah soon one of these days. It's been nearly two weeks now." Give me your coat . .

Sarah: Thank ye Mary . . . *(Removing it.)* I've only stopped by for but a minute . . . *(Nods)* . . . Hello Jeanie . . .

Jeanie: *(Quietly)* Mrs. McIver . . .

Mary: I do think it's turned colder again don't you? Either that or my blood's gettin thinner. You're just in time for a cup of tea Sarah.

Sarah: Like I say I can't stay long. I only dropped in to see if you'd heard the news of poor Mrs. Black?

Mary: No, I didn't. What happened to the dear thing?

Sarah: Had another attack, she did.

Mary: Ohhhh tch! How bad is it?

Sarah: She's no strength at all. The doctor said she's not to leave her bed.

Mary: The doctor was there an all was he? My goodness, who's looking after her?

Sarah: I was with her through the night, and Elsie said she'd do her best to spend most of today with her.

Mary: I'll take her some broth, and look in on her over the weekend and see if there's anything needs doing. Will they be notifying the boy I wonder?

Sarah: I don't think she knows where he is. He no writes her any more.

Mary: Someone's going to have to watch her. She's too old to be on her own anyway.

Sarah: Aye. Age is an unkind thing.

Mary: Well I'm glad you told me. The poor thing. Jeanie, fix the kettle, love.

Sarah: I really mustn't stay Mary.

Mary: Nonsense, you can't be leavin without at least havin a cup of tea to warm your innards. Sit down, sit down, Sarah.

Sarah: (Awkwardly, not knowing how to start.) I had wanted to ask you something as well . . .

Mary: (Suddenly nervous) Oh? What is it Sarah?

Sarah: (Embarrassed) To tell the truth I feel very silly even askin, mind you. Knowing my Sandy and the way he's always carrying on havin his jokes on people.

Mary: Aye. He's always been that way.

Sarah: He was to dinner last night, as he is most Thursday nights . . . Course he always comes on Sundays. First time he ever missed was last Sunday. (Her gaze falling on Jeanie.) He told me something very funny on Thursday. Said he wouldn't be coming nomore. (Nervous laugh) Said he and Jeanie there . . . were going to be married?
There is no answer. Jeanie looks away and Sarah's eyes come then to Mary questioning.

Sarah: Surely it's not true . . . ?

Mary: I'm . . . sorry Sarah.

Sarah: (Hushed) Jeanie and Sandy . . . ? I thought it was just a joke he was havin on me. (Faltering) Who would have ever imagined. (Staring at Jeanie.) God in heaven! (She stands just shaking her head.) Well I hope you're both very happy. May I please have my coat Mary.

Mary: (Weakly) No one meant to hurt you Sarah.

Sarah: (Getting her coat herself.) No, no, please, don't a no start offering me sympathy. It only just came as such a shock, that's all. Finding out people that you think are your friends . . . (Choking on the words.) have been carrying on behind your back.

Mary: It's not true Sarah.

Sarah: But it is the truth! (To Jeanie, losing all her composure.) You, you little scamp! What do you want with someone like Sandy? ? Why don't you get somebody younger like yourself? ! Disgustin cheap people, that's what ya are! ! (She bursts into tears.)

Mary: Sarah! !

Sarah: An you Mary . . . all these years, all these years . . .
Sarah exits sobbing. Mary follows, standing in the doorway and calling after her.

Mary: Don't ever come back here again, ya hear? ! You don't call us things like that!
Mary's voice trails off, and covering her face she crosses quickly to the sofa where she sobs quietly. Jeanie crosses and closes the front door.
Jeanie: Whew, she really flipped.

Mary: (Angered) Do you no see the trouble you've made for everyone Jeanie! She's been my best friend all my life.

Jeanie: It wasn't my idea to marry him!

Mary: I pray God it's a wise decision your father has made.

Jeanie: She can have him for all I care . . .

Mary: Hold your tongue! It's all been done for you!

A56

Jeanie: I'll make you some tea.

Mary gives a weary nod. Jeanie exits to the kitchen. The old woman blows her nose a few times and collects her composure. The front door opens and Jim enters carrying a large parcel.

Jim: Hi Tip, was that Sarah I just passed goin down the street? *(Mary nods.)* Thought it was. Didn't say a bloody word she didn't. Fact she never even looked up at me.

Mary: She was here asking about the wedding.

Jim: Ummmmmm. Well . . . can't be helped. She's a good woman. Always liked Sarah. Where's Jeanie?

Mary: Making the tea . . .

Jim: Don't be letting it bother you Tip, somes always got to be hurt by these things. Jeanie! *Jeanie cautiously enters from the kitchen.*

Jim: Come in here. Picked up a little something for you on the way home I did. *(Indicates the parcel.)*

Jeanie: For me?

Jim: Darn it, that's what I said didn't I! Well go on, open it!

Jeanie goes to the parcel and slowly unwraps it. Jim stands with a pleased smile waiting. She removes a white wedding gown, not boxed, but merely folded and wrapped in the brown paper.

Jim: Well . . . ?

Jeanie: Oh, it's beautiful. See mom?

(Mary rises, her attention completely captivated by the gown now.)

Mary: Aye . . . Where'd ya get it Jim?

Jim: Got it at the seconds on fourth street. It ain't brand new, but I'll be damned if I'll be payin out a whole lot of money for a dress you wear one day. The fellow there told me it cost fifty dollars when it was new.

Mary: *(Taking it.)* Here let me see Jeanie . . . *(She examines it closely.)* . . . bit soiled near the bottom, but spect we can clean that up easy enough.

Jim: Sure ya can! Go over it a bit with an iron an it'll look good as new. Only been worn once.

Mary goes to the full length mirror, and instinctively holds it up to herself. She is enchanted with the dress.

Mary: Aye . . . it is beautiful isn't it. *(Second thought)* Do you think it will be proper, her wearin this? I mean seein we're not having it in the church an all?

Jim: Hell a weddings's — a wedding and that there's a wedding dress ain't it!

Mary: I know, but . . . *(Dismisses it.)* Come here Jeanie and see how it fits on you.

Jeanie comes over and Mary holds it up to the girl.

Mary: Ahh . . . you'll look lovely.

Jeanie: Wait'll Dollie sees this! Dad can I have Dollie come?

Jim: I guess so.

Jeanie: *(Overjoyed)* Weeeeee! ! Thanks dad! ! *(She bounds off toward the phone.)*

Mary: O dear we're going to have to make a few adjustments. Upstairs now young lady and put it on.

Jeanie: I'm just going to call Dollie first!

Mary: Now don't be fooling about Jeanie! I've so much to do as it is.

Jeanie grudgingly consents and is followed up the stairs by Mary nattering behind her.

Jim: *(Calling after them.)* You help your mother now Jeanie! I want everything ship-shape. You'll be married at four pm tomorrow.

Quick curtain

A57

Scene four *(Late afternoon the next day — the Dougal home. The stage is empty and in semi-darkness. We hear the laughter of voices and singing, approaching, growing louder as they reach the veranda outside. The door flies open and Jim, quite high, enters, his arm around Sandy's neck. Sandy is very drunk. Three or four guards enter, all laughing and talking at once. Then Jeanie in her gown and carrying a small bunch of flowers. Dollie wearing some of her mother's clothes enters. She carries a small Brownie box camera with a flash on it. Mary is the last to enter. The entire scene hums with noise as everyone talks at once, removing their coats, etc. Dollie approaches one of the Vets and discusses something.)*

Tommie: *(Above all the noise.)* Well come on man, break out the drinks damn it!
(Loud approval from all the men.)

Art: Wait a minute everybody! Over here first! *(Starts herding them towards one end of the room.)* Come on, the little girl wants to take a nice photo of the whole bunch of ya!

(Loud "ohs" and "ahs" from everyone, reluctant to oblige.)

Jim: Oh to hell with it! I don't want my picture taken!

Another: Aye, me neither!

Mary: Please Jim, it's Jeanie's weddin photos!

Bob: Yeah come on Jim you have to be in em! You're the bride's father!

(Agreement from all. Jim grumbles and joins the rest, shuffling about awkwardly, forming a group. Dollie stands off to the side looking down into her camera, waiting.)

Art: That's right everybody. Wait a minute, I'll get in there myself!

Tommie: Fer Christ sakes, Sandy, you're spose to stand next to your new wife! *(Gives him a shove.)*

(Everyone breaks into laughter and Sandy is handled along by each person. Art places him

beside Jeanie then puts his own arm around Sandy and takes a pose.)

Dollie: Get ready now . . .

(They all freeze except Sandy who can't stop weaving. The flash goes off and the group instantly breaks, groaning about how they can't see, all talking and laughing again.)

Tommie: Well, where the hell are those drinks? !

Jim: Aye aye! Tip, come on give me a hand! *(He guides her off into the kitchen with him.)*

(Everyone starts talking and laughing again. Dollie and Jeanie pose with their arms round each other for Art to take a picture.)

Bob: *(To all)* Now listen everybody; we don't want to be staying too long! Sandy and his bride got things of their own they want to do!

(Loud round of laughter from everyone except Jeanie. Dollie whispers the meaning into her ear.)

Tommie: Ahh, you don't want to be saying them kinds of things! Look at the lass, she's embarrassed!

Another: She don't look bare-assed to me!

(Another round of laughter. Jim and Mary enter carrying several beers which are quickly handed about. A cheer comes from all.)

Bob: Give the girls one too Jim!

Jim: What? I'll be damned! They're too young!

(This is met with jeers from all. Reluctantly he hands Jeanie and Dollie each a bottle of beer. The group approves of him once more.)

Jim: Now I want you all to drink your share! There's a whole ice box full out there!

Bob: God bless you for your generosity Dougal!

Jim: Aye it's not every day a man gives away his daughter!

Tommie: Hear hear! and a finer man you couldn't have found! *(Agreement from all)*

Jim: Ahhh, love works in strange ways I'll tell ya. There he is . . . my best friend . . . my daughter. And I have nary an idea how they feel over each other. Then one day my Jeanie comes to me and she says, "Dad, I love Sandy." . . . *(Appreciative ohs and ahs from the group.)* . . . An there he is . . . not sayin a word! For obvious reasons of course. Because he's a deceitful old man! *(Round of laughter and clapping.)* . . . Well I got them together. And I said, "I'm a man of a few years myself ya know. And I hope I've gathered a bit of wisdom with it . . . Now Sandy," I says, "it's true you're a few years older than my lass, but! I know the man that you are too. I know you'll treat my Jeanie right . . . an them's the things that's important to me! " So I said to them, "You have my blessing". And a finer man it couldn't be, as you already said gentlemen . . .

(With this Jim gives a nod of the head and tilts back his bottle of beer. There is a loud round of "hear hear" and clapping.)

Tommie: Well I was the best man and I'm suppose to make a speech. But I'll be damned if I'm gonna!

Bob: That's a blessing!

Tommie: Enough from you Bob. Really I don't have much to say. Sandy's been a friend of mine for a good many years an . . . it's nice to see him settling down at last. I hope the both of you are very happy. I think I'm suppose to propose a toast to . . . ah to the bride. So gentlemen if you'll rise an join me in this toast. "To a very lovely bride."

All: Hear hear! *(They all drink up.)*

Bob: In case you don't know it, you're suppose to respond to that toast Sandy! *(Group laughter.)*

Sandy: I never been married before — how was I to know? *(Laughter)* But it's the truth anyway.

It comes a wee bit late for me in life . . . But I — I'll be a good husband you know. I want to thank you Tommie for what you said about my wee wife . . . (*Looks at Jeanie.*) . . . she's — she's a lovely thing alright . . . an I'm a lucky man. (*Awkwardly wipes the froth from his mouth with his cuff.*) An I think the drink's catching up on me too! (*Snorts with laughter.*)

Bob: There ain't enough drink in the world for Sandy Travers!

(*All agree! *)

Sandy: To hell with you too Bob!

(*Tommie has wound the gramaphone and put on a record of the anniversay waltz. He begins humming with it.*)

Tommie: Dahhh — dadada . . . dadadahhhh . . . dadada . . . You're supposed to dance with your bride, Sandy!
(*Everyone agrees and they drag Sandy over to Jeanie and Dollie seated on the sofa. Jeanie is embarrassed and, giggling, hides her face and turns away. Dollie tugs at her.*)

Dollie: Come on, Dougal, you're suppose to dance with him!

Jeanie: I don't want to. (*Gives Dollie a playful shove back.*) You dance with him!

(*Loud round of laughter and they pull her up and hand her to Sandy. The two of them stumble about awkwardly, Jeanie not knowing how to dance and Sandy too drunk. Everyone breaks into song, singing with the music. A Vet dances with Mary and Art takes Dollie for a few whirls.*)

All:
  So tell me I may always dance
  The anniversary waltz with you
  Tell me this is real romance
  An anniversary dream come true
  Let this be the answer to all future years . . .
  Millions of smiles and a few little tears . . .

(*Sandy suddenly loses his balance, falling flat on his face. Everyone begins laughing and teasing him.*)

Bob: Come on Sandyyy!

Tommie: Will you look at the fine groom now! ! That's the way you're suppose to be the morning after! ! !

(*All jeer with delight at this and coax Jeanie to make him get up and dance some more.*)

Sandy: (*On all fours.*) What I need is another bloody beer, that's all!

All: Give him a beer, Jim!

Jim: I'll give him a beer alright! Here ya're, my fine laddie!

(*He stands pouring it on Sandy's head. Everyone approves with laughter.*)

Sandy: That's a hell of a thing to do to a good beer!

Jim: An that's no way to be talking to your father-in-law!

Sandy: (*Falling back on the floor with laughter.*) I nay heard anything so funny! Help me up, for God's sake, Jimmie!

(*There is a good deal of grunting and wheezing and Jim helps him to his feet. Slowly the laughter subsides.*)

Tommie: I think it was time we was on our way. Leave the loved ones alone.

Jim: What the hell ya sayin man? We're just startin to have us a party here!

Tommie: Oh, I think Sandy's got other things on his mind Jim!

(*Snickers from everyone.*)

Jim: No, you can't go. Good Lord, I got all the drink in the cooler and Mary here prepared a lot of food an all!

Bob: It wouldn't be fair to Sandy, Jim. They want to be alone.

Jim: To hell with em!

Tommie: I tell ya what. We'll take it over to my place — how's that Jim?

Bob: It's okay by me! *(Others all join in agreement.)*

Jim: Well alright then. *(Starting for the kitchen.)* Come on, give me a hand. Good God, I thought you were all losing your heads for a minute!

(Some follow him into the kitchen to help; others begin to put their coats on. Sandy has been placed in a chair and sits in a stupor with glazed eyes.)

Dollie: Well I'll see you, kiddo. Everybody's going.

Jeanie: *(Suddenly frightened.)* Gee you don't have to go already. Mom, you're not going too are you?

(Mary stands helpless wanting to say something consoling to the girl at this time, but she cannot find any words.)

Mary: We must, Jeanie . . . *(Lost for words.)* . . . it'll be alright . . .

(The group suddenly sweeps back through carrying sandwiches, beer, etc.)

Jim: Come on Tip, we're going over to Tommie's!

(Jim is the first one out the door. The others follow, all bidding their goodbyes. Dollie whispers something to Jeanie and then disappears with the rest. Mary takes a quick look back and exits. Bob peeks back in before closing the door.)

Bob: Sandy, I don't want you misbehavin now! *(Loud snort of laughter.)*

(The door slams shut and the noise from the group quickly fades. There is a long silence. Then a few sniffles from Jeanie. It is so quiet you can hear Sandy wheezing as he breathes. He groans, belches loud and suddenly realizes everyone has left.)

Sandy: Where the hell . . . they all gone . . . ?

(His head bobs and he notices Jeanie on the far side of the room, sobbing quietly. He struggles to his feet, stands trying to get his co-ordination in check. He watches her.)

Sandy: Ahhh, you're not cryin are you? . . . *(He shuffles over toward her.)* . . . Ohhh Jeanie come on, come on . . . *(He reaches down and gently touches her arm. She pulls away. He speaks to her with kindness.)* Ohh now don't be frightened of old Sandy . . . come on . . . my head's splittin. I need ya to help me up the stairs, lass . . .

(She looks up at him now as she begins to regain her courage. She wipes away the tears.)

Sandy: *(Big smile.)* See. It's only me . . . *(She slowly stands)* That a girl . . . there's nothin to be scared of . . .

(He turns and shuffles towards the stairs. She walks hesitantly a few steps behind him. He stops when he reaches the stairs, and looks back to her for help.)

Sandy: Oh I don't trust meself on these stairs . . . will ye give me a hand?

(She stands beside him and he gently leans on her, his arm about her shoulder. He keeps purring in soft tones as they start slowly up the steps, their backs to the audience.)

Sandy: Easy now . . . that a girl . . . *(Pause)* . . . that a girl . . .

(Reaching the top of the stairs, his hand slowly slides down her back, and he gently caresses her buttocks . . . suddenly clutching them firmly.)

Sandy: *(Breaking into a loud hoarse laugh.)* That a girl!

(Quickly he pushes her into the bedroom and the door slams shut.)

Four beats of silence.

Slowly fade the setting to darkness.

End Curtain

Three Women

A trilogy of one-act plays

Hugh Garner

Hugh Garner was born in England in 1913, "into a family of Yorkshire woollen weavers, drunkards on the male side and temperance fanatics on the female," and came to Canada as a boy of six. Since then he has made his home in Toronto, a city that has served as the locale of most of his books and stories. He received his formal education in eight East End schools of the Toronto Public School System, and wasted three years in a technical high school, dropping out of school forever on his sixteenth birthday, from Grade Ten.

In his early years Garner made his living from "every kind of job listed by most other North American writers, from harvest hand and packer of Lux soap flakes to grocery store manager, magazine editor and public relations director."

After serving as an infantryman in the Abraham Lincoln Battalion of the International Brigades during the Spanish Civil War, and six years in the Royal Canadian Navy during World War Two, mostly on corvettes on the North Atlantic and North African convoy routes, Garner sat down in the winter of 1946 and wrote a novel, *Cabbagetown*. While this novel was going the rounds of disinterested publishers he wrote a second novel, *Storm Below*, which was accepted in two days by William Collins Sons, and published in March, 1949. From the day of its acceptance Garner became a professional writer, and has remained one ever since.

His later novels are *Present Reckoning, Waste No Tears, Silence On The Shore, The Sin Sniper* and *A Nice Place To Visit*. Four collections of short stories, *The Yellow Sweater, Hugh Garner's Best Stories, Men And Women* and *Violation Of The Virgins*, contain most of the more than eighty short stories he has written to date. He has also written a book of humorous essays, *Author! Author!* and an autobiographical work, *The Writing Years*.

Garner won the Governor General's Award for Fiction in 1963 for *Hugh Garner's Best Stories*, and has received three Senior Arts Fellowships and a Playwriting Fellowship from

A Trilogy Of One-Act Plays

the Canada Council. He is an Associate Fellow of Winters College, York University, and in 1972 was a recipient of an Award of Merit by the City of Toronto "For Distinguished Public Service."

His short stories and essays have been reprinted in more than fifty anthologies, textbooks and translations throughout the world, including *Best American Short Stories, 1952* and the *Oxford World's Classics.*

During the 1950's and early 1960's he wrote twelve successful television scripts that have been performed over the CBC, BBC, and Australian TV networks.

Garner has adapted three of his televison plays — each with a woman as protagonist — as one-act stage plays. This dramatic trilogy, which may be played as a repertory theatre, is titled *Three Women.*

Photographs courtesy of the Canadian Broadcasting Corporation.

Some Are So Lucky was presented as a half-hour TV play on the program "On Camera" over the CBC-TV network, Dec. 17, 1956, produced and directed by Ted Kotcheff, with leads by Anna Cameron and James Doohan. This production was re-telecast over the BBC-TV network on kinescope, Jan. 12, 1957.

The play was then re-cast, re-produced and re-telecast on the program "First Person" over the CBC-TV network on Aug. 17, 1960, produced and directed by David Gardner, with leads by Charmion King and James Doohan. This production was re-telecast over the CBC-TV network on the program "Summer Circuit" on videotape on Aug. 10, 1961, and again over the CBC-TV Pacific Network in 1966. The play was shot on movie film for the CBC-TV program "Canadian Short Stories", adapted by Brian Barney and starring Jackie Burroughs and Michael Tate in 1971. This adaptation was re-telecast on regional programs of the BBC in 1971. The play was adapted for radio by Len Peterson and broadcast as part of a program called "Four By Garner" on "CBC Stage", Feb. 21, 1964.

The Magnet was presented as a half-hour television play on the program "First Person" over the CBC-TV network on June 15, 1960, produced and directed by Harvey Hart with leads by Charmion King and Don Francks.

A Trip For Mrs. Taylor was presented as a half-hour television play on the program "On Camera" over the CBC-TV network on June 3, 1957, produced and directed by Leo Orenstein, with the lead played by Catherine Proctor. This production was re-telecast on kinescope over the BBC-TV network on July 12, 1957, and re-telecast over the Australian TV network in October, 1957. The play was then produced as a dramatized reading on the CBC-TV program "Take Thirty", starring Anna Cameron, on June 1, 1964.

This play was produced as a stage presentation by the Brockville Theatre Guild on Nov. 4, 1966.

Some are so lucky

Characters

Ethel Walton, 35, a wife and mother.
Rod Murphy, 38, an insurance underwriter.
Willie Barnard, 30, a Jewish disk-jockey.
Sue Barnard, 25, Willie's wife.
Waiter, friend of Rod Murphy's.
1st Businessman
2nd Businessman

Scene One *This scene takes place in front of the curtain, which remains down throughout.*

A downtown street on a cold windy evening in the fall. The time is 1955. There is a bus stop sign on a post, and the sidewalk around the bus stop is lighted by a streetlight. At the other side of the stage is a blinking neon sign spelling out "Cocktails".

Rod Murphy stands at the bus stop. People pass by on the sidewalk behind him, and a few join him at the bus stop. Ethel Walton approaches. She is clutching her upturned coat collar and has her head turned against the wind. Rod notices her, looks away, then quickly looks at her again. She joins the group at the bus stop, turning her back to Rod, who moves around trying to catch a glimpse of her face. When she faces him his face lights up with recognition, but she stares at him blankly. A little uncertain now he raises his hat.

Rod: Ethel? Ethel Walton?

Ethel: *(Without recognition.)* Why . . . hello . . .

Rod: You don't remember me, do you?

Ethel: *(Tentative smile, studies him.)* Your face looks familiar . . .

Rod: Rod!

Ethel: Rod . . .?

Rod: Rod Murphy.

Ethel: *(Steps back and looks him over.)* Oh . . . of course. *(Still no recognition.)*

Rod: It's been a long time.

Ethel: *(Her face lighting up and her voice becoming animated.)* Of course! Sure! Rod Murphy! *(Takes him by the sleeve, steps back and looks him over.)* You've certainly changed. Why, when I knew you, you were — well, just a kid. You've grown a lot heavier since then.

Rod: *(Laughs)* Some of us do. *(They move out of the way of a passing couple.)*

Ethel: *(Pulls him back from the group at the bus stop.)* What are you doing these days?

Rod: Oh, nothing much. I've been in the insurance business for years.

Ethel: Married?

Rod: *(With a cynical laugh.)* I'm too old to get married.

Ethel: Oh, you're not!

Rod: You know, Ethel, meeting you like this is just how I always pictured it would be. I've said to myself a thousand times, "Some day I'll run into Ethel Walton on the street."

Ethel: *(Surprised)* You mean you thought of me all this time?

Rod: I know it sounds corny, but I never forgot you — even if we only had three or four dates. I can still remember seeing you the first time — back in 1939. It was at the Masonic Hall — Remember, they had dance halls then? — down on Clayburn Street. I even remember the orchestra playing Darn That Dream and The Very Thought Of You. *(Laughs)*

Ethel: *(A pensive smile.)* Yes, I remember it now. *(Shivers and clasps her collar to her throat.)*

Rod: You're cold! Listen, Ethel, let's go and have a coffee, or maybe a drink?

Ethel: *(Obviously acquiescing.)* I really should go home.

Rod: You're married I suppose? *(They walk slowly away from the bus stop.)*

Ethel: Oh yes. I've been married now for fourteen years.

Rod: Any children, Ethel?

Ethel: One. My Bobby is twelve now — going on thirteen.

Rod: Did you marry anyone I know?

Ethel: I don't think so. My husband's name is Blanton — Ernest Blanton. Do you know him?

Rod: No, but I envy him. I always though that the man who married you would be one of the luckiest guys in the world.

Ethel: Thank you. I wish you'd tell my husband that. *(She shivers and stamps her feet. Rod looks up at the neon sign advertising the bar.)*

Rod: Listen, Ethel, let's go in here and have a drink. It'll warm you up. *(He starts to walk towards the sign, but Ethel hesitates.)*

Ethel: I'm not used to going to places like that.

Rod: It's just for a few minutes.

Ethel. *(Begins walking with Rod towards the sign.)* I really shouldn't. I promised Ernest I wouldn't be late tonight.

Rod: A half hour or so won't make much difference.

Ethel: *(Kittenish)* Don't you keep me too long. Promise?

Rod: *(Laughs)* I promise.
They exit.

B8

Scene Two   *The curtain goes up to reveal the interior of the cocktail bar. There are several small tables ringing a small dance floor. An out-of-sight jazz combo plays intermittently throughout the play. Some of the tables are occupied, one by the two businessmen and another by Willie and Sue Barnard.*

Rod and Ethel enter. Ethel is still wearing her coat, but Rod has checked his hat and coat. Rod takes Ethel's arm and steers her across the room to an empty table. A waiter follows them. They are picked up in a spotlight. The rest of the stage remains in a half-light in which the other occupants go through their actions in pantomime.

Waiter: Good evening, Mr. Murphy, what can I get you tonight?

Rod: Hello, Art. What'll you have, Ethel?

Ethel: *(Attempting to appear sophisticated.)* I guess I'll have a Collins — a Tom Collins. *(Rod and Waiter exchange glances.)*

Rod: Ethel, in this weather!

Ethel: I always drink Collinses.

Rod: I'll have a rye and soda, and the lady will have a Collins. *(The waiter nods and exits.)*

Ethel: *(Stares around the room.)* I've never been here before, although I pass it every night on my way home from work. Ernest and I do most of our drinking at home — or at parties.

Rod: Where do you work, Ethel?

Ethel: I took a little job in a department store for a while. I get so bored sitting around the house by myself. With Ernest away at business all day, and Bobby at school — you know.

Rod: Sure. I understand. *(The Waiter brings them their drinks.)*

Ethel: *(Glancing around her at the other customers.)* I should have ordered the kind of cocktail you get in those glasses with a stem. They look nicer, don't you think?

Rod: I'll order you a martini or manhattan next time.

Ethel: *(Sips her drink and laughs.)* Don't rush me, Rod. I'm not much of a drinker.

Rod: You haven't changed hardly at all. You're still as pretty as you were at seventeen.

Ethel: Me!

Rod: You don't seem any older than you were the last time I saw you.

Ethel: I feel older though.

Rod: Has your married life been happy?

Ethel: Are you kidd - -! I guess I can't complain. We have our spats now and again, you know.

Rod: It's hard to figure, isn't it?

Ethel: What is?

Rod: Well, the way things happen. The way we've changed. That first night I met you at the Masonic Hall I was out of work. My two-bits admission came from finding some empty milk and ginger-ale bottles under the cellar steps.

Ethel: *(Sips her drink.)* Nobody had any money in those days.

Rod: *(Laughing.)* I'll say we didn't! I remember Jim Sturdy and I rolling cigarettes at the dance-hall from Alex Myers' package of tobacco.

Ethel: *(Pensively)* I miss those days though. Boy, did we have a good time! My girlfriend Brenda Hastings and I used to go to three dances a week then.

Rod: I'd forgotten her name, but I remember her. She always hated me.

Ethel: I'd like to see her again. She got married and moved out West. She borrowed my overnight bag and never returned it to me. *(Rod smiles, they both drink.)* I'll bet you can't remember what I was wearing when you met me first?

Rod: *(Thinks for a moment.)* Yes I can. You wore a gray skirt and a red sweater.

Ethel: For crying out loud!

Rod: *(Hurriedly)* You wore your hair long and combed straight back. It ended in waves that you clipped together with a butterfly bow on your neck.

Ethel: *(Laughs)* You must have had it bad. *(They finish their drinks. Rod catches the Waiter's eye and motions him over with a finger.)*

Rod: *(To the Waiter.)* Art, some more of the same for me, and for the lady — *(Turns to her.)*

Ethel: I think I'll try a Manhattan. *(Waiter picks up their empty glasses and leaves.)*

Rod: I guess I did have it bad. You were the only girl I ever felt that way about.

Ethel: *(Places her hand on his arm but speaks laconically.)* That's sweet.

Rod: *(Not looking at her.)* I'll never forget that first night at the Masonic Hall. There I was, a skinny runt in a fifteen dollar hand-me-down suit, and socks that had knots of darning wool at the heels. I was so nervous I bumped into every second couple on the floor. I couldn't even talk. I wanted to ask you your name, and where you lived, but I was too scared. *(Ethel stares at his profile. She works her lips as if unable to make up her mind to remain serious or not.)* I wanted to let you see the things I had stored up inside me: the ambition and — and integrity, and plans for the future. I wanted you to hear the smart talk I'd learned and to know I'd read good books, and won a fifty dollar scholarship in my last year at school — *(The Waiter places their drinks in front of them.)*

Ethel: *(Skeptically)* You really wanted to say those things to me?

Rod: Yes.

Ethel: *(Picks up her drink and looks at it.)* It was a long time ago.

Rod: Yeah, I guess it was too long ago. *(Gives an embarrassed laugh and lifts his glass.)* To the pretty girl in the red sweater, and the innocent kid with the holes in his socks. *(Ethel touches her glass to his, then drains it.)* I thought you said you couldn't drink?

Ethel: *(Laughs and holds up the glass.)* There isn't much in one of these.

Rod: I forgot to ask you. How's the rest of your family?

Ethel: Dad's dead, you know —

Rod: Oh, I'm sorry.

Ethel: It was in the papers. He fell from a smokestack. He was a foreman steeplejack.

Rod: Golly, I'm sorry to hear it.

Ethel: He was only fifty-six. It was just after the war.

Rod: How's your mother?

Ethel: She hasn't been feeling too well lately . . . She lives with my Aunt May. Did you ever meet May?

Rod: No. Remember, I was only in your house once.

Ethel: I was thinking of somebody else.

Rod: How's your young brother and sister?

Ethel: Shirley's a dietician in a hospital in Cleveland, and Joe is married. He's got a good job; he's a machinist at McReady Gear and Tool.

Rod: I'm glad they're both doing well. *(Smiles)* Remember the night we came downtown to see Cab Calloway?

Ethel: *(Motions to the waiter as Rod did.)* I think so. Sure, I remember

Rod: I was the richest guy in the world that night. It was a couple of weeks after I started work with the insurance company, and my twelve dollar salary was the most money I'd earned in years. Remember when Calloway sang Minnie The Moocher and you started singing with him, and the woman in front of us in the show turned round and gave you a dirty look?

Ethel: How can you still remember those things?

The Waiter sets another cocktail in front of Ethel. She takes a drink.

Waiter: It's been a long time since you were here last, Mr. Murphy.

Rod: *(Laughs)* I guess it's been all of two weeks, Art.

Ethel drains her glass while Rod is talking to the Waiter. She signals to the Waiter, with a "cute" little smile, to bring her another. She eats the cherry out of the empty glass.

Waiter: The Paulsons were in here last night. They told me they're moving to the Coast.

Rod: I guess Fred got the job he was after out there.

Waiter: Yes he did.

Ethel: *(Gives the Waiter a ladylike smile.)* Rod, why don't you introduce me to your friend?

Rod: Oh, sorry! Art, this is Mrs. — This is Ethel, an old friend of mine.

Ethel: *(Offering her hand.)* How do you do, Art.

Waiter: *(Hesitates, unsmiling.)* I'm pleased to meet you.

Rod: How's business, Art?

Waiter: So-so, Mr. Murphy. It's always slow this time of year.

Ethel: I guess I didn't tell you, Rod. Ernie — Ernest and I went to the Mixing Bowl a couple of weeks ago.

Rod: That's pretty swanky.

Ethel: I never missed a dance, although my

B11

husband only danced with me twice. I'm crazy about dancing. I go dancing every week, even yet. *(The Waiter stares at her deadpan.)*

Rod: It's good for the figure I guess.

Waiter: Well, I've got to get back to work. *(Smiles at Rod then turns to Ethel unsmiling.)* And another one for you, Miss?

Ethel: Sure thing. *(A couple get up and begin dancing together.)* I never knew they had dancing in here. Do you dance much, Rod?

Rod: Not much, I'm afraid. *(Smiles)* My dancing is all pretty old-fashioned now. I guess I gave up dancing just around the time that the jitterbug was coming in.

Ethel: That was fun!

Rod: There used to be a little guy go to the Masonic that we called Seabiscuit. Remember him? He used to tear around the floor a mile a minute.

Ethel: *(Loud laugh.)* Seabiscuit!

Rod: I haven't seen him since.

Ethel: Do you ever see Bob Lawrence?

Rod: *(Puzzled)* I don't think I know him.

Ethel: All the girls were crazy about him. — I went with him after — after I knew you. He was swell!

Rod: I remember you like chopped olive sandwiches. You were the only girl I ever knew who ate chopped olive sandwiches. Both times we went into the Greek's on the way home from the dance you ordered them.

The Waiter brings Ethel another drink. Raises his eyebrows in a question to Rod, who shakes his head.

Ethel: I'm still crazy about olive sandwiches. *(Takes a long drink.)* You know, the waiter reminds me of a young fellow who roomed at our house last winter. His name was Ken. Ernie got jealous of him for nothing at all, and kicked

him out. I threatened to leave too, and that scared my husband all right. *(Simpering)* I feel that things would have been different if I'd married you, Rod. *(Rod's face lights up. Ethel stares as another couple begin to dance.)* Why don't we dance a while? It'd be fun.

Rod: But don't you have to go home, Ethel?

Ethel: *(Laughs)* I can phone Ernie and tell him we're stocktaking at the store.

Rod: But — *(Puzzled)* I don't want to cause any trouble for you. After all —

Ethel: *(Nuzzles his shoulder with her cheek)* There won't be any trouble, silly. After all, it's years since we were last out together.

Rod: I wouldn't want you to do that.

Ethel: *(Smiles archly.)* You wouldn't!

Rod: Well, I mean . . .

Ethel: Where's the phone?

Rod: *(Points)* Over there. There's a booth in the corner past the bar.

Ethel: *(Gets up, begins to walk away then returns and finishes her drink. Fishes the cherry from her glass, and chewing it leans over Rod, who has sat down again.)* I won't be a minute, dear. *(She walks across to the wings, a little seductively and a little unsteady, but not too much so. Rod watches her go, then finishes his own drink.)*

Waiter: *(Walks over and stands at Rod's elbow.)* Another one, Mr. Murphy?

Rod: *(Jarred from his thoughts.)* Hey! *(Looks up.)* Oh no, Art. I'm fine for now, thank you.

Waiter: Does the lady want another?

Rod: Probably. But don't bring her one right now. We may be going home.

The Waiter leaves. He sees Ethel coming back to her table and makes a detour to avoid meeting her. Ethel pauses beside Rod, who stands up.

Rod: *(Turns to her and smiles.)* Are you going home or are we dancing?

Ethel: *(Nudging him with her shoulder.)* What do you think?

Rod: For once in my life I don't know what to think.

Ethel: We're dancing. *(Takes off her coat and lays it carelessly over the back of her chair.)*

They join the two or three other couples on the floor. They both dance fairly well, but Ethel is getting slightly tipsy. When the brief number is over they return to their table.

Ethel: *(Throws herself down on to her chair. Sprawls.)* Whew! The old gray mare ain't what she usta be!

Rod: *(Laughs)* You can say that for both of us.

Ethel: *(Straightens up and picks up her empty glass.)* The service is lousy here.

Rod: *(Hurriedly)* I'll get some drinks. *(Turns and catches the Waiter's eye. Holds up two fingers.)* How old did you say young Bobby was, Ethel?

Ethel: *(Smiles fondly to herself.)* Going on thirteen. *(Gives a short laugh.)* He's a little devil! Since I been working he's been getting away with murder. His teacher sent the nastiest letter the other day — wait till I find it. *(Searches through her purse.)* I must have left it at home. Anyway, she didn't need to be so snippy. She claimed Bobby was being neglected ... *(The Waiter puts down their drinks and takes away the empty glasses.)* Neglected. I'll bet she never had a kid of her own in her life. *(Fans herself with her open hand.)* Is it getting hot in here or is it me? *(Takes a long drink.)*

Rod: It is a little warm. Tell me, did you get your husband on the phone? Did you tell him you were stocktaking?

Ethel: Stocktaking? No, I told him I was staying at my mother's place tonight. *(Winks)* She hasn't got a phone, so he can't check on me.

Rod: Did he believe you?

Ethel: *(Surprised at the question.)* Sure.

Rod: *(Shakes his head.)* It beats me.

Ethel: *(Snappishly)* Why shouldn't he believe me? I don't make a habit of this, you know! *(Finishes her drink.)*

Rod: I didn't mean that, Ethel.

Several people get up to dance. Ethel watches them critically, then turns to Rod.

Ethel: *(Now mollified)* Okay if you didn't mean it. *(Smiles)* What would a bachelor know about it anyway?

Rod: *(Leans across the table smiling.)* Nothing, I guess.

Ethel: I guess it's not so lonely for a man. You can always pick up a girl when you need one, can't you? *(Rod nods but straightens back in his chair.)* What business did you say you were in?

Rod: Insurance.

Ethel: You look pretty prosperous. I guess a lot of people are buying insurance these days? Of course, there's a lot of walking in it — ringing doorbells and things.

Rod: I'm not a salesman. Anyway, things have changed today. There's not so much door-to-door selling as there was when we were kids. Or weekly collecting either.

Ethel: There isn't? An insurance man'd have a hard time finding me in.

Rod: How much insurance do you carry?

Ethel: *(Places a finger to her lips.)* Let me see. I never was one for that kind of stuff. I think it's fifteen thousand dollars. Ernie has some group insurance from his union too.

Rod: *(Stares in disbelief.)* What does your husband do, Ethel?

Ethel: He works for a packing company. They wanted him to go on the road — selling, you know, but he'd sooner stay in the plant. He's got a good job. They've got a forty hour week and a pension plan.

Willie and Sue Barnard get up and begin to dance. One of the two Businessmen who share a table is emphasizing a point by banging his fist on the table. Ethel and Rod watch the dancers. Ethel catches the Waiter's eye and orders drinks.

Rod: I like that number.

Ethel: It's too fast for me. *(Holds her empty glass up and studies it. Simpers.)* I like these cocktails. Ernie always has a bottle of rye over the weekend. That is unless we go out to a party.

Rod: I guess you go out quite a bit?

Ethel: We do. We have quite a few — maybe I shouldn't say it — but influential friends. A couple of weeks ago we went to the Jackman's. Do you know Larry Jackman?

Rod: I'm afraid I don't.

Ethel: He's a district chief in the fire department

Rod: *(With a wan smile.)* Oh yes.
The waiter sets two drinks on the table. Rod looks up at him and he shrugs. Rod finishes his old drink, and the Waiter takes the empty glasses away. Ethel sips her drink.

Ethel: Don't you ever have to pay for drinks here?

Rod: Art'll give me a tab when I'm ready to go.

Ethel: *(Watches the dancers, then stands up.)* Let's dance, Rod.

Rod: *(Smiles and pushes himself to his feet.)* Okay.
The spotlight follows them as they dance. Ethel lays her cheek against Rod's chest so that he almost has to carry her. He wears a worried smile. Ethel staggers a bit and bumps into a couple. Another spotlight picks up the Barnards' table. Sue Barnard watches Ethel with bemused

disgust. *Spotlight leaves Barnards and settles on Businessmen's table.*

1st Businessman: *(Pointing at Ethel.)* That woman who was sitting over here *(Pointing to Ethel and Rod's table.)* is drunk, Sam. Look at her trying to dance.

2nd Businessman: *(With a disinterested glance at Ethel.)* Yeah, it looks like it. *(Turns to his companion.)* But about the price of the other block of property. The initial cost would amortize itself . . . (Voice fades as spotlight goes out.)* The music ends, and the couples go back to their tables. Ethel sits down with the flamboyant daintiness of the female drunk. Rod also sits down.*

Ethel: Whew! That made me feel a little woozy.

Rod: I'm not the boy I used to be. I think that'll do me for this evening.

Ethel: You'll have to dance with me again later.

Rod: *(Smiling firmly.)* No, Ethel, that's all for me tonight.

Ethel: *(Angry)* You know, now that I think back, you never were a very good dancer.

Rod: *(Laughs)* I admit it.

Ethel: Maybe you think I'm not good enough to dance with you?

Rod: Hey, listen —

Ethel: I never thought you'd try to act like a big shot.

Rod: I'm not a big shot.

Ethel: You're goddamed right you're not! I used to watch you sometimes hanging around the corner of our street. I could have twisted you around my little finger. *(Finishes her drink and motions to the Waiter.)*
Four laughing young women enter the lounge. They have obviously checked their coats, though three of them still wear hats. They could be office workers, nurses, members of a library staff. They stand in indecision near Ethel's table.

B16

The Waiter brings two extra chairs and they sit down at a table not too far from Rod and Ethel.

Ethel: *(Stares at the girls, sniffs.)* You know what they are?

Rod: Sure, Ethel, sure. They're girls from an office somewhere around here. Or maybe nurses.

Ethel: *(Curls her lip.)* That's what you think!

Rod: Watch out! They'll hear you.

Ethel: Who cares. What's it like to be a big shot, Mr . . . Mr . . .?

Rod: *(Quietly)* Murphy.

The Waiter puts a drink in front of Ethel, who ignores it.
Ethel: Your name's Irish, isn't it?

Rod: It was, away back.

Ethel: I guess you made your money during the war, didn't you, Mr. Murphy?

Rod: *(Quietly)* Let's not get involved in any arguments, Ethel, please. We came here to talk over old times. I thought it would be nice to remember them.

Ethel: Oh yeah! Who're you kidding! You haven't answered my question, Mr. Murphy. *(Straightens up in an effort to look dignified.)* Whad did you do during the war?

Rod: This is 1955. The war's been over for ten years. Does it matter?

Ethel: Sure it matters. My husband worked from nineteen-forty-one in the shipyards, see?

Rod: Fine, fine.

Ethel: What did you do? Sell insurance?

Rod: *(Angrily)* No, I didn't sell insurance, and I didn't work in a shipyard either!

Ethel: What did **you** do?

Rod: *(Controls himself)* I was in the P.B.I.

Ethel: Yeah? What's that?

Rod: The poor bloody infantry!

Ethel: *(Pouts and tries to be very dignified.)* You don't have to be vulgar. *(They turn away from each other, glancing around the room.)*

Second spotlight picks up Businessmen's table.

1st Businessman: I'm telling you, Sam, she's checking on me. When I went to the last convention she phoned me three times a day.

2nd Businessman: Look, Walter, with the Hillsdale place and the land to the west of it, we can . . . *(Voice fades as light goes out.)*

Ethel: *(Leans back and knocks her coat askew on the back of her chair. Rod looks at her.)* What do you think you're looking at?

Rod: I was just thinking back sixteen years.

Ethel: *(Smirks)* Do you remember the night you proposed to me? That was the funniest thing ever happened.

Rod picks up his glass and stares at it but does not drink. His face is suffused with anger and shame. Ethel glances around the room, spies Willie Barnard, her face lighting up with recognition.

Ethel: *(Stands up.)* Par'n me for a minute. I see somebody I know.

The spotlight follows Ethel as she walks with drunken exaggeration to the Barnards' table and leans over Willie Barnard. A lock of hair falls over her eyes but she brushes it back. Her speech has thickened as she sags once in a while but is making a desperate effort to look dignified. The Barnards are looking up at her and smiling.

Ethel: I met you at the Progress Packers' annual dance in September. I was introduced to you by Mr. Maybee, the advertising manager. Remember?

Willie: *(Not remembering at all.)* Oh yes! I remember now quite well. How d'ye do? Do you know my wife? Sue, Mrs. —

Ethel: Blanton . . . Ernest Blanton's wife. My husband's in production. *(Smiles and nods at Sue Barnard.)* I met your pretty li'l wife at the same time.

Sue: *(Not remembering her either.)* Of course.

Ethel: *(Coyly)* I'm quite a fan of your radio disk-jockey show, Willie. I haven't heard it much lately, but I never used to miss it. Of course, with TV now an' everything, radio's kinda pushed out, isn't it? I mean, nobody listens to it any more, do they? *(Sue gives her husband a quick look.)*

Willie: On the contrary, Mrs. Blanton, we still have quite a large audience.

Ethel: But not as many as you used to have though.

Willie: *(Trying to smile.)* Well, maybe not quite.

Ethel: And why don't you play more Liberace records? I heard you on your show one morning say you'd never play a Liberace record again. You know, there's thousan's an' thousan's of women crazy about Liberace.

Willie: I guess it was foolish of me to say that. I've had a lot of letters from listeners saying the same thing.

Sue: *(Smiles up at Ethel.)* I'm a Liberace fan myself.

Ethel: *(Sags as an arm gives way, but recovers, pushes her hair from her eyes.)* See, Willie, what'd I tell you!

Willie: *(Looks over at Rod.)* Your husband will be wondering what's keeping you, Mrs . . . Mrs. Blanton.

Ethel: That's not my husban'! It's jus' an old frien' . . . an old boy-frien' I didn't see for fift — for sixteen years. *(Sue stares in Rod's direction.)*

Willie: *(Stands and attempts to take Ethel's hand.)* It's been nice meeting you, Mrs.Blanton. I'll remember what you said about the Liberace records. *(Sue smiles a tight-lipped smile.)*

Ethel: *(Peering into Willie's face and wagging a finger at him.)* I'm not goin' yet, Willie. I come over here to say hello, an' I'm goin' to say it. *(Sue looks away in disgust.)*

Willie: I'm glad you dropped over —

Ethel: But now you wanna get rid a me, 'cause you think I'm a li'l drunk, eh? Don' worry, I won't embarrass you. *(Chummily)* You know why I won't? 'Cause I'm a lady, that's why.

Willie: *(Looks away, seeking succor.)* You're not embarrassing me.

Ethel's hand slips from the table top, and she recovers only after a supreme effort to regain her balance. She peers around for a chair to sit down on, as Willie and Sue exchange meaningful looks.

Sue: *(Trying to hide her anger.)* You'd better go back to your friend, Mrs. Blanton.

Ethel: *(Gives Sue an insolent look.)* I want you to meet my frien', Willie. His name's Murphy — Rod Murphy. He's a big 'nsurance 'xecutive. I've known him since he was — well, since a long time. He's always been crazy 'bout me, but I never gave him a tumble till tonight.

Willie: We'd love to meet him some other time, but I'm afraid —

Ethel: Wha's wrong with right now?

Willie: *(Resigned)* All right then. *(He sits down.)*

Ethel: *(Shouts)* Rod! *(Rod pretends to concentrate on his glass.)* Hey, Rod, come here! *(Rod gives her a startled glance, his face working with anger. Looks away.)* Hey, Rod!
Rod gets up and walks to the Barnard table, as the other customers stare at him. He gives Sue and Willie an embarrassed smile and takes Ethel by the arm.

Rod: Come on, Ethel, let's go back to our own table.

Ethel: *(Knocking his hand from her arm.)* I'd like you to meet a pair of ol' frien's of mine, Willie Barnard — you know Willie, the disk-jockey — an' — an' his wife. *(Willie and Rod shake hands.)*

Rod: How do you do. *(To Sue.)* It's a pleasure, Mrs. Barnard.

Ethel: Get a pair of chairs, Rod, an' we'll join Willie an' — an' Sue for a drink.

Rod: I'm sure they want to be alone, Ethel. We should go back to our own table.

Ethel: I'll go back when I'm good an' ready, Mr. Murphy. I said, get some chairs!

Rod: *(To the Barnards.)* I'm sorry. I guess Ethel isn't used to the drinks she's drinking. They're pretty potent when you're not used to them.

The Barnards: Yes.

Ethel: I guess I know when I'm not wanted. *(The Barnards make ineffectual gestures of denial.)* I guess I gotta go with him. You know, he's a pretty 'mportant man in the 'nsurance business. Always has to get his own way. *(Flips a languid hand at Rod.)* I 'member a time though when he di'n get his own way. *(Laughs)* D'ya know, he once proposed to me, an' I turned him down col'! Turned him down col'!

Rod: *(Gets a good grip on her arm)* Come on Ethel.

Willie: We'll see you both again, I hope.

Sue: Good night, Mrs. Blanton.

Ethel: *(Tries to shake Rod loose as she turns to the Barnards.)* Don't forget about Liberace, Willie!

Willie: *(Smiling with relief.)* No, I won't. *(Sue laughs.)*

Ethel: *(Struggles with Rod as she tries to return to the Barnards' table. Shouts.)* Are you laughin' at me, you little bitch! *(Sue stares open-mouthed.)* I know what you used to be! *(As Willie stands up again.)* An' don' think I don' know your right name, Mr. **Brodsky!**

Rod: *(Pulling her roughly by the arm.)* Come

on! *(The spotlight follows them back to their table, where they sit down again.)*

Ethel: I'll bet you didn' know he was a goddam Hebe, did you?

Rod: No, and I'm not interested either. I think you'd better let me take you home.

Ethel: *(Sneering)* Are you tryin' to get rid a me?

Rod: I have an engagement later, that's all.

Ethel: If it's money that's worryin' you, to-night's my pay night, an' I can buy my own drinks. *(Takes some bills from her purse and throws them on the table.)*

Rod: *(Sharply)* Put that away!

Ethel: I jus' wanted you to know I'm no cheapskate. I can pay my own way. I thought you an' me'd make a night of it. *(Gives him an oversized wink.)* Tha's why I tol' my husban' I was goin' to my mother's. We could go to your place, couldn' we?

Rod: I'm sorry but I've got to go, Ethel.

Ethel: *(Leans across the table and snarls.)* Runnin' out on me, eh? Go ahead, run home, li'l boy! Who needs ya? I got plenny of other boy-frien's! *(She straightens up and knocks her coat to the floor.)*

Rod: *(Stands up.)* I'm sorry things turned out like this, Ethel. I was hoping . . . well . . . Can I get you a taxi?

Ethel: No, I don't need nothin' from you. Get outa my sight, you cheap son of a bitch, tha's all!

Rod walks around the table and picks up her coat, placing it over the back of her chair. Then, with the spotlight following him, he walks to the bar where the Waiter is standing. Both of them look back at Ethel, as the spotlight swings back to her. She is wearing a crooked, hateful smile as she picks up her glass and stares into it. The spotlight swings back to Rod and the Waiter, who hands Rod the check. Rod glances at it,

B20

pulls some money from his pocket, peels off a bill and hands it to the waiter.

Rod: Keep it, Art.

Waiter: Thanks, Mr. Murphy.

Rod: *(Nods in Ethel's direction.)* Take care of her will you, Art?

Waiter: Sure will, Mr. Murphy. *(As the Waiter watches him, Rod walks into the wings, then returns putting on his hat and coat. The music continues and the people still dance, talk and drink.)*

Rod: *(Pulling on his gloves.)* You know, Art, I'm really sorry it turned out like this. *(A short bitter laugh.)* Until tonight I thought Ethel's husband was the luckiest guy in town.

Waiter: *(Cynically)* Some are so lucky.

Rod: *(Looks over to where Ethel is sitting, then shrugs.)* I always thought I'd meet Ethel again, and now it's happened, and now it's over. Maybe it's just as well. *(Smiles and turns to leave.)* Do you know, Art, suddenly I feel good. I feel good . . . I feel free . . . I feel sixteen years younger than I did an hour ago.

Waiter: Good night, Mr. Murphy.

Rod: Be seeing you. *(Walks off.)*

End of Play

The Magnet

Characters:

Grace Harding, 45, a farmer's widow.
Jake Barens, 30, a hired hand.
Shirley Cooper, 20, a neighbor's pretty daughter.
Mabel Doucette, middle-aged friend of Mrs. Harding.
Mark Doucette, Mabel's husband.
Rupert Cooper, middle-aged father of Shirley.

Scene one:

A northern Alberta farmhouse in the summer. Time, the present. A big kitchen opens to a rickety wooden porch, separated during the play by a screen door. Two bedrooms open from the kitchen. The kitchen is neat and clean, with a table and chairs, sink, wooden ice-box and large woodstove. Water is heated in a large kettle usually standing on the stove; cold water is dipped from a pail.

There is the sound of a truck pulling to a stop in the yard. Grace Harding, followed by Jake Barens, walks on to the porch. Grace is dressed up for a visit to town, and Jake wears work pants, an open-necked workshirt and a cotton windbreaker. He is carrying a small packsack and a paper parcel. As Grace goes to the kitchen door, Jake places his packsack and parcel on the porch floor and stands gazing out over the fields.

Jake: We're quite a way out from town, Mrs. Harding.

Grace: *(Turns)* Only nine miles.

Jake: That's quite a way. How often will I be able to go to town?

Grace: *(With a boss' brusqueness.)* As often as you want to — after the day's work's done.

Jake: How many acres did you say you had?

Grace: A hundred and seventy-five, but only ninety's cleared.

Jake: And your main crop is beets?

Grace: I believe I told you that in the employment office. *(Coldly)* Do you think beets are too much work?

Jake: *(Swings around on her.)* I didn't say anything about the work.

Grace: You didn't have to come if you didn't want to. I could have hired another hand you know. There's plenty in this part of the country who aren't afraid of a little work.

Jake: I'm not afraid of the work, and I need the job. I guess I'll be able to stand it as well as the next guy. *(Turns away from her.)*

Grace: The last two hands I hired lasted less than a week apiece. If you start I'll expect you to stay till after the harvest. If you want to change your mind now's the time to do it.

Shirley Cooper crosses the yard unseen by Jake. She wears a tight skirt and form-fitting sweater.

Shirley: Howdy, Mrs. Harding.

Grace: *(Without welcome.)* Hello, Shirley. *(Jake swings around and stares at the girl, his face breaking into a surprised smile.)*

Shirley: *(Answers Jake's smile.)* I been meaning to bring them magazines back, Mrs. Harding. I'll bring 'em up tomorrow.

Grace: There's no need —

Shirley: It won't be no trouble. *(Smiles at Jake.)* I'll be up. *(Exits)*

Jake: *(After watching the girl walk away turns to Grace.)* Who was that?

Grace: *(Biting it off.)* Just a kid who lives down the road. *(Opens the door.)*

Jake: *(With a leer.)* I think I'm going to like it around here. I'll take the job. *(Picks up his packsack and parcel and follows Grace into the house. Grace walks to the stove, lifts the lid and looks inside, then replaces it. Jake looks the room over, letting his packsack slip to the floor.)* This is a comfortable little house you've got, Mrs. Harding.

Grace: It'll do. *(Walks over and opens the door to his room.)* Here's your room. You can put your things in here. *(He picks up his packsack and enters the room as Grace stands at the door.)*

Jake: *(Comes out of the room without his pack and parcel.)* It's very nice. Yeh, very nice. *(Walks to the window and stares outside.)*

Grace: It's plain but it's clean.

Jake: *(Points through the window.)* Are they all beets?

Grace: There's some oats, hay and a bit of pasture. The beets need cultivating. You can start on them tomorrow with the team.

Jake: I'm used to driving a tractor, but I guess I can still manage a team. *(Turns and faces her.)*

Grace: I hope you can, that's why I hired you.

Jake: *(Looks her over.)* You live here all alone, Mrs. Harding?

Grace: Yes . . . since my husband died last year.

Jake: The other men you hired, what was wrong with them?

Grace: One of them was bone lazy, the other . . . he thought he could take over both me and the farm.

Jake: *(Laughs)* You won't have to worry about that with me.

Grace: *(Flings open the ice-box angrily and takes out a package.)* I'm glad we understand each other. *(Places the package on the table.)* Are you a Swede, Mr . . . Mr . . .?

Jake: *(Leaning indolently on the window-sill.)* Like it says on the job slip, ma'am, I'm a Polack and my name is Barens. Jake Barens.

Grace: We don't have any Poles around here.

Jake: *(With a wry smile.)* Well, Mrs. Harding, you've got one now.

Grace: *(Discomfited and angry.)* I've got to get supper ready. Do you want to unpack or — or anything. The convenience is out there beside the barn.

Jake: Convenience? *(Laughs as he leaves the house and exits. Grace goes to the stove and angrily begins jamming a length of wood into its firebox.)*

The following morning. Grace is sitting at the table finishing a cup of coffee. She gets up and peers through the curtained window, then admires herself critically in a small mirror hanging on the wall, arranging her hair and moistening her lips. She hears Jake whistling a snatch of song as he crosses the yard, glances quickly through the window and hurries back to her chair.

Jake: *(Crosses the yard and porch and enters the kitchen.)* It's going to be a hot day. I'll bet it's murder down in that employment office in town. I'm glad I hired out yesterday.

Grace: *(Her back to him.)* We can expect heat in July.

Jake: *(Stretching his arms over his head.)* Last night was the best night's sleep I've had in weeks.

Grace: That bed always did sleep good. *(Walks to the stove.)* Do you want more coffee? There's some left from breakfast.

Jake: Okay. *(Sits down at the table.)* I was looking at the team. Did you know there was a trace broken on one of the sets of harness, right near the hame?

Grace: *(Carries the coffee pot to the table and fills his cup.)* Yes, I knew about it. I'll show you later where the things are to fix it.

Jake: *(Stirring his coffee.)* I found them. That's a nice young team you've got.

Grace: You'll have to watch the mare. She's pernickity with strangers. *(Returns to the stove with the coffee pot.)*

Jake: *(Smiles)* Yes, I notices that. This place seems to be full of pernickity females. I heard you barring your bedroom door last night. What did you do, prop a chair under the knob?

Grace: A woman in my position can't be too careful. What do I know about you?

Jake: You know as much about me as I know about you.

Grace: Mmmmph! Knowing about a woman's different. There was a widow murdered by a hired hand over to Colbeck last year. All he got from her was fifteen dollars. You can't trust nobody these days. *(He looks up from his coffee.*) I've got a gun hid around here. I know how to take care of myself.

Jake: (*Smiles before taking another cup of coffee.*) I'm sure you do.

Grace: (*Sits down across the table.*) Were you born Poland?

Jake: No, but my mother and father were. They've been out here forty years. They farm a quarter section near Blackwood, Saskatchewan.

Grace: How come you're here in Alberta? Couldn't you work at home?

Jake: I've got brothers . . . the stay-at-home kind. How about you, have you any kids?

Grace: I had twins, but they died at birth. Twin girls. It was during a blizzard back in 'forty-eight. The doctor couldn't get through.

Jake: I'm sorry.

Grace: Were you ever married?

Jake: Who me! (*laughs*) No, ma'am.

Grace: (*Sarcastically*) I suppose you don't believe in it?

Jake: I think it's fine for those who like. Me, I've got plenty of time to think about it yet. I'm only thirty.

Grace: Most men that's thirty are already married . . . if they ever intend to be. How come you're not?

Jake: (*Laughs*) I've been lucky, I guess . . . so far. I been seeing the country. I've travelled everywhere since leaving home, out to the Coast, down East, all over. I never lit anywhere for long. I only hit Ferngrove yesterday morning . . . hitch-hiked up from Edmonton.

Grace: It doesn't sound like much of a life.

Jake: I'm independent.

Grace: How do you figure that when you're always working for somebody else?

Jake: (*Gets up and heads for the door.*) I'm free. I can always move on. I'm not tied down to a wife or a . . . well, a place like this.

Grace: Working for wages isn't like owning a place of your own.

Jake: No, but if I don't like a job I can always quit. (*Goes outside.*)

Grace: (*Shouts after him.*) You go easy on my horses! I don't allow them to be mistreated! (*Jake slams the screen door behind him and crosses the porch.*)

Shirley: (*Enters the yard.*) Hey, is Mrs. Harding in? (*She is dressed the same as she was the day before, but she now carries four or five magazines under her arm.*)

Jake: (*Grins at her.*) Hy'a, beautiful!

Shirley: (*Smiles*) Hi. Is Mrs. Harding in?

Jake: Sure. Right there in the kitchen. Say, this is pretty early in the morning for a social visit.

Shirley: I got some books to give back to Mrs. Harding.

Jake: (*Joins her, takes the magazines from under her arm and glances at the titles.*) You read this kinda stuff all the time?

Shirley: (*Defensively*) Why not?

Jake: (*Handing back the magazines.*) Do you do anything else for excitement?

Shirley: You got a nerve! What do you mean?

Jake: (*Glances at the door, then smiles.*) I mean what would a stranger like me do around here in the evenings?
Grace spies on them from behind the window curtains.

Shirley: You can do whatever you've a mind to, I guess. Some of us go down to Palmetter's store sometimes after supper. Then there's dances nearly every week over to North Forks or Colbeck, and there's the big dance on Saturday down to Ferngrove.

Jake: Where's Palmetter's store?

Shirley: Down the road a mile or so. You passed it coming in.

Jake: Will I see you there tonight, Shirley?

Shirley: *(Shrugs)* You might. Say, how come you know my name so quick?

Jake: I heard Mrs. Harding call you that yesterday. My name's Jake.

Shirley: *(Giggles)* It sounds sort of old.

Jake: Yeah. I'm kind of an old guy. Old before my time. *(They laugh together.)*

Shirley: You're not so old.

Jake: *(Glancing at the door.)* I don't figure to act like I am, either.

Shirley: Be seeing you. *(Shifts the magazines to her other arm and walks towards the door. Grace leaves the window hurriedly and sits down.)*

Jake: After supper at the store. *(Walks off stage as Shirley knocks at the door, then enters the house.)*

End of Scene One

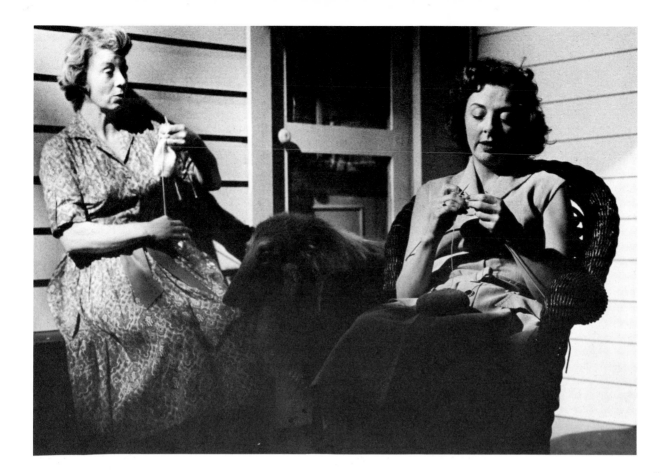

Scene Two:

An afternoon a week later. Grace and Mabel Doucette, a neighbor, are sitting on the porch. Grace sits on the floor, her back against a roof support, while Mabel occupies the rocking chair. Both wear housedresses, and Mabel also wears a pair of bobby-socks.

Mabel: *(Looking out at the fields.)* He seems to be a good worker anyways. He's got a lot of work done in a week.

Grace: His work gives me no cause to kick. He's . . .

Mabel: *(Suddenly interested.)* He's what?

Grace: I don't know, Mabel. It seems I don't trust him somehow. I guess I don't understand him.

Mabel: He seemed very nice when we was eating dinner. Maybe it's yourself you don't understand.

Grace: How do you mean?

Mabel: *(Smiling archly.)* It wouldn't be the first time a lonely widow fell for a hired hand.

Grace: Do you think . . .? *(Laughs)* Oh, Mabel, don't be a fool! Why, I'm fifteen years older than he is.

Mabel: That don't matter. You'd marry again in a minute, Grace, if the right man come along.

Grace: Maybe I would, but the right man isn't him.

Mabel: *(Teasing)* You're too late anyways. Mark seen him spooning with that Cooper girl down near the bridge the other night.

Grace: *(Sniffs)* She's welcome to him. I don't care what he does at night so long as he does his work during the day. *(Changing the subject.)* Tell Mark I'm going to bring my Guernsey heifer up to your place tomorrow night.

Mabel: I'm glad one female around here's gonna get fixed up anyways.

Grace: You silly thing! *(They both laugh.)*

Mabel: *(Wipes her eyes with her handkerchief and looks across the yard.)* Here he comes now. He's a good-looking man. What is he, a Ukrainian or what?

Grace: He says he's a Pole. *(Jumps to her feet.)* Do you want a cup of coffee or do you want to sit out here all day talking foolishness? *(Opens the screen door.)*

Mabel: No, Grace, thanks. I've got to be getting home or my old man'll shoot me. *(Gets up from the chair as Jake walks over to the porch.)*

Jake: What's the matter, ladies? Am I breaking something up? *(Grace enters the house without answering.)*

Mabel: Nothing important anyways, Jake. I've got to go is all. Time to be getting my old man's supper.

Jake: *(Unbuttoning his shirt.)* Be seeing you, Mrs. Doucette.

Mabel: *(Shouts through the screen door.)* 'By, Grace!

Grace: See you tomorrow, Mabel.

Mabel: *(Walks off the porch as Jake walks on.)* Be seeing you, Jake.

Jake: You bet. *(Takes off his shirt and carries it into the house as Mabel leaves.)*

Grace: *(Tearing up a head of lettuce into a bowl on the table.)* It's too hot to cook supper tonight. I thought we'd have a salad.

Jake: Sure, that'll be fine. *(Throws his shirt into a washbowl and places it in the sink. Takes a box of soap flakes from beneath the sink and sprinkles some on the shirt.)*

Grace: I've got all the salad fixin's, and we can have some sliced baloney with it.

Jake: *(Pours some water on to his shirt from the kettle.)* Great! I'm not a fussy eater. *(Pours some cold water from a pail into the washbowl.)*

Grace: *(Notices what he is doing and watches him for a moment.)* If you'd have asked me I'd have done your washing for you. Washing clothes is women's work.

Jake: *(Looks around, brushing back his hair with a sudsy fist.)* I'm used to washing my own things. Thanks just the same though.

Grace: *(Going on with her work.)* Now that the cultivating's nearly finished, I'd like to get the potatoes sprayed.

Jake: Yeah, I guess they need it.

Grace: I was looking at them today and they're full of bugs.

Jake: They need hoeing too. I'll be finished the cultivating by noon tomorrow; I'll get after it then.

Grace: I'm going to pick berries tomorrow with Mabel Doucette.

Jake: *(Scrubs his shirt and looks over his shoulder.)* I hear there's lots of 'em over at Fielder's Mill.

Grace: Who told you that?

Jake: Shirley Cooper. Shirley and her sister have picked nearly a hundred baskets the last two weeks.

Grace: Did she tell you that yesterday morning when you were wasting time talking to her down at the edge of the south field?

Jake: *(Grins at her.)* No. She told me that a couple of nights ago.

Grace: *(Tearing the lettuce savagely.)* I'd think you'd have better things to do with your evenings than hanging around the Cooper place. That Shirley Cooper hasn't a very good reputation around here.

Jake: *(Grinning)* So I heard. Larry Palmetter at the store told me she was considered fast. Isn't that why you call it around here? Fast?

Grace: We have worse names for her kind.

Jake: So how does that affect me? I'm not courting her.

Grace: You've seen her nearly every evening for a month though!

Jake: *(Laughs)* Seeing them and courting them are two different things. Don't worry, Mrs. Harding, I'm not going to marry her.

Grace: *(Swinging around.)* I don't care if you marry her or not! All I care is that you do your work, and that you don't bring that little slut around my house!

Jake: *(Leaning indolently on the sink.)* She came around here long before I did. Anyhow, I don't think she wants to come around here, Mrs. Harding. And any time my work doesn't suit, let me know. I figure what I do with my own time is my own business.

Grace: Nobody said it wasn't! It's my business though what you do in the fields during the morning! *(Drops the salad fixings and runs into her bedroom, slamming the door behind her.)*

Jake: *(Shouts)* I'm sorry, Boss! *(Smiles as he wrings out his shirt.)*

Later the same evening. Shirley Cooper walks towards the porch wearing a bathing-suit halter and skirt. A clothesline is hung with a man's workclothes. Shirley peers through the screen door, shading her eyes with her hand.

Shirley: Jake! Are you in there, Jake? *(Jake comes across the yard and sneaking up on her encircles her with his arms.)* Oh! Don't muss me up, you goddam fool!

Jake: *(Turns her around and kisses her.)* What are you doing up here? Don't you know Mrs. Harding wouldn't like it?

Shirley: *(Steps back and shakes out her hair.)* The hell with her! Anyways I just seen her going down the road past my place. I thought you were gonna meet me?

Jake: I was, sweetheart, but I had my washing to do first. *(Points to it on the line.)*

Shirley: Don't Grace do your washing for you?

Jake: She offered to, but I'd sooner do it myself.

Shirley: *(Pouting)* It's a wonder she'll let you. From what I hear she's pretty stuck on you.

Jake: *(Laughs)* You're crazy, sweetheart. Why she's — she must be nearly fifty. *(Tries to pull her to him but she twists away.)*

Shirley: She's not that old, and anyways when she's dolled up she's still a smart-looking woman. *(Looks angrily at the house.)* I don't trust you two living together in this house all by yourselves.

Jake: Don't be a little sap. *(Smiles)* If it was you it'd be different, but with her I'm just the hired hand.

Shirley: Honest, Jake?

Jake: Sure thing, baby. *(Tries to embrace her again but she resists and he lets her go, his face hardening.)* And what is it I hear about you going out with a guy that works with that oil-drilling rig?

Shirley: Who told you that! Has that old bitch been —

Jake: I didn't hear it from Grace Harding.

Shirley: *(Rubs herself against him.)* You jealous? *(Pouts)* Just because I got a ride to town with one of the drillers the other day. *(Stepping back.)* Those oil roughnecks make good money. Why don't you get a job like that, Jake, then you could take me riding in a big car and —

Jake: *(Pulls her around roughly.)* Baby, we don't need a car. *(Nuzzling her.)* Don't you like going out with me, eh? What's wrong with this?

Shirley: *(Breaking away.)* Tell me Grace Harding don't mean nothing to you.

Jake: Of course she doesn't. *(Takes her hand.)* Come on, sweetheart, we'll go down to the river bank and I'll prove she doesn't.

Shirley: *(Smiles teasingly.)* Maybe I won't let you tonight.

Jake: Then I'll rape you. *(She laughs as he pulls her along. They circle each other's waists as they leave the stage.)*

End of Scene Two

Scene Three:

Two months later. Grace Harding, wearing jeans and a man's shirt, is washing dishes at the sink. She walks to the table, picks up some dishes, and looks through the screen door before carrying them to the sink. Jake, wearing his work clothes, enters the kitchen from the yard and sits down at the table. He puts down a couple of letters and opens a newspaper he has also brought in.

Grace: Any mail?

Jake: Just a couple of business letters, one from the bank. I was reading here in the paper as I came up from the mailbox that they're putting a new highway into the Peace River Country. There should be work up there all winter. *(Grace turns from the sink, closes her eyes as if in momentary prayer, then turns to the sink again.)* I was never up in that part of the country. Those highway jobs pay pretty good.

Grace: I sort of figured you'd be staying on here for a spell, Jake. There's no cause to talk of leaving yet.

Jake: You don't need me around here now the harvest's finished. I've been here more'n two months now and I feel it's time to be moving on.

Grace: I was hoping you'd stay on after the harvest to clear some more land. My husband was always going to do it, but . . .

Jake: *(Gets up and stares out of the window.)* This wouldn't be a bad little farm with the rest of the acreage cleared. The soil's good and that second-growth wouldn't be hard to burn off.

Grace: I've been wanting it done ever since we came up here right after the war. Jack made a few starts at it but his heart wasn't really in farming. He'd have never come up here in the first place if he hadn't had his foot crushed on the railroad.

Jake: I've never asked you before, but did he get a pension?

Grace: A small one; not enough to live on. When he died I got a small lump sum, just about enough to pay for the funeral.

Jake: (Sits down again.) Why did you decide to stay here instead of going back to Edmonton?

Grace: I've thought about it a few times. I thought about it a lot last winter, even though I've always liked it up here. With a man on the place that was interested it could be made to pay. Not a fortune, of course, but enough to live comfortably on. That's why I sort of hoped you'd stay.

Jake: (Swings his chair around and faces her wearing a teasing smile.) How is it, Grace, that no single man around here, maybe a widower, hasn't tried to court you before this?

Grace: (Turns and rattles the pots and pans in the sink.) I could name some that wanted to, don't worry. I just didn't encourage them, that's all.

Jake: (Laughs to himself.) What's this I hear you've got your cap set for me, Grace?

Grace: (Swings around angrily.) Who's been telling you **that** cock-and-bull story!

Jake: (Smilingly raises his arm as if to fend her off.) Why, everybody says it.

Grace: Why . . . that's . . . that's . . . (Turns to the sink in confusion.)

Jake: (Stands and looks through the window again.) This'd be a perfect spot for anybody that wanted to settle down. A nice little farm and a nice little woman to boot. A man could live out the rest of his life here nice and quiet and peaceful. But for me . . . well, there's plenty of places I still haven't seen, and plenty of women I haven't met. Maybe in a few years' time I'll —

Grace: (Not facing him.) You're never going to get anywhere running around the country. It's about time you thought of lighting somewhere.

Jake: I'm not saying I mightn't change my mind. I've been thinking things out, and I'm more favorable to it now than I once was. If I do change my mind I'll say yes to your proposal.

Grace: (Swings around angrily.) You'll wait a long time before you hear a proposal from me!

(She holds a dish in her hand.)

Jake: (Grinning) I never met a woman yet that didn't want to tie me up in a neat little package and hide me away somewhere. (Grace curls her lip and turns back to the sink.) A woman isn't satisfied till she's got you locked up safe and sound with a married tag hung round your neck.

Grace: Watch out or Shirley Cooper'll have you tied up pretty soon.

Jake: (Laughs) You know, Grace, I think you're jealous.

Grace: Jealous! (Tries to laugh but it doesn't come off.) What makes you think I'd be jealous of that stupid little whore! Goddam you, as far as I'm concerned you can take her with you and the two of you go straight to hell! (She drops the dish which shatters on the floor. She looks down at it then begins to cry. She leans sobbing on the edge of the sink.)

Jake: (Surprised and chastened by her outburst walks out to the porch. He leans against a post staring off into the distance. Sees someone coming and opens the screen door.) Grace, here comes Mark Doucette. I'm giving him a lift into town in the truck. I've got to pick up that laying mash.

Grace: All right. (Wipes her eyes and begins to brush up the broken dish.)

Jake: And you might be interested to know I haven't seen Shirley for a week.

Grace: What's that to me?

Jake: I thought you might like to know. (Crosses the porch and meets Mark Doucette.)

Mark: Hi, Jake. Ready to go?

Jake: Sure thing, Mark.

Mark: (Looking into the sky.) Well, the weather held good this year till most of the harvest was in.

Jake: Yep, but it'll soon be cooling off I guess.

Mark: In this country it cools off fast come fall.

They exit together. There is the noise of a truck being started, then leaving the yard.

Grace has been watching the men leave through the screen door, and now she walks back to the sink and begins drying the dishes once again. Mabel Doucette crosses the yard and peers through the screen door.

Mabel: Hey, Grace, are you home?

Grace: *(Goes to the wall mirror and wipes away a vagrant tear with the dish-towel.)* Come in, Mabel.

Mabel: I waited up the road till Jake and Mark had gone. We had a little bit of a squabble up at the house. I hope Jake keeps that old fool outa the beer parlor. *(Stares at Grace.)* You been crying, dear?

Grace: *(Flustered)* Who me? No. No, I had something in my eye. Why should I have been crying?

Mabel: *(Sits down in a chair.)* What does it feel like to be washing up after a man again?

Grace: How should it feel?

Mabel: I shouldn't have to ask that. You look twenty years younger since Jake's been here.

Grace: *(A short sad laugh)* You're crazy.

Mabel: Don't try to fool me, Grace Harding, I've known you too long. You're alive again, woman. Why, you've even begun to smile again since he's been here.

Grace: *(Sits down across the table.)* I thought you'd have been going to town tonight with Mark?

Mabel: I told you we had a squabble. Anyways the last time I went with him he left me in the Chinaman's restaurant while he was supposed to be going to the hardware for a half-inch bolt for the binder. Instead he went to the beer parlor and didn't come out for two hours.

Grace: Have you heard from your daughter Elsie lately?

Mabel: I had a letter from her just the other day. Young Tommy's been sick. Nothing much, summer complaint I figure. Her and Eric have bought a new TV from the Hudson's Bay. They get good reception down in the city. Somebody told me they're putting a TV relay station over to Colbeck, that'll improve reception here. Mmmph! I'll be dead before that happens.

Grace: *(Smiles)* You'll outlive us all, you old fraud.

Mabel: *(Patting her hair.)* Not so much of the "old" business. *(Laughs)* I guess you don't need television any more now that you've got a good-looking man living in the house?

Grace: I see you're back on your favorite subject.

Mabel: Is he going to stay here all winter?

Grace: *(Shrugs)* He was talking about getting a job on the new highway up in the Peace River.

Mabel: If you don't do something soon it's going to be a toss-up whether the Peace River gets him — or Shirley Cooper.

Grace: Let's not talk about it. *(Getting angry.)* Especially about Shirley.

Mabel: I thought there was more to it than you been letting on there was. Don't worry, Grace. Why, you'd make that Cooper kid look silly in a bathing suit. *(Laughs)*

Grace: For the last time, Mabel, there's nothing been Jake and me. Why, I'm fifteen years older than him.

Mabel: That don't matter, I'm **twenty** years older than he is, but it wouldn't stop me if I was you. You musta scared him off at the beginning. Just show him you've changed your mind now, and that you're as eager as —

Grace: *(Jumping up.)* For Chrissakes, Mabel! *(Goes to the stove and moves the kettle over the heat.)*

Mabel: I'm sorry, Grace. I didn't mean to —

Grace: Supposing I did happen to like him. Just supposing. What good would it do me?

Mabel: Well, if you were lucky you'd get him to marry you, and if you weren't so lucky what would you lose?

Grace: (Laughs wildly.) My reputation.

Mabel: Maybe you've lost that already.

Grace: (Her laugh dying.) What! What do you mean?

Mabel: Grace, I mean people'll believe the worst no matter what. What do you think they believe now? They know you're living here alone together, don't they? It's only natural — what I mean is no young man and woman can live by theirselves like you and Jake do without —. It's just like there was a magnet drawing you together —

Grace: Maybe there is a — a magnet like you say, but it hasn't —

Mabel: (Holds up her hand for silence.) Oh, I don't believe there's been any namby-pamby — yet. You might have fought it up to now, but you won't be able to resist it forever. You'll have to give in finally.

Grace: I refuse to listen to any more. (Storms out to the porch, where she stands thinking and looking into the distance.)

Mabel: (Laughs, then shouts.) You're thinking about it though! (Glances towards the stove.) Grace, your kettle's boiling!
End of Scene Three

Scene Four:

An evening a day or two later. Jake comes out of his room dressed to go to town. Grace, still wearing jeans and a man's shirt, is sitting sewing in the rocking chair on the porch. When she hears Jake in the kitchen she goes into the house.

Jake: *(Puts his foot up on a chair and ties his shoe.)* I've been thinking of the things we talked about a couple of days ago, Grace. You know, about clearing more of the land and things. *(Smiles)* I was only kidding you then when I said you had your cap set for me.

Grace: That's okay.

Jake: Maybe I wouldn't mind sticking around here — that is if it's still all right with you?

Grace: *(With a shy smile.)* I wish you would, Jake. You could burn off most of the brush during the fall and then plow the new land in the spring. You'd be under no obligation — what I mean is you could leave any time if things didn't work out.

Jake: I don't think I'll want to leave.

Grace: I don't know how to say this, Jake. What about — what are you going to do about Shirley Cooper?

Jake: *(Laughs)* Shirley! I haven't even seen her lately, like I told you. Believe me, there wasn't anything serious between us. *(Wryly)* Besides, I found out she was going out with a guy called Will who worked on the drilling rig up the valley. She fell for his big car I think.

Grace: I'm — sorry.

Jake: *(Laughs)* There's nothing to be sorry about. Shirley and I — well — it was just one of those things.

Grace: I'm glad, Jake. I'm glad for you — for everybody's sake.

Jake: Look, Grace, how'd it be if I come back here from the store and drive you into Ferngrove? We could have a few beers or go to the movies or something. What do you say? It'll be sort of a celebration.

Grace: (Looks down at herself.) I'm not dressed.

Jake: You've got plenty of time. I'll be back in half an hour or so. What do you say?

Grace: I'd like that, Jake. (Goes to the stove and feels the kettle.)

Jake: I won't be long. (Takes her in his arms. She resists half-heartedly then presses herself to him and they kiss. He tries to push her to one of the bedroom doors, but she breaks away from him.)

Grace: Not now, dear.

Jake: Why not? Please, Grace! (Tries to pull her to him again but she escapes.)

Grace: No, Jake, the door's open!

Jake: I can easily close and lock it. (Strides to the door.)

Grace: Please, Jake, not now. Look, I'm not washed or anything. Let's wait till tonight, dear. I promise you —

Jake: (Goes back to her and she hangs her head.) Not even a little goodbye kiss?

Grace: (Lifts her face and smiles.) You silly fool! (They kiss again until she pushes him away gently.)

Jake: A half an hour or so. (Goes to the door.)

Grace: (Breathlessly) I'll have to hurry if I'm to wash myself and change. (Goes into her room as Jake goes out to the porch.)
Shirley Cooper and her father, Rupert, cross the yard to the porch. Rupert is wearing dirty work clothes, while Shirley is carelessly dressed and has been crying.

Rupert: I wanna talk to you, boy.

Jake: (Steps off the porch.) What about?

Rupert: (Turns to Shirley.) Now you're sure it's him?

Shirley: (Lowers her eyes.) Yes, daddy.

Rupert: (Angrily) I got something to say to you, Jake.

Jake: (With a quick glance at the house.) Okay. Let's get out of the yard

Shirley: What we've got to say we can say right here!

Jake: (With a frightened look towards the house.) I've — I'm going down the road anyway.

Shirley: I don't give a damn who hears —

Rupert: (Pushing her hard on the shoulder.) You shut your goddam mouth! It's just as much your fault as it is —

Mabel Doucette and Mark, carrying a newspaper under his arm, come across the yard.

Mabel: Hello, Rupert. Shirley. (Stares hard at Jake.) Is Grace in, Jake?

Jake: (Trying to hurry Shirley and her father away from the house.) Yes — yes, I think so. I'm — I'm going down to the store. I'll see you later. (Jake, Shirley and Rupert Cooper exit. Shirley very reluctantly.)

Mabel: (Standing watching the others leave.) I could have warned that young fool. He should never have got involved with that Cooper girl.

Mark: (Also staring after the departing trio.) I wonder what they want with him?

Mabel: (Grabs him and turns him towards the house.) Don't be such a stupid bloody fool, Mark! You don't think Rupert Cooper's with them just to make a happy bloody threesome, do you?

Mark: Oh. Do you mean — ?

Mabel: (Pulls him to a halt.) Now don't you go saying anything to Grace. Understand? (Mark nods as they go up to the door.) You home, Grace!

Grace: (Puts her head out of the doorway of her room.) Is it you, Mabel? Come in, come in! (Laughs) I'm just getting dolled up!

Mabel: I've got my old man with me. *(Gives him a warning look.)*

Grace: Okay, Mabel. You and Mark come in and make yourselves at home. I'll be out there in a minute.

The Doucettes enter the kitchen and sit down at the table. Mark opens his newspaper and begins to read it. Grace comes out of her room wearing a dressing gown, takes the dishpan from the sink and the kettle from the store.

Grace: *(Bubbling with happiness.)* I thought I heard voices outside, but I wasn't sure. I'm just getting ready to go to town with Jake. He's gone down to the store first, but he'll be back soon. I don't see how you missed him; he's just been gone a minute.

Mabel: We did meet him, Grace. We just come up from Palmetter's store ourselves.

Grace: Excuse me, you two. It won't take me long.

Mabel: Take your time, dear. *(Grace carries the dishpan and the kettle into her room.)*

Mark: *(Lowering his newspaper.)* I always knew there was no oil around here. Now they're even admitting it in the Ferngrove paper. Last spring it was all oil, oil, oil. Everybody was gonna be rich.

Mabel: Palmetter told me most of the gant from the drilling rig have gone already. There's only two men and a truck left. They're gonna dismantle the rig and truck it away.

Mark: Ain't it what I allus told you, Mabel? We were smart to sell the mineral rights when we did. There ain't enough oil under here to grease a sewing machine.

Mabel: Mmmph! It's no fault of yours. If there had have been oil you'd have kicked yourself the rest of your life. *(They hear Grace humming happily in her room, and exchange glances.)*

Mark: Grace shoulda sold her mineral rights too. Still, I guess she gets by comfortably enough on her beet crop. If that young fool Jake Barens has any sense he'll — *(Mabel leans across the table and shushes him angrily. He speaks in a lower voice, looking now and then to the door from which her humming is heard.)* Hey, Mabel, do you think Jake'll be marrying young Shirley? That boyfriend of hers that worked on the drilling rig has gone I hear. Now that he's out of the —

Mabel: Shut up! *(Points to Grace's door.)* If he marries that little slut, he's crazy! *(Walks over to the door as Mark begins reading his paper again.)*

The door to Grace's room opens and Grace, wearing her best dress, shoes, earrings and a string of pearls, and looking radiantly happy and beautiful, crosses the kitchen and empties the dishpan into the sink and places the kettle on the stove. Mabel turns to her from the doorway.

Grace: I'm sorry I can't offer you both a cup of tea. The fire's out and there's no water.

Mark: *(Looks up from his paper.)* By God, Grace, you look like a million bucks! Don't she, Mabel? *(Folds up his newspaper.)*

Mabel: You look lovely, Grace. Never mind about the tea.

Grace: Jake has decided to stay here, Mabel. *(Smiles from Mabel to Mark.)* I'm so happy! *(Pirouettes)* How does my dress look?

Mabel: *(Soberly)* Fine, dear. You look fine.

Grace: *(Laughing)* He's taking me into Ferngrove as soon as he comes back from the store. We're going to have a couple of beers maybe or go to the movies.

Mark: *(Looks from Mabel to Grace.)* Did you hear, Grace, that the drilling rig's pulling out? Most of the men have gone already.

Mabel: Come on, Mark, we'd better go.

Mark: What, alread — *(Sees the look on her face and gets up.)*

Grace: Listen, you two, stay until Jake comes back. He won't be long. What was that you said about the drilling rig, Mark? It's pulling out? *(Laughs)* Who cares! *(To Mabel.)* I'm so flustered! Like a young bride. I'm so glad, Mabel, that Jake's staying on. *(She is puzzled by the blank look on Mabel's face, and smiles tentatively.)* Of course, we'll get married. He hasn't exactly asked me yet, but I know he — *(Her happiness gives way to concern.)* What — what is it? *(Mark shoves past his wife and goes out to the porch.)*

Mabel: He's — Shirley — I'm not sure, Grace, but I think Shirley's in trouble. I heard something down at the store. *(Hurriedly)* It may not be him; she was going out with a drilling rig roughneck called Will at the same time. But when we come up to the house just now Shirley and old Rupert Cooper were walking up the lane ahead of us. Shirley'd been crying and her father had blood in his eye. When Jake come out of the house I heard Rupert ask Shirley if he was the one. Then Jake went with them — they went together down towards the road. *(Stricken, Grace sits down on a chair.)* Maybe I'm wrong about — about everything, Grace. *(She opens the screen door and backs out.)* I've got to go, Grace. See you later. *(On the porch she grabs Mark by the arm and hurries him off stage.)*

Grace stares unseeing at the door. Then slowly she kicks of first one of her shoes then the other. She unclasps one earring and then the other as she begins crying silently. She cups the earrings in her hand and removes the string of pearls from her neck. Then she picks up her shoes from the floor and carrying them in her hand goes to her room.

Later the same night. Jake enters the house and switches on the kitchen light. He is quite drunk, and he staggers to the door to Grace's room, tries to open it but finds it being held shut by something.

Jake: Grace. Grace!

Grace: *(From inside the room.)* I'll see you in the morning.

Jake: I'd like to talk to you, Grace. *(Rattles the door-knob.)* Let me in! *(Becomes maudlin.)* Grace, dear, I've got something to tell you. Listen, I couldn't make it back here like I promised. *(Shakes the door-knob angrily and shouts.)* D'ya hear me, Grace!

Grace: Go to bed! I'll talk to you in the morning!

Jake: *(Rattling the knob.)* No! Right now. Let me in! *(The door is opened and Grace stands before him wearing a dressing gown over her nightgown. She has obviously been crying.)*

Grace: What have you to say about you and Shirley?

Jake: *(Backs away.)* It's a lie. She was going with a fella called Will Sayers from the drilling rig. Maybe it was him.

Grace: Don't try to deny it. *(Curls her lip.)* At least stand up to it like a man!

Jake: *(With a drunken smile.)* You too, eh? *(Advances towards her.)* Listen, Grace, it doesn't need to make any difference to us. You and I can still get married like you promised —

Grace: Promised! *(Shakes her head in disgust.)* Please don't make things any worse. *(Draws back from him.)* Go to bed. We'll talk about it in the morning.

Jake: *(Laughs drunkenly.)* Let me tell you something, **Mrs.** Harding. You weren't always so goddam high and mighty. You promised me that when we came back tonight we'd —*(Shakes his head.)* I'm too young for you anyway!

Grace: Please leave it until morning.

Jake: *(With an air of outraged innocence.)* I'm not going to marry Shirley Cooper. She's not going to stick me with her kid! *(Laughs)* And you can tell old Rupert that after I leave this jeezly place in the morning.

Grace stares at him in disgust and slams the door in his face.

Jake; Don't forget to prop your chair against the door! *(Laughs and staggers into his own room.)*

The following morning. Jake, dressed as he was the night before, comes from his room carrying his packsack and paper parcel. He drops them to the floor, pours a little water from the kettle into the dishpan in the sink, and wets his face and hair. Grace, in her dressing gown, comes out of her room.

Grace: *(Without looking at him.)* You may as well stay for breakfast. You can't run very far on an empty stomach.

Jake: *(Wiping his head on a towel.)* Who's running! *(Shrugs)* What's the difference. Thanks, Grace, but I don't need any breakfast. *(Looks away from her.)* I guess I told you last night about Shirley?

Grace: *(Wearily)* Yes you did. *(Places some money on the table.)* Here's your wages up to yesterday.

Jake: *(Picks up his pack and parcel from the floor and the money from the table.)* I want you to know I meant it yesterday — about staying here I mean. *(Shrugs)* Funny how these things happen. *(Opens the door.)* Goodbye, Grace. *(Crosses the porch and the yard and exits.)*

Grace: *(Walks to the window and peers through the curtains.)* Jake! *(Turns from the window, trying to hold back her tears. She stares into the mirror on the wall.)* I'll always wonder if you were a fool or not. *(Covers her face with her hands and sobs. Looks at herself in the mirror again and backs away from it.)* You know what they say about an old fool. *(Sobs uncontrollably as she feels her way to a chair. She covers her face with her arms and lowers her head to the table.)*

End of Play

A Trip For Mrs. Taylor

Characters:

Mrs. Taylor, 75, an old age pensioner.
Mrs. Connell, 50, a landlady.
A Soldier, 21.
A Young Woman, 25, a young mother of two.
Gary, a small boy.
Newsy, a railroad news butcher.
Conductor, 60, typical railroad conductor.
Bus Driver, a city bus driver.

Scene One: *A cheap rooming house room with a door leading to an upstairs hallway. The furniture consists of a nondescript metal bed on which is an open suitcase, a scruffy kitchen table and two kitchen chairs, a dresser with a mirror and a low commode upon which is a single-burner electric hotplate holding a small kettle. A tall cardboard wardrobe stands beside the door, its top shelf holding a few pieces of chinaware and two or three cans of food. Hanging beneath the shelf are a couple of dresses and a winter coat. On the dresser is a cheap alarm clock, a large black bible, a milk bottle holding some drooping flowers, brush and comb and two framed photographs, one of a moustached workman wearing 1929 Sunday clothes, the other of two young men in World War Two army uniforms.*

Mrs. Taylor sits at the table eating a slice of bread and marmalade. On the table are a teapot, cup and saucer, a half loaf of bread, jar of marmalade, and a can of evaporated milk. Mrs. Taylor is fully dressed, wearing a high-collared black dress, black stockings and well polished but rundown black shoes. Her white hair is combed back into a bun.

There is a soft but authoritive knock at the door.

Mrs. Taylor: *(With a startled glance at the door, then around the room.)* Yes! Who is it?

Mrs. Connell: It's me. Mrs. Connell.

Mrs. Taylor: Just a minute! *(Scoops the bread and marmalade from the table and hurriedly shoves them on to a shelf in the commode, then opens the door.)*

Mrs. Connell: *(Enters, yawning.)* Why, you're all dressed up! What's the matter? *(She is wearing a dressing gown.)*

Mrs. Taylor: Nothing. I've been up since five o'clock. I hope I didn't disturb anybody?

Mrs. Connell: *(Looking around the room.)* I didn't hear any complaints, and you didn't disturb me, dear. I was awake anyway. It's my bladder again.

Mrs. Taylor: Oh, I'm so sorry.

Mrs. Connell: (*Transfers her inspection to Mrs. Taylor.*) Where you goin', to a funeral?

Mrs. Taylor: (*Looking down at herself.*) No.

Mrs. Connell: (*Stares at suitcase on the bed.*) Are you goin' away?

Mrs. Taylor: (*Hurriedly, with a smile.*) Not for long.

Mrs. Connell: Well, it beats all!

Mrs. Taylor: I'm just going on a little trip.

Mrs. Connell: (*Petulant.*) I thought at least you'd tell me. You were goin' without even lettin' me know.

Mrs. Taylor: No! No, it isn't — it isn't like that at all, Mrs. Connell.

Mrs. Connell: Well — (*Walks to the bed and sits down upon it, peering into the empty suitcase.*) Are you leavin' town? Takin' a bus?

Mrs. Taylor: No, I'm catching a train.

Mrs. Connell: (*Smiles.*) That'll be nice. I always like trains. Most of my travellin' has been on trains. They got busses beat all hollow. Joe and me went clear out to the Coast and back on a train once. That was when he was a company repersentative, of course. Back in the Depression.

Mrs. Taylor: Yes, it must have been nice. (*Pulls a small washbowl from beneath the electric plate and places it on the table. Puts her cup and saucer, knife, spoon, etc. in it.*)

Mrs. Connell. Did you hear the Graham's baby coughin' all night?

Mrs. Taylor: No.

Mrs. Connell: All night I heard it. Sounded like croup to me.

Mrs. Taylor: Poor little thing. (*Pours some water into washbowl from the kettle. Gets a dishcloth from the commode and begins washing her dishes. Mrs. Connell makes a useless gesture of fixing her hair.*)

Mrs. Connell: I musta nodded off comin' on mornin'. I didn't hear you gettin' up, nor washin' up neither.

Mrs. Taylor: (*Takes a dish-towel from a short piece of clothesline across the corner of the room and wipes her dishes. Then she begins putting them away on the top shelf of the wardrobe.*) I kept as quiet as I could. I only gave myself a lick 'n a spit as they say.

Mrs. Connell: (*Pontifically.*) In this weather it's no use tryin' to keep clean, Mrs. Taylor. If this heat wave doesn't let up soon I don't know what'll become of us. Joe said it was a hundred-'n-twenty down at the shop yesterday.

Mrs. Taylor: My goodness! (*She folds the towel carefully and places it back in its place.*)

Mrs. Connell: I read in last night's paper where six people died of the heat right here in the city. They say it's hard on them that's over fifty.

Mrs. Taylor: It doesn't bother me too much. I'm so thin now . . .

Mrs. Connell: Lucky you! You'll be gettin' away from it for a while.

Mrs. Taylor: (*Wiping the top of the table with the dishcloth.*) I'm so excited I don't know what I'm doing! (*Smiles happily.*) It's been years since I went away like this.

Mrs. Connell: It seems funny you didn't mention goin' away to me before?

Mrs. Taylor: (*Easing herself on to a chair*) I didn't think about it till yesterday. I was downtown for a walk and I went into the station to sit down for a minute — the streets were like an oven — and when I saw everybody going away I made up my mind to go too. I walked right over and bought a ticket.

Mrs. Connell: Did you win a sweepstakes or somep'n?

Mrs. Taylor: (*Laughs*) No. (*Looks into the past, wearing a beautiful smile.*) It came over me all at once. It reminded me of the times in the summer when me and Bert and the boys used to go up to my cousin Flora's in Jamesville. I got the same feeling I used to get then — a warm, picnicky feeling —

Mrs. Connell: Is that where you're goin' now?

Mrs. Taylor: To Flora's! No, she's been dead since the 'flu epidemic in 'nineteen.

Mrs. Connell: *(Petulant)* I'm not one to pry, Mrs. Taylor, you know that, but it seems kind of funny you won't tell me where you're goin'.

Mrs. Taylor: *(Stands up)* It — well, it's kind of a secret. I'll tell you all about it when I come back.

Mrs. Connell: *(Reluctantly)* Well, all right then.

Mrs Taylor picks up the dishpan and exits through the door to empty it. In the moment or two before she comes back, Mrs. Connell gets up from the bed and peers into the wardrobe. She shakes her head sadly. When she hears Mrs Taylor returning she rushes back to the bed and sits down on the edge of it.

Mrs. Taylor: *(Enters and glances at the clock on the dresser.)* I didn't need to get up so early, I guess. *(Places the dishpan in the bottom of the commode.)*

Mrs. Connell: I'm always the same way.

Mrs. Taylor goes to the wardrobe, takes down a heavy dress, and carries it to the side of the bed.

Mrs. Connell: You're not takin' that heavy thing with you surely?

Mrs. Taylor: *(Folds the dress carefully and places it in the suitcase.)* Why yes.

Mrs. Connell: But, my dear, it's too heavy for this time of year. What is it, velvet?

Mrs. Taylor: Yes. It's the dress Mrs. Eisen gave me last winter for helping her with her cleaning.

Mrs. Connell: *(Suspiciously)* You're sure you're not leavin' for good?

Mrs. Taylor: *(Stops on her way to the closet, turns.)* My goodness no!

Mrs. Connell: *(Hurt)* Any time you want to find accommodations somewheres else, you're always free to go, you know.

Mrs. Taylor: I'm not leaving, Mrs. Connell. *(Goes to wardrobe and takes down a blouse and skirt.)* It's just that I think packing up and everything is part of the fun of a trip. *(Carries blouse and skirt to the bed.)*

Mrs. Connell: I hate packin', myself.

Mrs. Taylor puts the blouse and skirt in the suitcase. Goes to the dresser and from a drawer takes some clean folded underwear, handkerchiefs and black lisle stockings. From another drawer a clean towel and a bar of soap in its wrapper. Carries these things to the bed and places them in the suitcase.

Mrs. Connell: *(Watching her)* That bag is too big for what you've got. Let me lend you the small one that Edna gave me last Christmas. It's a light one. *(Brags)* It's air-weight.

Mrs. Taylor: Thanks, but this'll do fine. I've got some more things to put in yet. *(Takes the two framed photographs from the top of the dresser, smiles at them for a moment, then cleans their glass with her sleeve.)*

Mrs. Connell: You takin' **them** too!

Mrs. Taylor: *(Places the photos in the suitcase.)* I couldn't leave **them** behind.

Mrs. Connell: *(Laughs and slaps her hands on her thighs.)* I've got it now! Johnny sent you the money to go see your grandchildren! Isn't that ni - -

Mrs. Taylor: I'm paying my own fare for this trip.

Mrs. Connell: *(Inquisitive)* But isn't that expensive? Now I know you won a sweepstake. *(Mrs. Taylor smiles and shakes her head.)* It must be nice to be rich. *(An exaggerated primping of her hair.)* When I get the old-age pension myself, I'm gonna take trips too.

B48

Mrs. Taylor: *(Sits down on a chair and becomes serious.)* Don't wish it on yourself, Mrs. Connell. It might turn out different for you, with your husband living and everything, but it's a struggle, let me tell you, when you're alone. It's nothing but scrimp and scrape all the time to make ends meet. *(Watches her hands as she twists them in her lap.)*

Mrs. Connell: Hey listen, Mrs. Taylor, I wasn't makin' fun of you! Listen, I know what a struggle you have gettin' along on a few lousy dollars a month. *(Angrily)* If I had my way I'd make the bastards up in - -

Mrs. Taylor: It's not only the money. There's the terrible loneliness too. You don't know what it's like to be cooped up month after month in a dreary little room, without even a radio to keep you company. Without even a cat or a dog or a — or a canary. Nothing but the four walls. *(Indicates them with a wave of her hand.)* And a bed, a dresser, and a — an electric plate.

Mrs. Connell: But my dear, I don't mind you havin' a radio or — or a canary.

Mrs. Taylor: *(Wry smile)* You know I couldn't afford them.

Mrs. Connell: Well, it seems to me that your son Johnny could help you out once in a while. There he is with a good job and everythin' —

Mrs. Taylor: *(Emphatically)* Johnny's a good boy. He's just — forgetful, that's all.

Mrs. Connell: *(Takes the photograph of the two young soldiers from the suitcase.)* I always forget which one of these is Johnny.

Mrs. Taylor: *(Gets up from the chair and sits beside Mrs. Connell on the edge of the bed.)* The one on the right.

Mrs. Connell: *(Points at the picture.)* I'll bet this one wouldn't have let you live like this if he hadn't — if he was here. That's Bert, isn't it?

Mrs. Taylor: He was young Bert. *(Smiles fondly at the photo.)* We named him after his father.

Mrs. Connell: *(Puts the photograph in the suitcase.)* He was a fine-lookin' boy.

Mrs. Taylor: Both my boys were fine. Johnny's a fine boy too.

Mrs. Connell: *(Puts her arm around Mrs. Taylor's shoulders.)* I know he is, dear.

Mrs. Taylor: Bert was no better than Johnny.

Mrs. Connell: I didn't mean anythin' by what I said. I do think though that after you sendin' him the pipe last Christmas and spendin' all the time you did crochetin' them runners for his wife, that he'd have sent you the fare to go and see your grandchildren. *(Mrs. Taylor walks to the dresser and takes a small tissue-wrapped package from a drawer.)* I'm sure you'd be happier livin' with your own kith and kin than alone like this. If it was me I'd write to him and —

Mrs. Taylor: Johnny asked me to go and live with him and Ruth right after the war, but I wouldn't. I've seen women who go and live with their sons and daughters-in-law. There's always squabbling, and they end up either as nuisances or a built-in baby-sitter. I was always independent, and I ran my own house when I was young. I'll run it now *(Gestures)* even as it is, now I'm old.

Mrs. Connell: Well, he could ask you down for a visit, and pay your way. *(Catches sight of package in Mrs. Taylor's hand.)* What's that you've got?

Mrs. Taylor: Just some old jewelry.

Mrs. Connell: *(Holds out her hand.)* I've never seen it before. Let's see it, dear. *(Mrs Taylor unwraps a gold locket and gold chain bangle bearing a small lock, shaped like a heart, and hands them to Mrs. Connell.)* They're lovely!

Mrs. Taylor: I've had them for years and years.

Mrs. Connell: I always say old jewelry's better than the junk they're peddlin' nowadays. *(Opens the locket and peers inside.)* My, who's the handsome gallant here!

Mrs. Taylor: *(Pleased)* That's Bert, my husband.

The picture was taken just after we were married.

Mrs. Connell: He looks like a banker.

Mrs. Taylor: *(Laughs)* When that was taken he was a teamster for a lumber company.

Mrs. Connell: It was honest work.

Mrs. Taylor: *(Takes the locket and stares at the photograph.)* He was always a good provider, till he took sick. It took all our savings. And with the boys being overseas at the time and all . . .

Mrs. Connell: You don't need to tell me how it is. *(Admires the other pieces of jewelry.)* This bangle is beautiful. My mother had one exactly like it, but she gave it to my sister Amy just before she passed away. Have you got the key for it?

Mrs. Taylor: *(Slips the bangle over her wrist.)* I lost the key a long time ago, but my hand is so thin now I can put it on without undoing it.

Mrs. Connell: Put the locket on too, Mrs. Taylor.

Mrs. Taylor fastens the chain of the locket around her neck, and admires herself in the dresser mirror. Mrs. Connell gets up from the bed and joins her in front of the dresser.

Mrs. Connell: Why, you look just like a lady! Like Lady — like Lady Godiva! You look real elegant! *(Mrs. Taylor takes a box of rouge from the dresser drawer and with a guilty wink at her companion rubs a bit of it on her cheeks.)* Whee! *(Both laugh conspiratorially.)* Don't be pickin' up no movie stars on the train! *(Mrs. Taylor takes a straw flower-bordered hat from the bottom drawer of the dresser. Mrs. Connell reaches for it, and then holds it in her hand, admiring it.)* My goodness! A new hat too!

Mrs. Taylor: *(Beaming)* I've had it for ages, silly. The flowers are new though. I bought them at the five-and-ten.

Mrs. Connell: *(Puts the hat on top of her uncombed hair and with her hands on her hips gazes at herself in the mirror. Pulling a face.)* Did you ever see anything so repulsive in your life?

Man's Voice: *(Coming from downstairs.)* Clara!

Mrs. Connell: *(Removing the hat and handing it to Mrs. Taylor.)* There's the bull-of-the-woods. *(Shouts)* I'm coming! Keep your shirt on! *(To Mrs. Taylor.)* Drop in on your way out. *(Looks at the clock.)* I hope I haven't made you late. What time does your train leave?

Mrs. Taylor: *(Places the hat on the dresser.)* Eight o'clock — that's eight Standard Time.

Mrs. Connell: What's that, seven our time?

Mrs. Taylor: No, nine.

Mrs. Connell: Why, you've got hours yet! Look, dear, you lie down for a while. As soon as I get his lordship off to work I'll come back and see you.

Man's Voice: *(From downstairs)* Clara!

Mrs. Connell: Oh shut up! *(She exits.)*

As soon as the landlady has gone, Mrs. Taylor checks the contents of her suitcase, smiling happily to herself. She begins to fasten the case then halts as she remembers something she has left out. She walks to the dresser and takes a large heavy bible from the bottom drawer. She weighs it in her hands in indecision, then brushes it lovingly with her sleeve before carrying it to the bed. She opens the suitcase and makes a place for the bible beneath the clothing. Then she fastens the case again with an air of finality and lifts it heavily to the floor. She lies down on the bed and stares at the ceiling, a pleasurable smile of anticipation lighting her face.

Curtain

B52

Scene Two   *The interior of a large city railroad station on a summer morning. There is an archway above which is a sign "Track 12." To the side of this archway a sign reads "Lakeshore Express" and beneath it, from top to bottom, are signs fitted in slots: Oshawa, Port Hope, Belleville, Kingston, Brockville, Cornwall, Montreal. The archway is flanked by a pair of waist-high iron railings, and a railroad gateman sits on a tall wooden stool. There is a queue of waiting passengers lined up before the gate.*

Mrs. Taylor comes on stage accompanied by a young soldier carrying her suitcase. They come to a halt away from the line of people. Mrs. Taylor wears her flowered hat and is carrying a worn leather purse. The soldier lowers her suitcase to the floor.

Mrs. Taylor: *(Excited and out of breath.)* I'm glad I made it in time.

Soldier: *(Glances at the queue and then at his watch.)* The train doesn't leave for a half hour yet.

Mrs. Taylor: I know, but I was afraid to miss it. You see, I've been looking forward to this trip for so long.

Soldier: Have you bought your ticket yet?

Mrs. Taylor: Yes, thank you. I bought it yesterday.

Soldier: That was a good idea. *(Points behind him at the gateman.)* You'll have to show it to him.

Mrs. Taylor: Yes. *(Glances at the gateman and back again.)* It was good of you to carry my bag from the street. I don't think I'd have been able to carry it all that way by myself.

Soldier: It was no trouble at all. It sure is heavy though. *(Smiles)* What are you carrying in it, goldbricks?

Mrs. Taylor: *(Serious)* Oh no! It's just my things. *(Notices he is joking and smiles.)* I've got my Bible in it. It belonged to my husband's family for years. I knew it would weigh me down, but I just couldn't go anywhere without

it. (*The Soldier nods.*)

Announcer's Voice: Mr. C. A. Staples, come to the Green Light please! Mr. C. A. Staples, come to the Green Light please!

Mrs. Taylor: You're pretty young to be in the army.

Soldier: I'm twenty-one. Starting my second hitch.

Mrs. Taylor: Are you taking the Montreal train?

Soldier: No, I'm going north to the camp I'm stationed at. (*Looks across the station.*) Everybody in the city seems to be taking my train. I hope I get a seat.

Mrs. Taylor: Oh, I hope you do too! Here I am gabbing with you, and —

Soldier: It's okay. I'll get a seat all right.

Mrs. Taylor: Have you been visiting your mother?

Soldier: My mother! (*Begins to laugh but changes his mind.*) No. That is — well, my people live in Red Deer, Alberta.

Mrs. Taylor: My goodness! Away out there?

Announcer: Last call for the northbound train! Passengers for Barrie, Camp Borden, Bala, Muskoka, MacTier, North Bay and Sudbury. Train now leaving on Track Seven! A-a-a-all A-b-o-o-oard!

Mrs. Taylor: That's **your** train! Don't miss it.

Soldier: I don't suppose it'll matter much whether I do or not.

Mrs. Taylor: Is there another one later?

Soldier: No, but I've overstayed my leave anyhow.

Mrs. Taylor: Well, they might let you off if you go back now. It'll be much worse for you the longer you stay away.

Soldier: (*Smiles down at her.*) Don't worry about me. I'll carry your bag over to the end of the line-up for your train. (*Picks up the bag and with Mrs. Taylor following him, puts it down at the end of the queue.*) Will you be able to manage with it now?

Mrs. Taylor: I'll manage fine now, thank you.

Soldier: Goodbye. (*Starts to walk away.*)

Mrs. Taylor: Son! (*The Soldier stops and turns.*) I didn't mean to butt into your business. For a minute . . . Well you see both my own boys were soldiers in the war. The youngest one, Bert — named after his father — well, he didn't come back. Just for a minute you reminded me —

Soldier: (*Walks over quickly and kisses her on the cheek.*) It's okay, ma'am. (*Smiles*) Goodbye — goodbye, Ma. (*Swings around and hurries away.*)

Mrs. Taylor: Goodbye, son — and thank you! (*The soldier exits.*) Good luck! Good luck to you, son. (*Stares after him.*)

The queue begins moving towards the archway. A man picks up Mrs. Taylor's bag and carrying it as well as his own walks past the gatekeeper. Mrs. Taylor pulls a small pasteboard ticket from her purse and shows it to the gatekeeper as she passes.

Curtain

A section of a railway day-coach. We see one line of seats, as if from the cut-away opposite wall of the car. On one of the seats sits a young woman holding a blanket-wrapped baby. Between her and the window, on the seat, are a pair of paper shopping bags presumably filled with food, baby bottles, diapers, etc. Next to her, near the aisle, sits a five-year-old boy. On the seat between the boy and his mother lies a large celluloid rattle. The boy is wearing light summer clothes, and is bored and restless. His mother is neatly but cheaply dressed in summer clothing, probably Levis and a blouse or sweater. She has the harried, tired look of a woman travelling with young children. People pass down the aisle of the coach searching for seats. A fat man carrying a suitcase makes as if to take the empty seat opposite the young woman with the children, then changes his mind and moves on. The young woman places the baby on the empty, opposite-seat, and places the shopping bags on it too. The young boy picks up the rattle and shakes it loudly while his mother is busy with the baby and the shopping bags.

Young Woman: Gary, stop that right now! *(Takes the rattle from him.)*

Mrs. Taylor enters the car, lugging her heavy bag, and pauses at the end of the seat holding the baby and the Young Woman's paper bags. She droops, leans against the seat end and lowers the bag to the floor. She smiles down at the sleeping baby, then at the Young Woman.

Young Woman: *(Lifts little boy to floor.)* Gary, you sit over there at the window and watch the choo-choos. Mind the baby now! *(The small boy moves to the seat opposite his mother, and presses his face against the window, staring outside. The Young Woman indicating the seat vacated by the boy, smiles up at Mrs. Taylor.)* You can sit here if you like.

Mrs. Taylor: Thank you. *(She shoves her suitcase along the floor between the seats and sits down gratefully.)*

Young Woman: Would you like me to put your bag up on the rack?

Mrs. Taylor: It'll be all right there. That is if it won't be in your way?

Young Woman: No. It's all right there.

Mrs. Taylor: *(Shaking the neck of her dress.)* It's awfully warm, isn't it?

Young Woman: I'll say! *(She bends forward in the seat.)* Gary, be still before you kick the baby.

Mrs. Taylor: *(Looking at the little boy.)* It's the heat that makes them restless.

Young Woman: *(Sits up straight again.)* He's been a little devil all morning. He thinks he can get away with it on a train.

Mrs. Taylor: *(Smiling at the other.)* I know. I had two boys myself. Is the baby a boy too?

Young Woman: Yes. Four months.

Mrs. Taylor: *(Bends to look at him.)* He's a big boy for four months, isn't he?

Young Woman: *(Smiling fondly at the baby.)* Yes. *(Both women smile down at the sleeping baby, then at each other.)*

Mrs. Taylor: *(Turning to Young Woman.)* Are you going far?

Young Woman: To Bathurst, New Brunswick.

Mrs. Taylor: My goodness! That's an awful long way.

Young Woman: You get used to it. My husband's got a job there with a mining company. I wanted my mother to see the baby, that's why I made this trip.

Mrs. Taylor: *(Wistfully)* I'll bet she was pleased.

Young Woman: Oh yes. We wanted her to come back with us for a month or two, but her arthritis is bad.

Mrs. Taylor: *(Nods)* It would have been nice for your mother. *(Changing the subject.)* My landlady has trouble with her back. Lumbago I guess it is.

Young Woman: *(Nods politely.)*

Mrs. Taylor: I love travelling, don't you? People seem more friendly somehow than they do at other times. I don't often get a chance to meet people like this. *(Looks around the car.)* The people are just like I hoped they would be.

Young Woman: They're always the same.

Mrs. Taylor: I was so excited this morning! I got up at five. *(Lowers her voice.)* Do you know, this is going to be my first train trip since my husband died.

Young Woman: It'll be a change for you. How long has it been?

Mrs. Taylor: Let's see — *(Stares at the ceiling as she thinks.)* Nearly fourteen years.

Young Woman: Fourteen years, my goodness! I suppose you live with one of your children?

Mrs. Taylor: No. I get my old-age pension. I have a room of my own, in a rooming house.

Young Woman: *(Sympathetically)* But —

Mrs. Taylor: *(Hurriedly)* My oldest boy lives in Montreal, you see. He's married with two small daughters. My youngest one, Bert, was killed in the war. In Italy.

Young Woman: It's none of my business, but can't you stay with your married son?

Mrs. Taylor: *(Her face dropping.)* Oh, I couldn't do that. My landlady, Mrs. Connell, is always saying the same thing, but I tell her I'm too independent.

The train gives a slight lurch, indicated by both women being jarred back against the seat. The Young Woman bends forward to guard the baby against being toppled to the floor.

Young Woman: *(Sitting up straight again.)* Well, we're on our way at last.

Mrs. Taylor: *(Beaming)* I can hardly believe it.

Young Woman: *(To Gary.)* You sit up straight, Gary, and watch the choo-choo trains.

Mrs. Taylor: *(Staring past the Young Woman and through the train window.)* I can hardly believe we're moving. It looks as though the station was sliding past.

Young Woman: *(Leaning over to listen to her son, who is whispering something to her.)* Oh no! Not already!

Mrs. Taylor: They're all the same. *(Smiles at the little boy.)*

Young Woman: *(With exasperation)* I've never known it to fail. Before we left home I —

Mrs. Taylor: You take him. I'll look after the baby.

Young Woman: Gee, that'll be swell!

The Young Woman stands up and carefully lifts the small boy from the seat and exits with him, holding him by the hand. Mrs. Taylor moves along the seat to the window, and gazes through it in rapt wonderment. Now and again she glances down at the sleeping baby.

News Butcher: *(Off stage)* Magazines, candy bars, peanuts, popcorn, soft drinks, Toronto and Montreal morning papers!

(Baby's cry)

Mrs. Taylor: *(Bends over and plays with the baby.)* There, there! Did the naughty man wake him up!

The baby continues to cry.

Mrs. Taylor: Oh, he's hot, poor little tyke! Wait till I loosen his clothes.

The baby continues crying as Mrs. Taylor fusses with him. After a moment or two she glances around indecisively, then lifts him into her arms and settles back in her seat. She smiles down at him in his blanket, rocking him back and fro. The baby's crying sinks to a contented gurgle or two, then stops. Mrs. Taylor looks triumphant at first, but as she stares down at him her smile fades and her eyes fill with tears. She stares through the window, trying to wipe her eyes unobtrusively with the knuckles of her hand.

Curtain falls momentarily to indicate passage of time.

Curtain rises again on same scene as before, but now Mrs. Taylor is sitting against the window with the little boy seated on her lap. The train is now moving at a moderate speed, as indicated by the swaying of the passengers, the sound of the diesel's whistle, and probably a passenger lurching along the aisle to his seat. In the aisle seat sits the Young Woman. She and Mrs. Taylor have obviously been engaged in conversation for some time.

Young Woman: . . . A friend of my mother's goes there. Mrs. Bellamy. Do you know her?

Mrs. Taylor: *(Shaking her head as she tries to remember.)* No, I don't think I do. *(Brightens)* Wait a minute! Is she a stout woman with bluish hair, that wears a Persian lamb coat in the winter?

Young Woman: Yes, that's her.

Mrs. Taylor: It's a small world, isn't it?

Mrs. Taylor squeezes the small boy's knee with her hand, and points through the window.

Mrs. Taylor: *(Turning to the Young Woman.)* The city has certainly changed, hasn't it? I was brought up right around here. *(Motions towards the window with her head.)* It was nice around here then. There used to be a nice little park where Bert and I used to walk in the evenings. That's where we did our courting. *(Turns to the window again, smiling to herself at the memory.)*

Mrs. Taylor: *(After a pause, and turning from the window to face the Young Woman.)* The city looks different from a train, somehow. You pass all the people's backyards, and wonder who lives in the houses. All the backyards with clothes on lines hanging in them, and the kiddies playing, and you think of the women in the houses washing up after breakfast, and — You must think I'm crazy!

Young Woman: No I don't, Mrs. Taylor.

Mrs. Taylor: I guess that's what I miss most of all — the feeling that I **belong** with all this. *(Hugging the small boy to her.)* I envy you, Norah, with your kiddies still young and everything. I guess I'd give up every one of the rest of my days just to be young again just for an hour or two, with my boys crawling round on the floor.

Young Woman: *(Laying her hand on Mrs. Taylor's forearm.)* I know what you mean.

Mrs. Taylor turns away quickly to hid her embarrassment, and whispers to the boy as she points through the window.

Young Woman: I'll be glad to see this day go. We'll be in Montreal before supper time. It must make you glad too.

Mrs. Taylor stares at her, suddenly realizing that the other doesn't understand.

Young Woman: You must be looking forward to seeing your grandchildren?

Mrs. Taylor: *(Trying to make light of it.)* I'm not going to Montreal today. I can't afford to go that far.

Young Woman: *(Surprised)* Well — well, where are you going then?

Mrs. Taylor: Just up the line apiece. It's just a short trip.

Mrs. Taylor turns and stares through the window again. The young woman begins to say something, but then changes her mind.

Conductor: *(Off stage.)* Tickets please! All tickets. Please have your tickets ready.

Young Woman: *(Picking up her purse from the seat beside her.)* Here's the conductor coming for the tickets, Mrs. Taylor.

Mrs. Taylor takes a small piece of pasteboard from her handbag. It is in contrast to the long ribbon of paper that the Young Woman takes from hers.

Mrs. Taylor: *(Turns to the window, then back to her companion.)* They're certainly building the

city out in every direction. I can remember when all this (Nods to the window) was all farmland. And now it's well within the city limits.

Young Woman: We won't be out in the real country for miles yet.

The Conductor appears, and begins punching and collecting tickets along the car. Mrs. Taylor stares through the window. The Young Woman looks down at the sleeping baby, moving the blanket from its face.

When the Conductor reaches their seat the Young Woman hands him her ticket. He punches it, tears off a section, and hands it back to her. Then he reaches across the women and places a small slip of cardboard in the window blind. He then takes Mrs. Taylor's ticket, and places it in his pocket.

Conductor: (To Mrs. Taylor.) We'll be at your station in a minute, ma'am. In fact we're slowing down now. Will you get off at the front end of the car please.

Mrs. Taylor stands up with the little boy in her arms. She kisses him and sits him down in the seat where she has been sitting. She picks up her suitcase from the floor. The Young Woman is staring at her openmouthed.

Conductor: (Surprised) You have luggage, Ma'am!

Mrs. Taylor: (Apologetically) Just this bag.

Conductor: (Takes the bag from her.) Here.I'll carry it for you.

The conductor exits, carrying the bag.

Mrs. Taylor: I'll have to say goodbye to you now. You don't know how much I've enjoyed being with you and the kiddies.

Young Woman: (Still surprised.) We've enjoyed it too.

Mrs. Taylor rubs her hand over the little boy's head, then bends down and kisses the baby.

Mrs. Taylor: You be a good boy now, Gary, won't you. (To the Young Woman) You must think I'm crazy just coming this far. You see I've wanted to take a trip for so long, and this was sort of — pretending.

Young Woman: (Holding back her tears.) No I don't, Mrs. Taylor. I just wish you were coming all the way. Thanks so much for helping me with the children.

Mrs. Taylor: (Suddenly shy.) Goodbye, dear, and God bless you. Have a nice journey. (She walks along the aisle of the car.)

Young Woman: (Shouting after her.) Thanks! Thanks a lot! (To the little boy.) Say goodbye to Grandma Taylor, Gary.

The small boy mumbles a goodbye and waves his hand. Mrs. Taylor turns and waves in return before she exits. As the train begins to move again the Young Woman and little boy crowd against the window waving at someone on the platform.

Curtain

Scene Four: *The interior of a city bus. We are facing the driver from his rear, and he is in profile to the audience. He is collecting fares from two or three passengers, but the bus is almost empty. The driver is wearing a uniform cap, but his uniform jacket is hanging on a hook beside his seat.*

Mrs. Taylor climbs the steps, out of breath and obviously weighted down with the heavy suitcase. She places the suitcase down on the floor, and searches in her purse for the fare.

Bus Driver: *(Smiling at her.)* You look happy, Ma. You must have had a swell vacation.

Mrs. Taylor: *(Abandons her search in her purse and looks up.)* Oh yes. I had a wonderful trip. I'm a little tired though.

Bus Driver: I'd never come back to this heat. *(He removes his cap and wipes his forehead on his sleeve.)* Did you just get off a train?

Mrs. Taylor: Yes, the Montreal train.

Bus Driver: *(Enviously)* Montreal, eh? *(Sighs)* It's nice to travel, but it's pretty expensive I guess.

Mrs. Taylor: *(Smiling at a secret thought.)* Yes, but it's almost as expensive staying put these days. *(She finds the fare and deposits it in the fare-box.)*

Bus Driver: It must be nice to get away from this heat once during the summer anyway.

Mrs. Taylor: *(Picking up her suitcase.)* Yes it is. *(On a sudden, boastful impulse.)* I'm taking another trip next month. But that one'll be on the Winnipeg train!

Mrs. Taylor comes downstage towards the audience, limping a little and lopsided from the weight of the heavy bag. She has to steady herself with her hand on the rear of the seats. Her face lights up and her smile widens as she comes down the aisle of the bus. It is a smile of achievement and triumph beyond happiness.

Final curtain.

The Devil's Instrument

Instrument

W.O. Mitchell

The Author

W. O. Mitchell was born in Weyburn, Saskatchewan, and educated at the Universities of Manitoba and Alberta. Following a brief spell of European travel, during which he held a number of odd jobs — not the least odd of which was a short stint as an organ-grinder's assistant — he returned to Alberta where he worked for a while as a teacher before finally settling in High River to devote all his time to writing.

In the intervening years, W. O. Mitchell has produced an impressive body of work for radio, television and films, and has had the distinction of contributing to anthologies in both Canada and the United States.

In Canada, however, he is perhaps best known for two outstanding works: the novel "Who Has Seen the Wind", and the famous series of stories "Jake and the Kid", which ran for many years on both radio and television.

"Who Has Seen the Wind" — an account of the development of a young boy in a small prairie town — is a sensitive prose work of lyrical beauty. In this novel, W. O. Mitchell held in check his enormous talent for comic characterization — but gave himself full rein in the "Jake and the Kid" stories, a collection of which was awarded the Leacock Medal for humour in 1962.

To these nationally-known works may be added a third: "The Devil's Instrument" — written originally for television — is a short but intensely dramatic and moving play about the rebellion of a young Hutterite boy against the restrictive life of the colony in which he was born and raised, and from which his older brother has already escaped.

This now-famous work was produced recently by Ontario Youtheatre, a group which had the great good fortune to have as their advisor none other than author W. O. Mitchell himself. This critically acclaimed production not only marked the beginning of a stable and successful existence for Ontario Youtheatre, but also gave added lustre to the name of one of Canada's most celebrated writers.

"Theatre is not a happening. It must be nurtured, disciplined, worked at a long time." These words, spoken on the occasion of an adjudication by Guy Beaulne, Director Général of Le Grand Théâtre de Québec, can be applied equally well to the underlying concept of Ontario Youtheatre.

For those who study theatre as a part of their curriculum, it presents a unique opportunity to find out once and for all if they have made a good choice of a profession and if, indeed, they have the talent and the stamina for it. At a most critical time in their development, young people are given a chance to decide whether they wish to become performers, choose involvement in the technical aspects of the theatre, or create part of an intelligent audience.

A concept originally developed by George Merten of the Youth and Recreation Branch, Ontario Department of Education, Ontario Youtheatre came into being in 1970 under the guidance of **James Colbeck** who, as their General Manager, steered the fledgling company through its first difficult seasons. The beginning was marginally successful. The second season was a greater achievement.

In 1972, the third season, the group found a base of operations — the Guildhall in Peterborough. In this well-equipped theatre, owned by the Peterborough Theatre Guild, new Artistic Director **Ron Hartmann** trained and rehearsed his company of thirty-two young actors, designers and technicians. Their production of W. O. Mitchell's "The Devil's Instrument" resulted in critical acclaim. After visiting eight major cities in Ontario, the tour ended its run with sold-out performances in the Studio Theatre of the National Arts Centre. In December, 1972, staff member **David Barlow** became General Manager. Training and rehearsals for Summer Company '73 again are taking place at the Guildhall under Artistic Director Ron Hartmann.

More than five hundred young people have been involved in Ontario Youtheatre's summer programs; plans for 1973 now include support of local training programs — in winter and summer — plus the establishment of four regional companies as well as a graduate company.

Where will it go from here? Well, in 1971 the National Youth Theatre of Great Britain, which was the inspiration for Ontario Youtheatre, moved into a theatre of its own. Ontario Youtheatre surely deserves no less . . .

Production photos by Karin Trapper.

Cast of Characters

Jacob Schunk, 16, Hutterite
Darius, his older brother
Marta Schreiber, 16, Hutterite
John the Blacksmith, her father
Peter, the Goose Boss
Preacher
Vogel Unger, young Hutterite
Bone-Setter
Marta's Mother
Susan ⎤
Rachel ⎬ Hutterite women
Anna ⎦
Mike ⎤
Otto ⎬ Hutterite men
Joe and Jake, two truckers
Wong, Chinese café proprietor

Scene one   *Small town in Alberta. Palm Cafe.*

Jacob Schunk, 16, Hutterite, stands by juke box, completely lost in the music. He is quite unaware of Wong, proprietor of the cafe, who stands behind the counter, annoyance visible on his face. He leans across to Jacob and taps him on the shoulder.

Wong: *(As Jacob starts guiltily)* What you want? You want buyee something. You buyee . . . ha!

Jacob: Nothing, thank . . .

Wong: Doesn't pay me some kinda money . . . Listen my juice box . . .

Jacob: I do not want to buy anything, thank you.

Wong: You kinda peopah nevah buyee nothing . . . nevah buyee dinnah . . . ham ' egg . . .

Two truckers, Joe and Jake are presenting their bill at the counter.

Joe: Costs money. Hooterites too tight to spend.

Wong: *(Jabbing at cash register viciously.)* Nevah buyee . . . nevah buyee . . . ice cream . . . vanillah . . . mapo wa'nut . . . nevah smoke . . .

Jake: Sinful. They ain't sposed to smoke. Them bosses . . .

Wong: . . . Nevah buyee plug . . . seegah . . . you like plug?

Jacob: Nothing . . . I would like only to . . .

Wong: *(Shoving chewing tobacco plug across counter.)* You like plug . . . Black Judas . . . you chew some . . .

Jacob: I would only like to listen to the music out of the little box.

Wong: *(Slapping Joe's change down on the counter with disgust.)* You like music. Make music. Make you own.

Joe: He ain't even sposed to whistle.

C4

Wong: Make you own. Mouth ohgan. I got lots mouth ohgan. You buyee one . . . make you own music . . . make religion music.

Joe: Send him straight to hell, blowin' a mouth organ. Better watch out, you fellow, one of them beardy bosses comes in an' catches you listenin' to that juke box . . .

Jake: Aw, let him alone. Here . . . *(Hold out a nickel.)* Have one on me kid . . . *(As Jacob hesitates.)* Go on . . . stick it in the slot. Push that there lever down . . .

Jacob: No thank . . .

Jake: Come on . . . it won't hurt you. Any the bosses show up I'll give you the high sign. They're all over in the Royal Beer Parlour suckin down beer . . .

Joe: You folks so religious . . . won't smoke . . . drink tea . . . coffee . . . chew . . . when she comes to beer . . . look out.

Jake: Stick that nickel in.

Jacob: No thank you.

Jake: What's wrong? *(Shoving the nickel at Jacob.)* Here! First time I ever saw one of you people didn't . . .

Jacob: No . . . thank you . . . I don't . . .

Jake: . . . jump at the chance a gettin' somethin' . . .

Jacob: Please . . . no.

Jake: Take it!
Darius has come up during this.

Darius: If he doesn't want to, he doesn't have to!

Jake: Who the . . . I ain't tryin' to force nothin' on him . . . I just . . .

Darius: He doesn't want it . . . obviously.

Jake: I just offered him a nickel for that juke box an' he . . .

Darius: He's told you at least three times . . . he doesn't want it.

Jake: *(Shrugs and swings away.)* No skin off my . . .

Wong: Alla time Hooterite come in . . . nevah buyee . . .

Darius: *(To Jacob)* Don't let it . . .

Wong: Nevah buyee . . . nevah buyee even comb . . .

Joe: Too tight.

Wong: Ice cream comb. All he do . . . listen my juice box on othah peopoh nickoh . . .

Jake: Then when you offer him a nickel to play . . .

Jacob: Excuse me . . . I will go away outside now.

Darius: No . . . No. Sit down. Will you have a dish of ice cream with me?

Jake: Ain't gonna listen to music on my nickel . . . sure as heck ain't gonna eat ice cream for a tee-total stranger.

Darius: Will you . . . please?

Jake: He's gonna disappoint you stranger.

Jacob: Thank you.

Jake: Well, I'll be . . .

Darius: Thank **you.** *(As they move towards booths.)* What kind? Pink? Vanilla? Chocolate?

Jake: Look at that, will you. Hooterite for you.

Joe: Contrary.

Jake: Touchy as a cut calf . . . won't take my nickel . . . some stranger from outa town, he . . . *(They go.)*

Jacob: Pink.

Darius: Pink.

Wong: Pink.

Darius: You . . . you from the hook and eye . . . the Cash River colony?

Jacob: Yes.

Darius: What is your name?

Jacob: Jacob. Jacob Schunk.

Darius: Jacob! Jacob Schunk!
Wong arrives with two dishes of ice cream.

Darius: Jacob Schunk!

Wong: Pink. Thirty cen'.

Darius: Oh . . . yes . . . yes . . . thank you. *(Wong goes.)* Jacob Schunk. Your father . . . your mother . . . they live in the colony?

Jacob: My father and mother are dead.

Darius: Who looks after you?

Jacob: I work and I sleep with Peter, the Goose Boss. He is my grand-uncle.

Darius: Goose boss! Isn't that women's work?

Jacob: *(With some spirit.)* No, it is not! It is important!

Darius: And . . . will you be goose boss when you get older? *(Jacob works on the ice cream.)* I should think it would be much finer to be a Horse Boss or the Oats and Barley Boss . . . or . . .

Jacob: I would like to be a Goose Boss when I get older.

Darius: How old are you Jacob?

Jacob: Sixteen.

Darius: I see. Then you do not go to school anymore?

Jacob: No.

Darius: For it was from the tree of knowledge that the apple came for Adam and Eve's first sin . . . I know.

Jacob: Where are **your** father and mother?

Darius: Mine? *(Pause)* They are dead. Like yours.

Jacob: And have you any sisters?

Darius: One brother.

Jacob: How old is he?

Darius: He is your age, Jacob.

Jacob: *(Suddenly)* Is it hard to blow music out of a little mouth organ?

Darius: Do you like music?

Jacob: Oh yes! No! I don't know how to say it. It . . . hurts me.

Darius: Hurts you!

Jacob: But not bad. It . . . I . . .

Darius: How does it . . . hurt?

Jacob: Like when I come home . . . when the hills are dark . . . only high on top there is light there yet, and I see that die . . . and it leaves me like . . . like . . .

Darius: Sad . . . Jacob.

Jacob: Like I am the only one left in the whole world. It is like I am left hanging. And it hurts . . . in your throat. I want to . . . to cry, for something is lifting up in me, and I want to cry.

Darius: Is it the same with music?

Jacob: I think so . . . the feeling. When you want something so you ache and it hurts . . .

Darius: And you know it's sinful.

Jacob: Yes! Yes! It is the devil's music! It . . . *(Suddenly realizing the importance of what he has said and making a noble effort.)* I do not love . . . like . . . anything of the devil.

Darius: How do you know it is the devil's music? How can you know it isn't . . .

Jacob: I know.

Darius: Because the bosses tell you? Because old men with their . . .

Jacob: I know.

Darius: . . . dry old hearts . . . their very ordinary hearts . . .

Jacob: I know it with my own heart.

Darius: . . . their gross materialistic hearts . . . tell you it is sinful?

Jacob: It is wicked and sinful!

Darius: Do you think the devil likes beauty?

Jacob: It would send me to ever-lasting burning.

Darius: Jacob, that is not true.

Jacob: I know.

Darius: It is not true!

Jacob: The Preacher says it is true. The Chicken Boss says it is true. Otto, the Oats and Barley Boss . . . He is head boss over all the bosses. He is just like Moses.

Darius: Is he?

Jacob: Yes. His beard is black and he is not afraid of anything. He is not afraid to look into the face of the Lord. He is not afraid.

Darius: Is he not?

Jacob: John, the Blacksmith . . . when I was a child, I used to think he looked like Christ. His beard is lovely. It is soft. His eyes are blue . . . and Marta's . . .

Darius: Marta's?

Jacob: He is Marta's father . . . Marta Schreiber. Her eyes . . . they are blue too.

Darius: Are they now?

Jacob: Yes. They are blue . . . like a crocus is blue. The little braids, they . . . do you know something?

Darius: What Jacob?

Jacob: If you had a beard, then . . . then you would look a lot like John, the Blacksmith. *(Rises suddenly)* Thank you for the ice cream.

Darius: That is nothing. *(Stopping him.)* Wait. About this . . . mouth organ.

Jacob: No thanks. I am going to be a good boy like Vogel Unger.

Darius: Is he a good boy?

Jacob: Oh yes. He is going to be the Preacher when he . . . *(He sits down again.)* He has faith.

Darius: Has he?

Jacob: He has tested it. He tested it two years ago, when he was shingling the new horse barn. He laid down his shingling hatchet and he told me he said to himself when the noon bell rang for dinner: "Our Christ walked upon the waters. Why not Vogel Unger, son of the Pig Boss?" Do you know what he did?

Darius: No Jacob.

Jacob: The peak of the new horse barn is seventy-five feet up in the air. That is high.

Darius: That is high.

Jacob: Vogel Unger walked off it on to the air.

Darius: To test his faith.

Jacob: He told me he started walking towards the kitchen behind the spinning building where the women work.

Darius: I don't imagine he reached it Jacob.

Jacob: *(Slowly shakes his head.)* No. The air did not hold him up. He fell fifty feet and onto a load of hay Joseph Martin had just driven up.

Darius: But he is still going to be the Preacher some day?

Jacob: Vogel cannot say his esses very well now.

Darius: Can he not?

Jacob: When he landed on the hay he bit the tip off his tongue.

Darius: It is quite probable that Vogel will become the Preacher.

Jacob: The Bosses said he was vain of his faith. They said he was setting it above his love of God.

Darius: Still . . . the Lord did save him. And Joseph Martin. Oh . . . and the load of hay.

Jacob: I am going to be a good boy. I am not going to ever blow music out of a little mouth organ.

Darius: *(Rising)* Wanting to make music with a little mouth organ . . . that is not sinful. Come over to the counter with me, Jacob. *(They go to the counter.)* See them. *(Wong appears.)* They are very splendid. There is one taken out of its scarlet box and placed upon the lid.

Jacob, in spite of himself, has bent over and is peering at them intently.

Wong: *(Lifts mouth organ from counter.)* Buyee mouth ohgan . . . buyee foh make music . . . not listen my juice box on othah peopoh nickoh.

Jacob: Oh no . . . please.

Darius: Jacob, I am going to give you something.

Jacob: No . . .

Darius: How much are they?

Wong: Lovely mouth ohgan. Dollah fi'ty cen'.

Darius: We'll take this one. *(Handing mouth organ to Jacob.)* Music is not wicked. I want you to have this Jacob. I want you to learn to play it.

Jacob: I . . . I must . . . *(Takes it.)* Thank you . . . *(Wildly)* Peter, the Goose Boss, will be waiting . . . I have kept him long after he will have his teeth. The dentist made his new teeth . . . we came in today for his teeth!

Darius: Don't be afraid of the Goose Boss, Jacob.

Jacob: *(Moves to the door.)* I must go before he comes to look for me . . . thank you for the little mouth organ.

Darius: Hide it away from the Bosses. Play it when you are alone. Be a good boy and do it. If there is a devil in that . . . If he is in it . . . I can tell you this . . . He's a little devil Jacob . . . Such a very unimportant little devil.

Jacob rushes out.

Scene two

Peter the Goose Boss is waiting. He sits hunched over and is a little sour and disconsolate. He works his mouth as he tries to acquaint his gums with his new teeth. He has a long and flowing white beard. Jacob appears and climbs up beside him.

Peter: It was not right to keep me waiting, Jacob.

Jacob: I am sorry Uncle Peter. I thought you would be longer. I thought you would still be in the beer parlour . . . at the dentist's.

Peter jerks the reins of the buggy and it runs away. Jingle and creak of harness. Pock Pock of horses hooves quickens. Town sounds fade away during this scene and prairie road sounds take over.

Peter: You be a good boy, Jacob. The devil don't like good boys, so you be a good boy Jacob.

Jacob: Yes, Uncle Peter.

Peter: The devil is a lot like a weasel, in his thirty-six inch thrashing machine he thrashes souls. He likes fat Hutterite souls . . . mixes them with others to bring the grading up. He is a lot like a weasel.

Jacob: Your new teeth . . . (Tries for better look.) They look nice.

Peter: His breath is hot. His eyes are red. He is pure evil.

Jacob: They shine very white. They are whiter even than your beard.

Peter: Are they? When he steps from his weasel hole, he leaves behind his footprints of drought scorching the prairie for miles . . . They pinch a little.

Jacob: They are lovely and white like an egg. After you have peeled it. Your beard is so white . . .

Peter: You be a good boy . . . like Vogel Unger.

Jacob: Vogel says a beard could not be so white as yours unless there was some blueing . . . (Meadow lark.) He says it is not right to be so vain about a beard. He says . . .

Peter: Let Vogel talk about beards when he is old enough to be married and grow one himself . . .

Jacob: . . . just a little blueing in the wash water when you wash your beard . . .

Peter: Do not listen to such talk! You are easily led in the ways of wickedness as it is! Darius was so too. Remember Darius when you are tempted.

Jacob: Yes Uncle Peter.

Peter: The soul of your brother Darius is doomed to damnation and everlasting hellfire. Remember that!

Jacob: Yes Uncle Peter. Do they still hurt?

Peter: The top ones. At the back. It is like a saddle sore where they rub and rub.

Jacob: Could you not take them out?

Peter: I will keep eighty-nine dollars and fifty cents in my mouth where it is safe.

Jacob: The Chicken Boss says he has not had any teeth for fifteen years.

Peter: The Chicken Boss is jealous.

Jacob: Just his bare gums he said.

Peter: It was the Chicken Boss himself who said to send your brother Darius away to . . .

Jacob: Yes, Uncle Peter.

Peter: . . . the teachers' training school so we could have our own kind of teacher for our own kids. And how did he come back from the city? How . . . what did Sodom and Gomorrah do to him fifteen years ago? Your brother?

Jacob: He smoked.

Peter: Yes . . .

Jacob: He hanged pictures on the schoolhouse walls.

Peter: You did not see. You were not old enough to remember.

Jacob: But you have told me often enough, Uncle Peter.

Peter: You did not hear him teach the kids to sing songs. The devil got his finger into our colony that time. The devil won't get **your** soul, Jacob.

Jacob: No, Uncle Peter.

Peter: And there will be no more about blueing.

Jacob: No, Uncle Peter.

Peter: In the water for washing my beard.

Jacob: No, Uncle Peter.

Peter: Or about loving my white beard and my new teeth more than the Lord, My God?

C10

Jacob: *(He is sneaking a look at mouth organ.)* No, Uncle Peter. *(Meadow lark.)*

Peter: The devil is like a weasel . . . very like. And the devil is in women. He is pure evil, Jezebel!

Jacob: Ah . . . do they . . . do they still hurt now, Uncle Peter?

Peter: Yes . . . they do. There is no reason for them to stop.

Music.

Scene three

Susan: Such a good well — it was . . .

Old Woman: No glauber salts at all . . .

Preacher: Faith we need — with our faith Mike will find water . . .

Mike: No — no — not there . . .

Bone-Setter: Ninety-nine percent faith — one percent Mike, the pig boss . . .

Mother: I hope he finds it —

Otto: So the kids got no excuse for not taking the bath any more.

Mother: So there is water for the garden again . . .

Vogel: Praith the Lord for the water thign he may thend through the willow wand . . .

Bone-Setter: The witching of water is at best a superstition.

Mike: It moved — it moved there . . . !

Otto: Superstition it is not . . .

Mother: No — no!

Peter: What you using, Mike?

Mike: Willow.

Peter: Hazel's better . . .

Mike: I got some movement already — see . . .

Otto: Willow grows near water always -- willow wand works better because it loves water . . .

Peter: Willow's water logged — belly full of water it's got — Hazel's thirsty for water . . .

Mike: Hah — hah! That's it! Strong . . .

Susan: Look at it — look at it!

Rachel: Pulling right down . . .

Vogel: Mutht be loth of water thuckin' it down tho thtrong . . .

Mother: Such a pull — a flowing well . . .

Old Woman: Flowing well . . .

Vogel: Praith Hith Thweet Name for thending uth . . . Praise Mike, the pig boss.

Otto: Best water witcher west of the Hairy Hills!

Peter: Pretty strong . . .

Bone-Setter: From down below the power pulls . . .

Peter: For willow.

Bone-Setter: . . . down below and that is where the powers of darkness lie . . .

Preacher: Stick to the back bone, Bone-Setter! Spiritual to the Preacher belongs. God is everywhere — above — around us — below and He has shown us here pure water in abundance once more. Take the wand from Mike — see for yourself . . .

The Bone-Setter steps back involuntarily. The Preacher holds out his hands to Mike, who turns it up and placed it in the Preacher's hands but after he has gone round behind the Preacher's and with arms around his shoulders is placing the Preacher's hands on the arms of the wand with thumbs in the upright position. Mike's hands still cover the Preacher's as the wand quivers and then dives down. Not only does it dive but it brings the Preacher with it to his knees.

Preacher: Praise God — Praise His Holy Name!

Cast: *(Reverent Assent)*
Praise the Lord . . .
Blessed Jesus . . .
Praise His Name . . .
Amen — amen . . .
Hallelujah . . .
Mike the Pig Boss done it again . . .

Preacher: Let us pray —

Some kneel — some stand for prayer tableau — all put hands together for prayer — all have heads down except Preacher who looks aloft to where God is. Looking sideways Vogel sees this so as he usually does he squeezes his eyes tightly shut and raises his attention aloft like the Preacher's.

Preacher: Heavenly Father, we thank Thee for showing us where Your water lies — through Mike the Pig Boss and his willow divining rod — for we have sorrowed that our old well was getting low and Thy children and Thy children's children's flocks and Thy children's crops were thirsting bad. Now they shall flourish again — especially if you can arrange for a half inch of rain as well now that the wheat and the oats and the barley are in the shot blade stage.
As he has prayed the sun has been setting and the sky is red and the faithful are silhouetted against the foothill and the prairie sky.

Scene four

Sleeping quarters. Jacob and Peter sleeping.

Music: Mouth organ up softly softly.

Jacob: *(Dreaming: Voice over.)* I wonder — I wonder — why did he give me the little mouth organ — ice cream — pink — he was kind to give me the mouth organ and the ice cream. Why should he ask all those questions?

Music: Into subtle hell stuff.

Lights: Devil effect as Darius appears. Hell stuff.

Darius: *(Voice over)* Your father — your mother — they live in the colony? Who looks after you, Jacob? How old are you, Jacob? I have one brother, Jacob. He is your age, Jacob. How do you know it's the devil's music, Jacob? Does the devil like beauty, Jacob? Who am I, Jacob — the devil is pure evil, Jacob . . .

Music: Hell and turmoil.

Jacob asleep and tossing.

Jacob: *(Voice over)* No — no — no he isn't — the devil is like a weasel. He was not like a weasel — he gave me the mouth organ.

Music: Softly the mouth organ takes up.

Jacob: I will make lovely music. I will blow all the songs. I will blow all I have ever listened to. I will play tunes that have never been played before. I will play them first. They will be beautiful tunes. Beautiful tunes. They will . . .

Music: Mouth organ up in Jacob's dream — music then into unlovely snoring note.

Peter: *(Tossing; voice over)* His breath is hot. Be a good boy Jacob. Don't be — Darius . . .

Lights: Dream effect fades to black.

Music: Up full with mouth organ, then into hymnal stuff.

Scene five

The colony — morning.

A montage of scenes showing the colony awakening.

From the TV script — two scenes.

The patriarchs at the breakfast table — the Preacher in his intense head-back act of prayer — the other heads lowered along the table. Prayer finishes. As one they dive into their porridge.

Kitchen with Hutterite women busy at breakfast preparations ladling oatmeal into bowls and handing them to the girls who carry them into the dining hall. One woman is handing Marta the large steaming kettle from the stove. Marta walks towards the corridor door.

Scene five A

Men at the finish of their prayer . . .

Preacher: Amen . . .

Other: Amen . . .

Mike: An' pray God — no more lumps in the porridge.

Peter: Mash with the back of the spoon.

Preacher: Lord helps those who help themselves.

Otto: . . . mash their own porridge lumps out . . .

Peter: . . . with the back of the spoon. *(It was his wise crack.)*

Women have been bringing on their stove, etc.

Mother: Careful — careful with the lid — steam burn is bad. . .

Old Woman: Steam is bad . . .

Rachel has come on later . . . braids flying . . .

Susan: Here — here — your hair loose . . .

She swings daughter over to the table end and begins on the one untidy braid . . .

Susan: Shame — shame — sleep late and no time for the hair . . . Shame — shame . . .

Old Woman: Shame — Shame . . .

Susan: Just like the devil your hair it did — make you look like a young witch . . . or worse — girls in the town and the city . . .

Women in the kitchen . . . Marta's mother is the woman in charge of the breakfast preparations —

Mother: For lumps — no excuses — never.

Woman One: Never.

Mother: Always the same — lumps come — they from too fast adding the oatmeal . . .

Woman One: Too fast adding . . .

Mother: I told you that — stirring is important too, Ruth.

Ruth: I didn't stir it — Rachel . . .

Rachel: You said you would — you said you would when I had to leave . . .

Woman One: Never leave the porridge — it burned last week . . .

Ruth: Not bad.

Mother: No — but the black taste was in it — Vogel Unger complained . . .

Rachel: He always complains . . .

Ruth: Without all his tongue he can't taste anyway . . .

Other girls all laugh and possibly it is during this that Anna gets through to Marta. Marta's mother notices.

Mother: Marta — come — from her — away!

Laughter of the girls is quelled . . .

Woman One: Oatmeal is so simple. Not like noodles.

Marta's mother simply hands Marta the kettle and Marta knows she is to take it out to the washstands for the men.

Mother: You have your turn on the bread today, Ruth — this time — punch down hard . . .

Woman One: Punch down hard.

Rachel: Pretend it's Vogel's face . . .

All laugh . . . Mother sends Marta off.

Mother: Marta — more wash water for the men maybe and make sure they didn't waste it.

Scene six

A rough wash-stand of two-by-fours, holding a wash basin over which Jacob is bending. With one blind hand he is feeling for the long towel hanging on a nail in the wall.

Marta is standing there by Jacob holding the kettle. His reaching hand touches her kerchief — she steps back — he sees her for the first time.

Marta: Water. *(Breathless)*

Jacob: Uh. *(Speechless)*

Marta: Water — hot. *(Afterthought)* Jacob. Here is a towel too. *(Holding one out)* It is clean . . . Jacob.

Jacob: Thank you.

Marta: It is a fresh one . . . Jacob.

Jacob: I am all done.

Marta: Oh.

Jacob: Er . . . except my neck . . . I will need it for my neck. *(Takes the fresh towel from her.)* It is very dirty still . . . it . . . *(Clutching at the kettle which she holds.)* I will need hot water too.

Marta: Yes? *(Still holding the kettle.)*

Jacob: For . . . for . . . my neck . . . my dirty neck.

Marta giggles.

Jacob sees that they are both still holding the kettle handle. Marta releases it. With his eyes still on her he absently pours it into the basin.

Jacob: It gets dirty working the summer fallow.

Marta: Yes, Jacob.

Jacob: *(Unaware that as he still pours, the basin is flowing over its sides.)* Your eyes . . . they . . . they are . . . they . . .

Marta: Yes?

Jacob: Blue. Very blue . . . I should not . . . it wasn't right for me . . . I . . . I . . .

Marta: No? *(Giggles again)*

Jacob: Yes looking at them. It was looking at them . . . Marta . . . that . . . that . . .

He drops the emptied kettle with a clang. He turns from her and plunges his face into the basin and begins furiously to wash his face.

Marta laughs. She picks up her kettle and walks towards the kitchen door.

Scene seven

Kitchen with women. Marta enters still laughing.

Marta's mother looks back over her shoulder from the stove where she is stirring something or other.

Mother: Marta . . . here . . .

Marta: More water, Mother . . .

Mother: Where have you been . . . what have you . . . you **got** water, girl!

Marta: It spilled . . .

Mother: You be a good girl, Marta. *(Taking kettle from Marta.)* You were not talking to Walter or Anna?

Marta: No, Mother.

Mother: What is wrong with you?

Marta: Nothing is wrong, Mother. He spilled the water . . .

Mother: Who spilled the water?

Marta: Jacob.

Mother: Jacob Schunk! Now you be a good girl, Marta. You look at poor Anna and you be a good girl.

Marta nods acquiescence.

Mother: That was how it started with Anna . . . giggling and laughing with Walter. And look how it ended with Anna . . . look . . . straw stacks and three months of no talking. Don't you talk with her, Marta! It will be isolation for you too! Do not go near her or Jacob Schunk! You hear?

Marta, with head down, nods obediently.

Scene eight

Music: Mouth organ's rather crude efforts at hymn tune.

Straw Stack: Jacob seated with knees up and wide . . . elbows resting upon them as he leans against straw stack in evening light.

He finishes the last bars of the hymn tune, and lowers the mouth organ slowly.

Jacob: Ahhh . . . there is music from the little mouth organ and it was not so hard. It was not so hard at all . . . just the hymn tunes . . . that cannot be sinful to play hymn tunes only . . . that is not the devil's music. It cannot be wrong to feel this way . . . this strange *(Lifting elbows and mouth organ.)* feeling that is so daring and so fine and . . .

Jacob begins the rolling chords of hymn-like music. Orchestra takes it up in a sort of mouth organ concerto. Carried away by his music, Jacob rises.

Music: Hymn music breaks and slips into bouncing bawdy earthy Red River Valley, picked out by mouth organ. Orchestra breaks off to leave mouth organ alone carrying the tune. Mouth organ breaks off.

Jacob: No! No! That is the devil's music.

Scene nine

Women spinning.

Rachel: Spinning I don't mind, carding I hate. Grease all over the fingers.

Ruth: Dirt.

Rachel: It is all for the good of the colony.

Susan: Rachel is right, our young girls can learn a lesson from Rachel.

Ruth: Like snooping into peoples' hope chests.

Susan: Kleinsaucer the sheep boss says the shed is full and another shearing is ready.

Ruth: *(Whispering to Rachel.)* Kleinsaucer the Sheep Boss does not look like a sheep — he looks like a she goat.

Mother: Girls, girls we must keep ourselves free from worldly things.

Rachel: You mustn't say things like that.

Mother: Not listening again girls?

Ruth: Yes — oh yes . . . *(Parrotting)* We are free of worldly things . . .

Mother: But it was something else Ruth said to you . . .

Rachel: *(Female version of righteous Vogel.)* She said . . .

Ruth: Rachel!

Rachel: What she said . . . she said the Sheep Boss . . .

Ruth: Tattle-tale!

Rachel: The Sheep Boss does not look like a sheep.

(She turns and smiles sweetly at Ruth who is utterly relieved that Rachel has not squealed on her.)

Rachel: Instead — *(Very quickly as she stabs her dearest friend.)* He looks like a goat!

All laugh . . .

Old Woman: Girls — girls! that is disrespect!

Susan: Very like — very like . . .

Old Woman: Susan!

Susan: With his little red chin beard that wags when he talks and when he talks — *(She cannot repress a giggle.)* He bleats . . .

Mother: Girls — girls — Susan — no more — not nice it isn't . . .

Girls' laughter subsides and just as it has died down . . .

Ruth: Baaaaaaaaa!

All burst into a gale of giggling — but then as they look over to Anna they turn it off like a cold water tap.

Mother: *(To Marta)* Away from Anna Kleinsaucer.

Scene nine A

Community kitchen. Spinning building, Women are chatting — working cleaning wool. (Spinning)

Mother: Marta! More wool girl! Marta . . .

Marta: Yes. I am going — now . . . *(She moves off.)*

Mother: Go straight to the shed — no fooling on the way — and on the way back, Marta. Straight there and straight back now! Just remember Anna and Walter if you think about stopping maybe. Jacob Schunk is no better than Walter Staebler — it was not long ago that maybe Anna was giggling just with Walter, and look at her now. *(Pause)* Straight there — Straight back, Marta.

Scene ten

Wool Shed. Jacob waiting. Colony yard.

Marta crossing yard sees Jacob and responds — surprised — a little frightened . . .

Marta: Oh! It is you — Jacob.

Jacob: Yes. — I was — Just — Uncle Peter — On my way — the — the geese . . .

Marta: *(Pointing back beyond Jacob.)* But they are the other way — Beyond the horse barns.

Jacob: Oh. Are they? Are they. Yes. — I should — they are.

Mother: *(From kitchen)* Marta — the wool! Girl . . . the wool . . . we are waiting!

Marta: Yes! In a moment. Jacob.

Mother: Marta!

Marta: In a moment. Jacob — you must not do this — we will be seen and it is not right!

Jacob: Seen!

Marta: No one speaks now to Anna or Walter!

Jacob: I know — but . . .

Marta: Two weeks of isolation, already! She is in there now and no one dares speak to her.

Jacob: It is bad for Walter too . . .

Marta: No one dares look at her even, for it will mean as bad for them.

Jacob: Today at lunch, Vogel was laughing and he saw Walter's face and he stopped right in the middle, and . . .
Behind Jacob stands the Oats and Barley Boss.

Marta: *(In terrified warning.)* Jacob! ! Jacob!

Oats and Barley Boss: What is this! What is this! Jacob Schunk — You are not with Peter, the Goose Boss . . .

Jacob: I — he has sent me — I came to — I was going to . . .

Oats and Barley Boss: Marta Schreiber — you are not with the women.

Marta: I came outside to . . .

Oats and Barley Boss: I can see that.

Marta: *(In a rush)* And I saw Jacob pass — and I was to tell him to bring wool from the sheep.

Oats and Barley Boss: Profit by the sight of Anna, the Preacher's daughter, and Walter, son of the Wine Boss. See them as they move through days that are hushed and lonely. See conversation cease at their approach. See laughter and all eyes turned from them. For they have been now gifted with the power to blight: The shadow of their straw stack sinning does travel always before them. The wrath of the Lord had descended down upon them. His angered hand lies upon their smothered hearts. — Now — about your work — both of you *(Meaningful pause.)* No — straw stacks!

Scene eleven

Dining Hall. Evening Worship.

Preacher: Always we must watch — we must be ready, for he is waiting to get into our colony. Til now he has not got into our colony but he has new ways — last year he tried to ride into our colony on a self-propelled combine — and he **did** ride into the hook-and-eye colony on the four tractors they bought. These are machines of the devil! *(Various degrees of assent from the other bosses.)* He will sneak into the colony through the radio and he will sneak into the colony any way he can. But we must watch — and we must guard. It is the devil speaking through the Massey-Harris agent trying to sell us machinery and what does his machinery do? All it does is take work away from the men and from the boys so they have all kinds of time to hide a radio in the straw stack and listen to the devil's music out of there. All it does is give them time to think of other things they should not think about. These are machines of the devil. Mostly, the devil tries to sneak in through the young ones — the ones that have the flesh to itch — the unmarried ones — like Anna and Walter now in isolation. The devil does not like married men — *(The other patriarchs agree to this.)* — so we must watch — watch for the boys and girls that are looking at each other — watch for the ones that blush and the ones that laugh too much — watch for them and remember them and watch them more carefully. *(Pause)* These are the ones that the devil is making to blush and to laugh — these are the ones that will marry in the fall — before harvest.

Scene twelve

Straw Stack: Jacob with knees up at his straw stack in evening light. He stares down at the mouth organ held in his hands ... he lifts it to his mouth then takes it away — he stares at it with distaste — then rises to his feet with sudden determination — he crouches and scoops a hole in the straw stack. Begins to bury it there — hesitates — then buries it and turns away — seats himself — stares out disconsolately — then back and takes out mouth organ to his mouth ...

Music: As in previous scene — hymnal at first ... his foot keeping time to the music.

The music slips and slides into quite unreligious stuff ...
Jacob's eyes are closed. He is lost in the bouncing ecstasy of his cowboy ballad.

Breaks suddenly.

Jacob: No! No!

(Jacob falls to his knees. Hands up. His eyes tightly shut.)

Jacob: Our Father: The Stranger gave me the little mouth organ and I have used it. I blew through it and played music. Forgive me and I will not do it again — ever — I will not blow through the wooden teeth to make songs. I will not even blow the hymns, O Lord, let alone "The strawberry roan and the death of Pete Knight" and — "Going to go to Heaven on a streamline train". I will not. I promise. Amen — Lord.

Lights fade out.

Scene thirteen

Lights fade up.

Jacob and Peter sit against the straw stack set ... daytime.
Sound: Meadow lark a couple of times the gabble of geese from flocks off — BG.

Peter: Jacob. Jacob.

Jacob: Yes, Uncle Peter.

Peter: *(Bending forward and pretending great interest in Jacob's chin.)* What is that on your face?

Jacob: *(Alarm)* On my face!

Peter: *(Smiling)* In no time at all you will be growing a beard. By Fall perhaps. Marriage and a beard — they go together, Jacob.

Jacob: Marriage! A beard!

Peter: In fall . . . there will be marrying. The devil don't like married men so good. Marta.

Jacob: We have not been . . .

Peter: There was a meeting of the bosses last night. The bosses are not blind, Jacob.

Jacob: But we had not . . .

Peter: Marta is a good girl. You could have lots of kids. In fall, Jacob. If you wish — if Marta wishes . . .

Jacob: I do — I do — she — oh — Uncle Peter.

Scene fourteen

The yard: Back end of wagon box — on a trip to town they would use an ordinary wagon box and team — piling in as many as possible — perhaps a visit to the town dentist — perhaps to the liquor vendor's with permits to get the month's supply of liquor — for the most part there is no feeling about liquor though there is about tea, coffee, tobacco.

We see Hutterites of all ages and sizes piling out of the wagon — the last one comes over the end, seat first . . .
Vogel Unger, he stands looking about — then as he sees Jacob in the distance . . .

Vogel: Jacob — Jacob — there was a man! Do you know he wanted to see you! He asked to see you in town, Jacob!

Jacob: Man — wanted . . .

Vogel: He is not one of the people from the town. He had just come, he said. Do you know — he is staying at the hotel. Do you know he wants to see you?

Jacob: But why — who is he? What did he say his name . . .

Vogel: He just came where we were doing the machinery. Do you know Jacob Schunk, he said — do you know whether he is coming into town? Do you . . .

Jacob: Was he tall? Did he look like John, the Blacksmith?

Vogel: He had no beard, — of course, he hadn't any at all . . .

Jacob: I know — but with a beard — then would he look like John, the Blacksmith? Did he?

Vogel: I couldn't tell.

Jacob: Are you going in tomorrow? Are — could you let me go in your place, Vogel?

Vogel: We are going all this week, but I could not — you couldn't.

Jacob: Just tomorrow — that will be enough. Tell them — ah — you could have a — tell them you do not feel well tomorrow.

Vogel: But — it doesn't — they — that would be lying!

Jacob: Vogel — you do not feel well at all — your head aches — your back hurts.

Vogel: But — it doesn't — it does not! They don't — at all.

Jacob: They will tomorrow! You will have to go to the Bone-Setter and tell him . . .

Vogel: Oh, no I won't! Do you know — I never felt better?

Jacob's ominous face.

Jacob: If you do feel well tomorrow, Vogel — do you know, Vogel — then you are going to have to go to the Bone-Setter anyway!

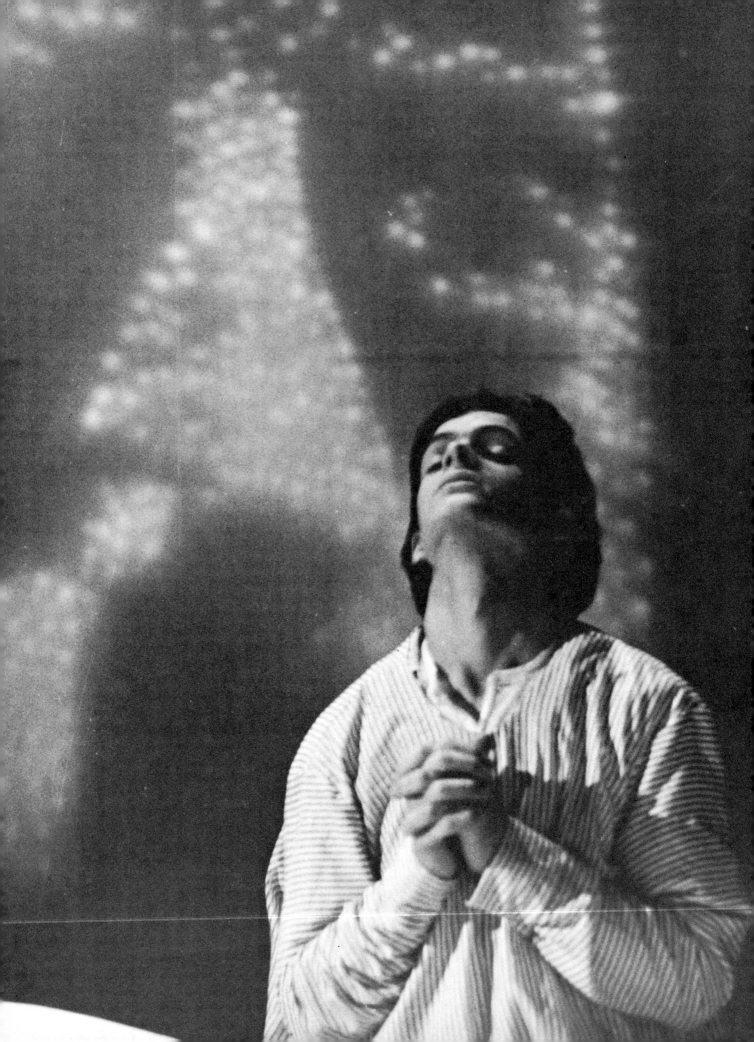

Scene fifteen

Palm Cafe: Darius at the counter, buying a package of cigarettes.

Darius: Small please — cork tips.

Wong: *(Reaching down for cigarettes.)* Oh yeah — oh yeah — thirty-four cen' — make thirty-fi' you take match. *(Tosses Darius packet of matches.)* Why bothah peipoh penny — why thirty-four why not thirty-five cen'. Make law — no penny law so peopoh don't fool with penny all time.

Darius: I guess so.

Wong: Everythin — fohty-nine — fifty-nine — thirty-foh — dollah seventeen — nasty penny — *(Picks up Chinese paper he's been reading behind counter — mutters into paper.)* No more penny law! Utterly no more penny law against pennies all ovah Canada!

Darius moves back to a booth. There he sits looking up anxiously from time to time.

Jacob: *(Enters)* I am looking for somebody . . .

Wong: Oh sure — sure — no kind you peopoh here today —
Darius rises

Darius: Jacob. Jacob — Jacob Schunk!

Jacob: *(Pause)* Hello.

Darius: Well, how are you, Jacob?

Jacob: *(Going towards him.)* I played the little mouth organ.

Darius: That's nice, Jacob. *(Darius sits down.)*

Jacob: *(Sitting down with him.)* You told Vogel Unger you wanted to see me.

Darius: Yes. Yes, Jacob. *(He does not know quite how to get on with it.)* You see ah — I have a special interest — I — I am *(Weakening)* I was once — I once belonged to our — your people. I was twenty when I left the colony — twenty years, Jacob, is a long time to eat the

bread of security — to have all your decisions made for you by the bosses. Perhaps I have not lost — all that — that weakness. *(Pause)* Outside the city — just outside — where I live — there is a colony . . .

Jacob: There isn't any colony near the city . . .

Darius: Not the same kind, Jacob. In this one they have different prisoners. Each morning they take the men out in the trucks to work the beet fields. Each night they take them back to sleep inside. It is called a jail, Jacob. When I have passed the camp, I have thought of you, Jacob. Each time. There are guards there with guns instead of bearded bosses. The fence is higher. But those are slight differences. They — are — so — slight.

Jacob: Who are you?

Darius: My name is Darius. I — I — am your brother, Jacob. I am Darius.

Jacob: You say it like that. You are my brother.

Darius: Yes. I have dreamed of coming for you and taking you away with me, but when you told me who you were that day I could not do it.

Jacob: Could you not?

Darius: I wanted to, but I couldn't. When I returned to the city I cursed myself for not bringing you back with me.

Jacob: That was all right — Darius. I guess it was all right — Darius.

Darius: Because you are not free either, Jacob — it — you are not free in body or in soul. None of you are — not even the Oats and Barley Boss.

Jacob: Oh no — it is not like that . . .

Darius: None of you are! The colony is not God's way! It is wicked!

Jacob: Not wicked, Darius!

Darius: Freedom is light, Jacob! The way of the Lord is a shining light — the way of the wicked lies in the shadow and darkness of ignorance and bondage!

Jacob: Our people are not wicked!

Darius: There are three things. There is truth and that is the best thing. There are freedom and beauty too, and the devil hates all these things. Truth and beauty are the same — and that's all you need to know, Jacob. A poet said that, and he is not one of our — your people. Our people have no poets . . . for the colony kills what is beautiful . . . it will not let beauty grow . . . it cannot grow without freedom!

Jacob: But — I have found . . .

Darius: *(Over-riding him with all stops out.)* The devil wears hook-and-eye fasteners right down his ugly home-spun jacket! He has a long beard and he is Boss over all the Bosses!

Jacob: No — No — that is not true!

(The fire fades slowly from Darius' face then quite gently.)

Darius: I am sorry Jacob.

Jacob: You say there is no beauty in the colony. *(Pause)* There is Marta.

Darius: Marta?

Jacob: John, the Blacksmith's daughter.

Darius: Oh.

Jacob: The first time — here — you asked me if I was happy in the colony. Well — I am happy . . . now.

Darius: I see.

Jacob: I do not — not play the little mouth organ — *(Pause)* now.

Darius: Did it make you unhappy, Jacob?

Jacob: Are you happy outside the colony, Darius?

Darius: Happy? **I am free!**

Jacob: Are you happy Darius?

Darius: Happiness is not everything. I must be honest with you. I am free. Anyway — I am free.

Jacob: *(Blurting it)* I am going to be married. *(Pause)* I am going to marry Marta.

Darius: Are you? Are you Jacob?

Jacob: Soon.

Darius: That is their hold — that is the bosses' strongest hold. They make that work for them too.

Jacob: You do not understand, Darius. Last night I walked with Marta from the pump to the kitchen. We did not talk. We came to a patch of mud. We both stepped aside — in the wrong direction. She touched me, Darius. I felt her hand against the back of mine. It was lovely — it was aching lovely. I could not breathe, Darius.

Darius: You will never leave. *(Pause)* After you are married. I am married now. I met her soon after I left the colony to go to the teacher's school. Women are important, Jacob. They are not weak. One takes me from the colony. Another holds you to it.

Jacob: *(Slowly and gently — his voice almost breaking.)* I am sorry — Darius. *(He gets up and walks away from the table.)*
Darius gets up as though to go after him and bring him back, then sinks back into his seat. Wong comes to the booth. He looks down at Darius a moment — the other man staring at his hands before him on the table.

Wong: He go. *(Pause)* no ice cream. *(Pause)* Mouth ohgan. *(Long Pause)* *(Darius looks up.)* I remember — long time here — I remember — you buy too befoh — you don't buy mouth ohgan then. Don't smoke cigarettes then too. *(Pause)* You smoke cigarette now. *(Long pause — he shrugs.)* Same thing China — all kinds peopoh — come along — all kinds peopoh do different — after while change —

Scene sixteen

Straw Stack evening . . .

C22

Jacob burying mouth organ — when he has finished he stays on his knees and looks up to wherever the Hutterite God hangs out.

Jacob: *(Half to himself, half to God.)* Like I promised — I keep it. No more music out of the mouth organ — not any more. It is a trade and I will marry Marta and not play the mouth organ. I buried away the mouth organ for Marta Schreiber, daughter of John, the Blacksmith, because she is more beautiful than any music out of a mouth organ and it is a good trade. I have traded with You for good — the mouth organ for the soft brush of her hand — for the curve of her cheek. And I would please want another thing. My brother is a good man, he is not wicked. Do not turn your face from him — save him from doom and eternal damnation. *(Pause)* And — and — *(He looks back to where the mouth organ is buried.)* — give me a little help — to let it stay buried — perhaps I can see Marta once before we are married — just once alone . . .

Scene seventeen

Kitchen: Women — Marta — Anna sits alone from the others as they prepare the supper meal — Marta carries a pail of potatoes over to Anna, seated — she stoops low as she sets down the pail.

Marta: *(Whispering)* Hello Anna — it will end, Anna — they will not be silent to you forever . . . *(She looks up.)*

Mother: Marta! Here —

(Marta straightens up — leaves Anna . . . heads for door.)

Anna alone and tragic — begins to peel the potatoes, if that can be a tragic act.

Outside the yard — Jacob standing — obviously waiting — Marta appears in door.

Jacob: Marta — Marta — Please may I see you — alone?

Marta: Oh, no — Jacob — we must not! We . . .

Jacob: Tonight — the straw stack! Please!

Marta: It is only a month now Jacob!

Jacob: Please, Marta! You must — you must!

Marta: The Preacher — the Sheep Boss — they are coming — we will be seen!

Jacob: I will be there, Marta! I will be there!

(Marta is wildly shoving Jacob away.)

Marta: No — no — go now — I won't — you shouldn't — it is not fair, Yes, Jacob — Dear God — yes!

Jacob joyful exits — Marta watches him leave — she turns and goes across the yard on her errand.

Scene seventeen A

Anna: *(Whispered fiercely)* Marta O — oh, Marta . . . *(Marta does not leave her but she doesn't answer her.)* . . . You were my closest friend, Marta . . .

Marta: Sh — sh, Anna — don't . . .

Anna: Just touch me Marta — my hand . . .

Marta: *With glances towards the older woman — Marta does — hiding the friendly touch from the older women . . .*

Anna: I — it is so terrible, Marta — I am alone in the whole world — or else in the world — I'm not any more — at all . . .

Marta: All right — all right, Anna — you aren't — I think of you — so I keep you alive in myself . . .

Anna: I can't stand it any more!

Marta: It will end — they will not be silent from you for ever . . .

John The Blacksmith: Marta!

Marta is startled since she had not seen her father come up.

John: Be a good girl, Marta. *(A gesture of his hand sends her off — he turns and stares down at*

Anna, who has turned her head down to the potatoes. She is crying now — John The Blacksmith places his hand on her shoulder.)

John: Little Anna — be a good girl too — your punishment is almost over — the silence will lift from you soon.

The Preacher comes over to them. John turns to him.

John: I've told her — just now.

Preacher: You were not told to tell her.

John: Someone told me to tell her . . .

Preacher: I didn't tell you to . . .

John: No not you — somebody from the meeting — I was alone and His Voice came to me in the wind that travelled in a funnel over the summer fallow — and His Voice told me to tell her — and the wind was gentle and warm —

Preacher: You have disobeyed . . .

John: I obeyed His Voice that was in the wind. I obeyed Him when he told me to tell Anna — I think you must listen to that wind better, Preacher — when it blows through our colony. It is the wind of compassion.
The Preacher has no answer to this. John takes his hand from Anna's shoulder and turns away from her and from the Preacher.

Scene seventeen B

Just outside the kitchen where the old well is Mike and Otto are taking out the pump to go to the new well.

Mike: Just new leathers and she will be working like new — good deep well double piston pump . . .

Otto: Sure — over twenty years we didn't have to prime much . . .

Mike: Almost as old as the colony here — don't drop it, that little brass plug . . . work better in the new well, even . . . just like us — works good — he must have been Hutterite, eh?

Otto: Who?

Mike: Mr. Wisconsin — Hutterite made good religion back there with Martin Luther — Simon Mennon — Jan Huter . . . Mr. Wisconsin made good good piston pump too.

Then John and Preacher have come out of the kitchen and are carrying on their exchange from where they were in with Anna . . .

John: They are spirit but they are flesh too . . .

Mike: But I guess Moses made the first one when he hit the rock with his staff, eh?

John: . . . and they must grow to beauty and goodness . . .

Preacher: Not to wickedness — the world will seduce them into it — we must shield our children from the ways of the world — they must fear God.

John: . . . Love God.

Preacher: Do not rely on love too much! Without fear — there is danger! We have done for Anna Kleinsaucer a great thing to save her soul from eternal damnation — we will do it for others — I warn you, John, the Blacksmith — the Anna Kleinsaucers can be father — to the sin that are clear to others — sin signs in his own flesh and blood. They are not easy to see always!

Mike: Preacher's right . . . sometimes I think it's too bad we didn't have some kind of wand — like my willow for divining the water — a wand we could hold in our hands and pass it over them and tell us where the sin welled strong. *(Brings himself up as he realizes this is ridiculous.)* But of course what kind of wood — could do that?

Preacher: That which the Lord used, Pig Boss — in the garden of Eden — apple tree!

Scene eighteen

Jacob: Marta — oh, Marta . . .

Marta: Jacob! It is wrong! You shouldn't . . .

Jacob: I wouldn't ask you to do wrong, Marta! I don't want us to do wrong at all!

Marta: We have done it now . . .

Jacob: I have — you haven't I will not any more — because of you! You are everything now. I told God —

Marta: You shouldn't ask me to . . .

Jacob: I had to see you —

Marta: I'm afraid Jacob! I don't want to be like Anna — I don't want to die from everyone like Anna . . .

Jacob: You won't — you won't — I promise you won't . . .

Marta: Maybe Walter said that to Anna.

Jacob: It's all right, Marta!

Marta: Not for Anna . . .

Jacob: No one will know . . .

Marta: What did you tell God?

Jacob: I told Him — I told — I told Him I love you more — I told Him I loved you more than the little mouth organ — (*Catching himself up.*) Not more than Him — but Marta — it is a lot I love you! I had to tell you that Marta! I had to! Is that wicked to tell you that — just to tell you that!

Marta: (*Pause*) I don't think it is.

Jacob: Oh, Marta!

Marta: Jacob — I love you a lot too.

Jacob: Marta, Marta — . . .

Clinch

Scene nineteen

Straw Stack: Morning

Morning Sounds: Geese

Lights fade up — to discover Jacob lost in reverie.

Peter: (*In his own reverie.*) The devil don't like married men. (*Long pause*) You want to marry Marta. (*This is a statement of fact.*) You want to grow a beard — have kids. Be a good boy, Jacob. (*Long pause*) You were not. (*Shaking his head sadly.*) You were not — (*Pause*) last night.

(*Jacob is startled from his reverie.*)

Peter: I do not sleep so well, Jacob. (*Pause*) You left.

Jacob: (*Seems about to protest, then lowers his head in admission.*)

Jacob: Yes, Uncle Peter.

(*Peter is sadly shaking his head.*)

Peter: Straw stacks.

Jacob: Yes — no! I tell you it is not like that. (*Springs wildly to his feet.*) I did see Marta last night — but it's not what you think — we — we just stood — . . .

Peter: Yes, Jacob?

Jacob: I — we could feel the night air cooling against our cheeks — it was — the smell of hay and the wild mint — it was beautiful, Uncle Peter.

Peter: Was it, Jacob.

Jacob: It would make the spit come to your mouth.

(*Peter stares with understanding at Jacob — gently nods his head . . . reaches up to take Jacob by the arm and gently pull him down beside him . . .*)

Peter: I had my straw stack too, Jacob. When I was young . . . before I could grow a beard, the devil came to me in the city one day. He found me on the street with a bag of money in my hand. It was colony money. The devil told me to buy a new suit for myself. (*Wistful — Ah, wistful this whole confession of youthful folly many*

many years ago.) The pants had creases in them. It was a sort of green suit. Pretty. I wore it that day. Right out of the store. I met a woman with red hair. She wore a blue dress like a violet. She lived with a lot of other Jezebels on the edge of the city and she called me her little geranium flower. I was going to take her away from that place, but in the Chinaman's cafe she unscrewed the top from the stool and hit the waiter over the head. *(Still the incredibly gentle and sweet reverie.)* She screamed very loud — long — she swore wicked too — she threw their spittoon through the whole window. Twenty dollars for the green suit with creases in the pants. Ten dollars for the wine. Five dollars for the Jezebel. Fifteen dollars for the window. Thirty dollars for the Chinaman. Fourteen dollars for the judge. *(Long and contemplative pause.)* Sin comes expensive, Jacob. A sinful life could run a man as high as two hundred dollars a month. *(He turns his head to look at Jacob and see how this astronomical figure strikes him.)* There are worse things, Jacob, than being lonely in the colony. You could be lonely outside the colony too. Like your brother — Darius.

Jacob: I know, Uncle Peter.

Peter: Be a good boy, Jacob! *(This is a fierce plea.)*

Jacob: I will, Uncle Peter! *(This is just as fierce a promise.)* *(Sound: meadow lark's four notes above the BG gabble of goose . . . as light fades.)*

Scene twenty

Straw Stack: Night — Night Sounds
Jacob arrives at the Straw Stack — drops to his knees.

Jacob: I do not see her — I am not meeting her any more by the pump — I do not even look into her eyes when she serves at the table. I will wait till we are married. I have been good two weeks — but — *(He falters.)*

(Jacob's hand on the straw — it feels around — goes into the straw — comes out with the mouth organ — he looks down at it.)

Sound: Coyote howls distantly, and train shoops on the night silence . . .

Jacob lifts the mouth organ — puts it hesitantly to his mouth — Makes it do the long interrogative Whoooooooo — Whoooooooo of the train. He lowers it and sighs as with relief. He gives in and begins to play, hymn-like, sad . . .

Jacob stops playing — lowers his elbows — knocks the organ against the side of his palm to shake the condensed saliva from its space teeth. His elbows rise up and out again. Closes his eyes. Plays again.

Music: Orchestra now with mouth organ riding high and lyric.

Jacob lets mouth organ buck, his feet tap. His body sways ecstatically with the music.

Peter comes on. He grabs Jacob — wrenches the mouth organ from his hands.

Peter: I told you! I warned you, Jacob! I told you to be a good boy!

Scene twenty-one

Oats and Barley Boss: *(Clears throat portentously.)* Jacob Schunk — you have sinned. *(There is the deep assent of male voices.)* Peter, the Goose Boss, say before us what you know and let him deny it.

Peter: *(Rising to his feet by the Judgment Table.)* I wakened in the middle of the night. I had to go outside. I am not a young man any more. I heard a sound. It came from (old horse barn?) south forty straw stack. I went there. *(He turns and throws out an accusing arm.)* I found him! He had that in his hands. *(He points to mouth organ.)* I called to him. He did not hear me. He was blowing into it, so music came out of it.

There are clicking sounds of disapproval from the Bosses. The Preacher hawks in his throat — sounds die down to utter silence.

Sound: Rooster off — crows loud and clear and long — the sound stretching like an elastic band.

Oats and Barley Boss: Jacob Schunk, you have sinned. Let Peter say before us again what he knows; let Jacob deny it.

Peter: Four years ago, he set a trap line. He caught four weasels and a skunk. He turned in to the Hide Boss three weasel pelts and a skunk. He took the weasel pelt hidden in his jacket, to the hide buyer in town. He got fifty cents for it. He bought a bag of Maple Bud candies. He also bought five ice-cream cones from Wong, the Chinaman at the Palm Cafe. He ate three and he gave one to Vogel Unger and another to Otto, the Sheep Boss's Son. Behind the livery stable.

The members of the court who make their deep male herd sounds again. The Bone-Setter belches accusingly.

Oats and Barley Boss: Jacob Schunk, you have sinned. Let Peter say further what he knows. Let Jacob deny it.

Sound: *The second clear call of the outside rooster.*

(Peter his head is thrown back. He has been working himself up into evangelistic fervor. For the first time since his fall from grace with the Calgary hooker of his youth, he is now one of the orthodox fold. It is a fine and wonderful feeling and the moment of his greatest triumph.)

Peter: He sneaked out in the middle of the night. He met Marta, the daughter of John the Blacksmith. It was at the straw stack in the south forth. He kissed her on the mouth. She kissed him back. I saw them do this. I saw them.

The court murmuring again.

Oats and Barley Boss: Jacob Schunk, pay attention. We are not angry with you. We want you to know that. We wish only to turn you back from the path of wickedness. To save your soul from eternal damnation. Your punishment is this. You shall be apart. No one shall come near you. Everyone shall turn his eyes from you. No one shall speak to you — for three months. To do any of these things shall be as great a sin as those you have committed. *(Many of the court nodding slow approval of the sentence.)* You shall not blow through the mouth organ again. John the Blacksmith, shall place it on his anvil and he shall smash it. Marta, daughter of John the Backsmith, shall have one month's isolation. When the Fall marrying comes, she shall not marry you, Jacob Schunk. We will not lose a soul — another — soul.

Jacob: *(As this part of the sentence sinks in.)* Marta! It is not fair to punish Marta . . .

Oats and Barley Boss: *(Rising)* We will sing now a hymn.

Jacob: She had nothing to do with the mouth . . . *(Oats and Barley Boss begins first line of old chanting German hymn)* . . . organ. She — the weasel pelt . . . *(Two deeper voices join the voice of the Oats and Barley Boss.)* — It is not fair that . . . . *(Louder to make himself heard)* . . . it is not fair that . . . *(More voices in the relentless hymn.)* . . . she should be punished too . . . *(All voices now in the chanting hymn)* — *(Jacob is fairly screaming to make himself heard.)* Listen — listen to me! I will not stay — if you do this to Marta, I will — damn your black fat souls — I will — OOOOOOOOOOOO! (He is lost now in the full strength of the men's singing.)*

Mother: Don't touch the lid after the dough is dropped . . .

Susan: It makes the dumplings sad . . .

Old Woman: Makes them sad . . .

Susan: Nothing's worse than sad dumplings . . .

Old Woman: Nothing's worse . . .

Possibly it's Ruth, who is looking over to the lonely Marta.

Rachel: Yes, there is nothing worse than sad dumplings . . .

Rachel: Sin is worst — wicked wicked — straw stack sin . . .

Anna: Stop it — stop it . . .

Rachel: You ought to know, Anna . . .

Anna: Leave her alone . . .

Rachel: Yes — that's just what we are to do . . .

Woman One: Girls — girls —

Scene twenty-two

The kitchen. A bustle of activity — but over by herself, Marta sits with hands in her lap, apart from the others. A woman pauses by her . . . she looks up to speak, then realizes she must not — woman passes her — her mother comes and hands her a pail silently — indicates the door with a silent nod of her head. Marta gets up slowly with the pail — moves to the door . . .

(Jacob is waiting outside for her) . . .

Jacob: Marta — Marta! *(Stricken and frightened — she turns away and runs past him — Jacob runs after her.)* Please — Marta! *(She struggles to be free from him.)* Marta — I am leaving — I want — Marta, come with me — my brother, Darius — (He seizes her by the shoulders — she struggles.) Marta — Marta — please Marta — please — just listen. *(She breaks away and runs back towards kitchen.)* — you don't have to talk — All I want you to do is listen! *(He reaches her half-way to kitchen door and grabs at her again.)* There is nothing wrong with listening, is there! You don't have to say anything . . . *(She breaks from him again and runs to kitchen door and inside.)* Marta — I am going away . . . *(He brings up against the slammed door.)* Please, Marta — *(He beats against the closed door.)* Marta — listen — *(Beating again.)* You will listen to me! All of you — listen to me! I am going! Leaving! All of you — this is your chance to hear! Can your ears hear this — damn you all! Oh damn you, all of you — I leave you all!

Scene twenty-three

Wong's Cafe: (Wong and Trucker at counter — Trucker paying bill — Goes to Juke Box — makes selection and inserts coin — then leans against counter to listen to the record play. Jacob enters — sees Trucker — goes to him — Trucker turned slightly away and wrapt in music. After a couple of false starts — Jacob plucks at his sleeve . . .)

Jacob: Please — *(Trucker turns and looks at him.)* Excuse me —

Trucker: Uh-huh?

Jacob: I — wondered — would — are you leaving?

Trucker: Huh?

Jacob: Are you going to drive away now? Right now? *(Trucker simply nods his head.)* To the — towards the city?

Trucker: Yep.

Jacob: *(After an awkward pause.)* Would you let me ride?

Trucker: Uh-huh. *(Looks steadily at Jacob.)* No beard. No beard, so you ain't married. *(Laughs)* No beard down your hook an' eye jacket, so you ain't . . . *(Sees the boy is distressed.)* No offence, kid — sure — I can give you a lift. Sixteen — y'ain't old enough to get married yet — or grow a beard.

Jacob: *(Dully)* I am old enough.

Trucker: What you goin' to the city for — long ways — over a hundred miles . . .

Jcaob: I have left the colony.

Trucker: *(Surprised)* Oh — now — I wouldn't do that. You — *(Grins)* won't never grow a beard you do that.

Jacob: No — I will never grow a beard now. Poor Marta . . .

Trucker: Your girl?

Jacob: They punished her too — she would not — she could not talk to me again — she was afraid.

Trucker: That why you're leavin'?

Jacob: Yes.

Trucker: Awful holt over you folks. Never heard of one of you to cut loose before.

Jacob: My brother Darius did.

Trucker: Why'd he leave?

Jacob: He hanged pictures on the schoolhouse

walls. He smoked cigarettes.

Trucker: Catch you smokin?

Jacob: No. I played some music out of a little mouth organ.

Trucker: That all! Just for blowin' a mouth organ! What you gonna do?

Jacob: If you give me a ride in your truck to the city, I am going to my brother. *(Pause)* He wants me. *(Pause)* He will buy me another mouth organ.

Trucker: Come on, then.

(Music: Mouth organ alone in a simple happy air, possibly built on four-note meadow lark song — orchestra takes it up for crashing and triumphant finale. Jacob Schunk may not know it, but this is victory . . .)

The Pile,
The Store,
Inside Out.

Mavor Moore

The Author

Mavor Moore was born in Toronto in 1919, the son of the distinguished actress-director, Dora Mavor Moore. Now Professor of Theatre at York University, he has been a notable part of the Canadian dramatic scene since he first starred in a radio series at the age of fourteen — although he wrote (and saw produced) his first stage play three years before that.

In the intervening years — besides acting and directing for theatres across the country — he has been chief producer for CBC Television, executive producer for United Nations film and television in New York, drama critic for the Toronto Telegram, founder of the Charlottetown Festival, chairman of the cultural committee of the national Centennial Conference, and general director of Toronto's St. Lawrence Centre for the Arts.

"When I began seriously to write plays in the 1940s," he recalls, "there were no professional companies left to put them on; that was how I got into the production business." And few men have done more to provide their fellow playwrights with an opportunity to see their work produced. In 1946 he joined his redoubtable mother in launching the New Play Society, which — before the days of government subsidy — successfully mounted plays by Morley Callaghan, Andrew Allan, Harry Boyle, Mazo de la Roche, Lister Sinclair, John Coulter and others, as well as the phenomenally popular annual revue *Spring Thaw*.

At CBC-TV he commissioned new works from many young writers; and in 1964, when invited to Prince Edward Island to run the new Confederation Centre in Charlottetown, he seized the opportunity to institute a festival of Canadian musicals. (The first commission went to Donald Harron and Norman Campbell for the now legendary *Anne of Green Gables*.) As first head of Toronto's 1967 Centennial project, the St. Lawrence Centre, he initiated a policy of presenting Canadian plays, but resigned before it opened to take up his present position at York University — where he now teaches playwriting to another generation of young Canadians.

He himself has turned out more than a hundred radio plays, some thirty for television, two full-length stage-plays (*Who's Who, The Ottawa Man*), word *and* music for two musical comedies (*Sunshine Town, The Best of All Possible Worlds*), the book and lyrics of another (*Johnny Belinda*), and the libretto for the outstanding Canadian opera *Louis Riel*, with music by Harry Somers.

It was after completing *Louis Riel* in 1967 that he turned to writing a series of short plays for radio, television and the stage. The CBC International Service has recorded a group of these *Enigmas*; several of them have been performed in the U.S.A. and Britain, and translated into Italian, Swedish, Finnish and Italian. At present, in addition to adapting several 19th Century plays for CBC Television, he is bringing out a book on four of his fellow Canadian playwrights and editing an anthology of Canadian plays.* And at last, he says, he has another full-length play "in progress."

* New Press

A foreword by Mavor Moore

These three short plays were neither written in sequence nor intended to be performed together. But they do have in common a working-out of certain ideas about ambiguity with which I was much concerned at the time (1970-71). And each is a kind of *reductio ad absurdum* of one aspect of theatrical ambiguity.

The Pile is a play about responsibility in which the main factor (the "pile" itself) is so abstract that any member of the audience can see in it anything he wishes. Since it also lies, physically, in front of the stage, it can even stand as a metaphor for the theatre audience itself, or for the theatre today. And since the play can only work by virtue of the completing response brought to it by each viewer, its very form exemplifies the idea of responsibility I wanted to get across — that it only works, like radar, by virtue of resonances bounced back from others.

The Store, equally naturalistic on the surface, deals in similar fashion with our ideas of sanity — only here, instead of having a totally abstract symbol for the viewer to interpret as he likes, the audience is intentionally led to believe one thing and then gradually persuaded (I hope) to believe another. At first the Manager seems to be eminently rational and the Woman what is referred to in stores as "a nut-case"; later it becomes clear that she is in fact only a figment of his own unbalanced mind. But his world is not entirely a fantastical one: surely all managers — even God — would be driven mad by being blamed for everyone else's sins. It is not the case, as some psychologists and playwrights would have us believe, that in a mad world only the insane are sane, but rather that sanity consists in confronting the ambiguity in ourselves. The theatre, it seems to me, is a good place to do this.

Inside Out is, obviously, a play about levels of reality — a subject which one might think had been done to death, if not by Plato 2,000 years ago then by Pirandello in this century. But a still unexplored theatrical level occurred to me one day when the Canadian Broadcasting Corporation commissioned me to write a work for television to be performed by myself and my actress daughter Tedde: a level of *known* reality (in this case an actual relationship) altogether outside the play and, indeed, the medium. The multiple levels of role-playing within the drama could then be totally subverted by the final introduction of a demonstrably real reference point. Ideally, the play should therefore be performed by a father-daughter acting team; that way the point is made that despite all the ambiguities with which life confronts us, there are here and there bases of reality which we can touch.

These are all, then, I am afraid, inescapably "idea plays". But since the ideas are about people, and since I (like most theatre-goers, I suspect) like having fun with ideas, I hope these little pieces are also entertaining in their own right.

D3

The Pile

Characters in the play

X, a businessman
Y, an engineer

A vacant lot, on the shore of a lake. Sounds of lapping water and the occasional cry of gulls come from the back of the theatre. Offstage an automobile drives up and stops. The door opens and shuts. X and Y come on slowly, down to the very front and centre of the stage; X carries a folding canvas stool and Y a seat-stick; X wears dirty construction shoes, Y wears galoshes. Both, as they approach down centre, seem to be scanning the audience — or scanning something which lies where the audience sits.

X: Well, there it is.

Y: Yes. There she is.

(*They survey, with a touch of possessive pride, what lies before them.*)

X: Maybe we should say, there it lies.

Y: No. IS is the word. It exists.

X: You're existing if you just lie there.

Y: That's not the point. If it was just lying there, hurting nobody, we wouldn't have to worry. It would be . . . passive. The fact that it exists, actively, is the problem.

X: How . . . actively?

Y: It'll begin to stink.

X: I see what you mean.

(*Solemnly, each erects his sitting apparatus, and they sit — still contemplating what lies before them. A pause.*)

Y: (*Finally*) What are we going to do about it?

Y: You mean, what are we going to do **with** it.

X: What's the difference?

Y: You could leave it right there and still do something **about** it . . . like walking away.

X: Well, why don't we?

Y: Because we can't. It's ours. We have to do

D5

something **with** it. It's our responsibility. With it.

X: I guess you're right.

(A long stare out front, increasingly glum.)

X: What?

Y: I didn't say anything.

X: I mean, what do we do with it?

Y: That's the problem.

X: Then **what**?

Y: Hmmm.

X: Why don't we just . . . get rid of it?

Y: How?

X: I don't know . . . dump it somewhere?

Y: With what?

X: A dump truck.

Y: A dump truck wouldn't take it . . . all that.

X: Several loads? Back and forth, back and forth?

Y: Back and forth! How would you get it in, in the first place?

X: There must be some way.

Y: As the fat lady said to the midget. *(Pause)* Where would you put it?

X: I don't know. The lake?

Y: Can you imagine that in the lake? With all this talk about pollution?

X: Nobody'd see us.

Y: They'd soon find out. How long do you think you could keep a thing like that secret? They're always digging, dragging, analysing . . .

X: *(Rising, and going to look at the pile from a different angle.)* Well . . . you come up with something better, then.

Y: I will if you'll let me think.

(He thinks, silently: comes up with an idea, and discards it. Then he thoughtfully fills and lights his pipe.)

X: I wish we'd never done it. *(He paces.)*

Y: Spilt milk.

X: I wish we'd never got into the whole damn business.

Y: It seemed like a good idea at the time.

X: It wasn't my idea.

Y: I wondered when that was going to come up.

X: Well it wasn't.

Y: What's that got to do with anything?

X: Well, I mean, you were the one who —

Y: You went along with it. You thought it was a great idea. Terrific, you said. Colossal. A stroke of genius. I planted the seed; you grew it. Instead of implying it's all my fault, you should be grateful.

X: All my life, I've wanted something we could do together. Your scientific knowledge, and my business know-how. Think of it, I used to say to myself: his scientific knowledge, and my business know-how.

Y: Well, we got **your** scientific knowledge and **my** business know-how. Think of **that**.

X: I am. I am, I am, I am. *(He sits again.)*

Y: Now we're stuck with it.

X: Yes. *(He extracts a cigar, unwraps it and lights it.)*

(Y rises, folds his seat back into a stick, and strides back and forth with it.)

X: Speaking of science . . .

Y: I wasn't. You were. *(Continues pacing.)*

X: Well, what I mean is, isn't there some way we could just . . . make it vanish?

Y: That's not science, that's magic. *(Lifting his stick.)* If this were a wand I'd have waved it long ago.

X: I meant disintegrate it . . . scientifically. Like . . . well, burn it.

Y: You think I haven't thought of that?

X: I'm not a mind reader. You never mentioned it.

Y: It won't burn.

X: Pour kerosene over it.

Y: It still wouldn't burn.

X: You mean it's inflammable?

Y: Inflammable means it **would** burn.

X: No it doesn't — that's flammable.

Y: There's no such word. Inflammable means what you think flammable means: you can in-flame it, ignite it, burn it up.

X: You sure about that?

Y: Allow me to know my business. Look it up if you want.

X: *(Aggressively)* All right then: is it **non**-inflammable?

Y: That's what I said.

X: That's not what you said. You said it wouldn't burn.

Y: That's clear enough, for god's sake! — or would be to anyone less thick-headed.

X: People in glass houses, et cetera. How am I supposed to know whether you mean that in its present state it isn't likely to catch fire — because it's too wet, or too gooey, or not gooey enough, or too hard, or too something — or that it literally can't be burnt up in whatever state it eventually gets to? Right? How am I supposed to know?

Y: Because I tell you. Nothing whatever will make that stuff burn — ever! Now have we got that straight?

X: Don't snap at me — I'm only asking . . .

Y: And I've told you!

X: I haven't asked you yet.

Y: Haven't asked me what?

X: Whether it could be used for non-inflamma-bility — you know, instead of asbestos, or whatever.

Y: Christ. No.

X: Why not?

Y: Because you'd never — you can't cut it up; you can't fit it into places; you can't — well, it's not the right kind of material. It just isn't. The fact that it won't burn doesn't make it a candidate for anything special. There are lots of things you can't burn in the ordinary way. They're no special use to anybody. The point about asbestos is that you can **do** things with it. You can't do anything with **that**.

X: I've thought of something else.

Y: What?

X: There isn't enough of it.

Y: Well, that's another thing.

X: I suppose we could always get more.

Y: Not on your life. We've enough trouble now getting rid of this lot.

X: Yes, that's the problem: getting rid of this.

Y: Precisely.

(Emphatically, he opens the top of the seat-stick and props himself on it.)

X: What about . . . couldn't we disintegrate it?

Y: With what?

X: Well, acid.

Y: Honestly. That's only another form of burning.

X: I thought it was eating. Acid is eating. Eating isn't burning.

Y: I wish to god you'd leave the chemistry to people who know something about it.

X: All right — but isn't there some way of . . . breaking it down? I mean, **you** tell **me**. Won't acid do that?

Y: I really don't know where you get these fairy stories. If you could put it bit by bit in an acid bath for several days, you might. And how would we do that? We haven't got an acid bath, and even if we had we couldn't get it there to wherever the bath is that we haven't got. Right out here in the open, all of it, not a chance. So forget it.

X: I was just trying to help.

Y: Forget it. *(His pipe has gone out: he lights it.)*

(X now has a deep thought, and rises to frame it, eventually, into words.)

X: When I was a boy, I used to build puppet theatres. You wouldn't think there was much money in puppet theatres, would you?

Y: No.

X: There was then, for a kid. I got this commission to build a puppet theatre for a rich girl. They wanted to give it to her as a Christmas present, to go in the playroom, in the basement. They wanted all the trimmings, lights, curtains, everything. I made a beautiful theatre, spent all November and December on it, even with school and everything. It was to be a surprise. I got my older brother to rent a truck and we took it up there on Christmas Eve, up to their mansion in the suburbs. We couldn't get it in.

Y: How do you mean, you couldn't get it in?

X: It wouldn't go. It was too big. We couldn't get it through the front door, or the back door, or even the basement window.

Y: What the hell has this got to do with anything?

X: They wanted us to saw it in half. But if we'd sawed it in half that would have ruined the curtain tracks and the lighting circuits and a lot of other things. (Pause) They wouldn't take it. (Pause) Have you ever wondered what to do with a five-by-eight-foot puppet theatre nobody wanted?

Y: Can't say I have.

X: Well . . . I took it apart again, piece by piece, and used the pieces on something else. Disintegrated it. That's all I was asking. *(He sits again. His cigar has gone out: he relights it.)*

(They look at the pile, then at each other, then away.)

Y: I didn't say you couldn't break it up and use some of it.

X: Yes you did.

Y: I did not. You asked about making it vanish.

X: Breaking it down.

Y: Down is not up.

X: What's the difference?

Y: You break something down and you separate it into its constituent parts. You break something up and you get accidental pieces, like shattered glass.

X: Well . . . if we could break down —

Y: I'm not saying we could and I'm not saying we couldn't.

X: But you said we could! That was the whole idea in the first place . . . that if we went into this, we could make something of it, and get rid of it. That was the whole idea.

Y: I said it was a reasonable risk. That's all I said. I said IF we could make something of it, and IF you could get rid of it, it represented a reasonable risk.

X: How can I get rid of it unless you figure out something to get rid of in the first place?

Y: What's the use of my figuring out something unless you've already figured out a way of getting rid of it after? Try to be logical.

X: I am trying.

Y: The problem is basically logistical.

X: I'm **trying** to be logical.

Y: I said logistical. Logistics has nothing to do with logic.

X: But you said —

Y: Logistics has to do with lodging. Finding lodgings for . . . whatever it is. This is a problem in distribution, and that's not my specialty, it's yours. Now: there she is. Never mind your crying over spilt milk, never mind your recriminations — the question is, purely and simply, how do we get rid of it. And that, my friend, is **your** responsibility.

X: Yes.

(Y rises: moves closer to the pile, examining it.)

Y: Why couldn't you palm it off on a contractor?

X: What for? *(Rising to join Y: peering closely.)*

Y: Don't they need something . . . just to fill things with?

X: Not just anything. You can't fill things up with just anything.

Y: Then **what**?

X: Well, if you could grind it down, make a material that would set . . .

Y: Dumping it back in **my** lap, are you?

X: Well . . . I mean, I don't know what you'd come up with. So how can I tell whether a contractor would need it?

Y: If you just **give** it to him — give it to him if he'll only come and take it away. Then let him figure out what to make of it.

X: Why would he go to all the trouble and expense of carrying it away unless he wanted it for something?

Y: Can't you think of something he would want it for?

X: No.

Y: There you are, you see. Negative thinking.
(X is about to reply, but thinks better of it and walks away. Y is thinking furiously.)

X: I suppose it's ridiculous to ask, but what about fertilizer?

Y: What about it?

X: I was wondering about the farmers. I mean I could flog it to farmers if you could think of a way to make it into fertilizer.

Y: It's a thought.

X: You mean we — it could . . .

Y: Not really.

X: But is it possible?

Y: Possible but not probable.

X: But if there's a possibility . . .

Y: Theoretically possible, but practically impossible.

X: But you said —

Y: How would you handle it? What process? What equipment? And what would you have when you were finished?

X: Fertilizer.

Y: Like drinking a double martini to get the olive pit. A waste of time and effort. *(He walks away.)*

X: No good, eh?

Y: No.
(Leaving X to think furiously, Y goes to the extreme right, and then to extreme left, studying the pile from the sides.)

Y: I'm wondering . . .

X: About breaking it down?

Y: About breaking it up.

X: Into what?

Y: Toys.

X: Toys? !

Y: They make toys out of amazing things these days: sticks, stones, shells, rags, nuts, berries . . .

X: Be serious. You think we're playing games?

Y: Games could be bloody serious. Now put your mind to it: couldn't one **play** with it . . . somehow?

X: For fun?

Y: Of course.

X: I don't see how, looking at it.

Y: Use your imagination.

X: I am.

Y: Take a **good** look.

X: *(Having done so, from several angles.)* You mean, paint it up? . . . red, yellow, blue — that sort of thing?

Y: Little pieces of it. Toys are little.

X: Some toys are big. If you made a park around it and painted the whole thing bright red —

Y: I'm not talking about painting the whole thing.

X: How would you break it up, then?

Y: Trying to put it onto me again, eh!

X: I just want to know how you'd break it up.

Y: It's just a hypothesis. IF we could break it up . . .

X: Well IF we could break it up, what about sculpture?

Y: What about it?

X: You've seen what they use these days: scrap metal, chunks of this and that, old chairs, pieces of anything. They come and pick it up, carry it off, weld it all together and sell it for a mint.

Y: I don't exactly know how you'd weld **that**.

X: But if you could break it up, you could put it together again.

Y: That doesn't follow at all. Half the things in the world, you smash them up and that's that. Humpty-Dumpty. Besides, how many sculptors are there anyway? Put them all in one room and you couldn't have a party.

X: They might take **some** of it.

Y: Then what do we do with the rest of it?

X: I hadn't thought of that.

Y: Hmph. *(He opens his stick and sits again.)*

(Sadly shaking his head, X sits and picks dirt off his shoes.)

X: In all my life, I never thought I'd have to handle a thing like this. Where did we go wrong?

Y: You expect justice in this life?

X: No. But there's no escaping judgment. I've worked hard, I've tried to do the right thing . . . and now to have it end like this.

Y: This isn't the end.

X: We'll never get out of this one. This one's done it.

Y: Never say die until you're dead.

X: It's that sort of silly optimism that got us into this.

Y: Now you're blaming me again.

X: I'm not blaming you. I'm to blame.

Y: I never said that.

X: I'm saying it. I've had it coming. It's all very well for you, working away in your lab or wherever, sitting up in your ivory tower . . . but you don't get far in business without cutting a few corners now and then. I've got away with a good deal, so far. Now it's caught up with me. It's as if that . . . out there . . . is what I've been piling up all my life . . . a little bit here and a little bit there . . . until it's got too big to ignore. Too big to get rid of. And even if you could, **how** could you? Where do you hide it? You can't even break it up and do something with the pieces. We're stuck with it. There it is, starting to stink, not just lying there — you're right — swelling out of its own rot . . . indisposable. We're the disposables.

Y: We're not disposed of yet. *(He rises, walks about with the stick.)*

X: It's what we deserve.

Y: Speak for yourself. How do **you** know what we deserve?

X: It's a judgment.

Y: It's nothing of the kind. Superstitious nonsense, that's what it is. Next you'll be telling me it's an Act of God, who arranges the way you part your hair, or would if he'd seen fit to leave

you any . . . that there is providence in the fall of a sparrow, let alone yours truly, and that we'd better like it or lump it. Well, I don't like it and I don't propose to lump it, God or no God.

X: It wouldn't hurt to pray.

Y: It wouldn't help to pray — unless it gives you some sort of lift to grovel. We got ourselves into this, and we'll get ourselves out of it.

X: How?

Y: I'll think of a way if you'll stop drivelling about judgment and give me a **chance** to think.

X: Go ahead. God helps those who help themselves.

Y: And they're precisely the ones who don't need his help. Now shut up.

X: All right . . . but I can think too, can't I?

Y: If you can refrain from passing judgment long enough.

X: We'll both think. Hard.

Y: Right. *(He pauses, leaning on the stick in front of him.)*
(They both think furiously. X takes out a notebook, consults it, shakes his head and returns it to his pocket.)

X: Have you thought of anything yet?

Y: I'm getting there.

(X rises and paces.)

Y: You can't think of any single thing it could be flogged for?

X: No.

Y: And you can't think of any single thing it could be given away for, if only someone would come and take it away?

X: No. Unless . . . *(Stops)*

Y: What?

X: *(Lamely)* Unless you can think of something useful that could be made out of it. Can you think of **anything** useful that could be made out of it? Or from it? Or with it?

Y: *(A glint in his eye.)* What you mean is, is there a way of breaking it up . . . or down . . . so that what's left over might be put to some useful purpose for someone?

X: If you like.

Y: Well, I can't think of one.

X: *(Aggressively)* That's the first time you've said that. Earlier you said perhaps. You said you couldn't say yes and you wouldn't say no.

Y: I did not. That was only about breaking it down or up. I didn't say anything whatever about distributing the residue as a useful product. That's not my department, it's yours.

X: All right, then: can it be broken up or down?

Y: Possibly. In the long run, of course, everything disintegrates. The whole world is disintegrating — a process known as entropy. In the long run it's neither here nor there whether it's here or there.

X: Never mind the long run. What about the short run? What do we do today so it'll be gone tomorrow?

Y: Can't you see I'm trying to come at it scientifically, by a process of elimination?

X: We've eliminated everything except the thing we're trying to eliminate.

Y: No we haven't. Not yet. We've got bogged down in a chicken or egg conundrum, whether we start with how to get rid of something, or with the something you get rid of. The real problem, if we may please avoid these irrelevant philosophical blind alleys, is that it exists, as such, and a way must be found of putting an end to its existence. It is, and it must not be.

X: Where do we go from there?

Y: We must eliminate the positives before we examine the negative. If there is no earthly use to which it can be put, then — and only then — should we look at the alternative.

X: Right.

Y: Now then. *(Indicating the pile.)* It becomes apparent that it cannot be burnt up, broken up, sold up, or even given up. It's a question of it or us.

X: You forgot one up.

Y: Pardon?

X: You left out one kind of up.

Y: What are you talking about?

X: You never mentioned **blowing** up.

Y: What: you mean with dynamite, or something?

X: Why not? We could drill a hole down the middle, way down into the ground, drop in a stick of dynamite, and blow it up.

Y: That would make a worse mess than we've got now.

X: How would it be worse?

Y: Some of it would be under, but some of it would be on top.

X: It would depend.

Y: That's not the **main** problem, anyway. You haven't even thought of the main problem.

X: What?

Y: We don't own the land. We only rented it. You can't blow up property you don't own.

X: We own what's on it.

Y: That's not the point.

X: *(Turning away.)* Well, you come up with something better, then.

Y: Just let me think, that's all. *(He makes the seat, and sits where he is.)*

(X sits, coolly: the responsibility has been lifted from his shoulders.)

Y: When I was at college, we did an experiment . . . with plastic. We were supposed to fill a few molds with the stuff. We had all the makings there for the whole class, which was quite a lot. The mix went into a large tube which fed into the molds, and you shut it off after each fill. Well, the spiggot stuck and we couldn't turn the damn thing off. It overflowed all the molds, the tables, the equipment, everything . . . and set. Not a thing we could do except break everything off and throw it out. Nothing you could do with the plastic. Not a thing. *(He rises and walks away.)*

X: *(After a bemused pause; expecting more to have followed.)* What was the point of all that?

Y: I'm thinking it through. A hypothesis.

X: Thinking what through? What hypothesis?

Y: At least it's more to the point than you and your puppet theatre.

X: That was just . . . a parable.

Y: So is this. You were stuck with it, so you broke it up. You couldn't very well break up the house it was supposed to go into.

X: Hardly.

Y: We've been concentrating on the contents instead of the container — don't you see? There are **two** ways of getting rid of anything: throw away the contents, or throw away the container.

X: I'm trying to follow you . . . *(Rises, joins Y.)*

Y: We've got to forget about that, out there, and put our minds to what contains it.

X: Contains it?

Y: The land — don't you see? The moment you brought up the land it's sitting on, I should have got it.

X: But you said we couldn't. You said —

Y: I said we couldn't leave it in a mess. But if we did it neatly . . .

X: I wish you'd just tell me.

Y: I'm wondering . . .

X: Yes . . .

Y: I'm wondering if there isn't some way to bury it.

X: Bury it where?

Y: Right here.

X: Just dig a hole and bury it?

Y: Yes.

X: It would have to be a big hole.

Y: Well?

X: And you said it wasn't our property.

Y: Well?

X: An awful lot of digging.

Y: What would that matter? We're not burying treasure, we wouldn't want it back again. Once it's dug, the hole wouldn't be ours, it would be his.

X: No. The hole would still be ours. *(Searching for a document in all his pockets.)* If he didn't like it he could insist we take the hole away.

Y: How can you take away a hole? It's what's in it that matters.

X: But you said to forget the contents and concentrate on the container. The container would be the hole.

Y: No! The land would be the container.

X: *(He finds the document.)* But the land isn't ours . . . it says so right here!

Y: Look! We dig a hole, put it in, put the earth back on top, and leave the land just as it was — it's as simple as that! Why worry about the hole?

X: Because you can't just dig a hole and leave it there on someone else's property!

Y: You're not just digging a hole, you're filling it up!

X: Yes, but look what you're filling it with, and it isn't even your hole!

Y: You said it was! That was the whole point of your objection: that the hole would still be ours. Now you say it would be his.

X: *(Searching through the document.)* I meant the land that was **making** the hole would still be his. We'd be making our hole on someone else's property, and he'd have a perfect right to come along and tell us to take OUR hole off HIS land. I'll find it — I'll **show** you.

Y: Once and for all, it's not the hole, it's what's in it.

X: — Including what's in it.

Y: How do you mean, including!

X: He'd have a perfect right to come along and tell us to take the hole and what's in it off his land.

Y: *(Sighing)* Not if it's buried. Not if it's down under.

X: Why not?

Y: What does he care what's underneath?

X: *(Pointing to the clause he has finally found.)* He owns the mineral rights.

Y: Why in the name of god bring that up!

X: Because it's here in the lease.

Y: But the stuff is worthless! We've already established that. What we'd bury there is absolutely worthless. It's no good to us — what good would it be to him?

X: That's not the point. He'd have mineral rights over something that's ours.

Y: But we don't want it!

X: Then why would he want it?

Y: He wouldn't want it. He'd be stuck with it.

(X slowly takes this in: looks at the document again, and then nods in worry. The light thickens.)

X: That . . . wouldn't be fair.

Y: I didn't say it would be. We took a risk, he took a risk when he rented the land to us to put it on. Even-stephen.

X: It wouldn't be right. It's only a six-month lease.

Y: With an option.

X: That doesn't change anything. When he comes along and finds out what we've buried here . . .

(X shakes his head and puts the document back in his pocket.)

Y: Maybe he'd never find out. Maybe he'd use it for something that didn't need digging.

X: But what if he did find out?

Y: Maybe he'd be able to figure out some way of using it . .

X: **We** couldn't.

Y: Still, **he** might.

(Y knocks the ash out of his pipe. X comes over with a gleam in his eye and nudges Y.)

X: Then . . . why bury it?

Y: What?

X: I mean, if he could figure out a way of using it . . .

Y: He might.

X: Or if he could figure out a way of getting rid of it . . .

Y: He might.

X: . . . why not leave it right out there in the open! We wouldn't need to go to all the trouble of burying it, and he wouldn't need to go to all the trouble of digging it up again.

Y: Hmmm.

X: And another thing. If he couldn't figure out a way of using it . . .

Y: We couldn't . . .

X: . . . And if he couldn't figure out a way of getting rid of it . . .

Y: We couldn't . . .

X: . . . Then what could he do but bury it?

Y: And if HE buried it, on his own land . . .

X: Then the hole wouldn't be ours . . . it would be his.

Y: And then . . . he'd be . . . stuck . . . with it.

X: Yes.
(Slowly, they both fold up their seats, and look again, fondly, at the pile.)

Y: I guess that's the solution.

X: Just to leave it. Walk away, and leave it.

Y: Not do anything.

X: After all, it isn't really our responsibility.

Y: That's right. I mean, there it is.

X: Yes — there she is.
(They take a last look out over their erstwhile property.)

Y: Let's go.
(They drift off, turning to look back as they go.)

The Store

Characters:

The Manager
The Assistant Manager
The Woman
The Secretary (voice off)

The office of the Manager of a large department store. The essential elements are his large desk, on which stands an inter-com box along with telephones, and the usual desk accoutrements including an elaborate letter-knife; a stuffed owl which sits atop a filing-cabinet in a corner; his desk-chair and two others facing him for visitors; and the single entrance door.

Whenever the door is opened we hear the clamour from the store: busy crowds of shoppers, cash-register bells, etc. — and whenever the door is shut it ceases abruptly.
As the house-lights dim, we hear the clamour from the store. It comes up full in the darkness, then fades out as the stage lighting comes up. The door is shut.

(The Manager is seated at his desk, a pile of papers in his hand. Standing facing him is the Assistant Manager. The Manager is outwardly a very solid, commanding executive without a trace of the neurotic even when angry — which he is at the moment. The Assistant is a harried man who has risen within the firm by being a faithful servant.)

Manager: Complaints! Complaints! Complaints! Can't you bring me anything but complaints?

Asst. Manager: I'm very sorry, sir —

Manager: What's an assistant manager for if he can't assistant manage?

Asst. Manager: But sir, this clergyman was irate. He invoked Jesus Christ several times.

Manager: It won't do him any good. The discount for clerics has been discontinued, and that's that.

Assistant: He says the whole moral order of man is disintegrating.

Manager: Let him! That's his job. It's our job to look after the store. And the way men are messing things up, these days, we've both got our work cut out for us.

Assistant: *(Going to door)* Yes sir. I'll tell him that. *(He opens the door)*

Manager: *(Turning away)* That'll be all, Mr. Pontifex.

(While Pontifex is at the door, and unseen by the Manager, the Woman slips into the office, ending up behind and beyond Pontifex.)

Assistant: Yes sir. I'll try not to interrupt unless it's something essential. *(He goes, closing the door behind him. The Manager droops with fatigue. Then he flicks on the intercom.)*

Secretary: *(Female, over intercom)* Yes sir?

Manager: Miss Chang, I am not to be disturbed. Please hold all calls unless they're urgent.

Secretary: Yes sir.

(He flicks off the intercom. Then he girds his loins, picks up a pen and starts to check off a list of items on his desk. Angrily he crumples one and throws it in the wastebasket.)

(The Woman steps forward. She is middle-aged, over-dressed, aggressive and clearly unbalanced. The Manager, on the other hand, is just as clearly in command of the situation.)

Woman: I want to see the manager, please.

Manager: How did you —

Woman: I've been waiting for a long time, and I want to see the manager.

Manager: *(Rising)* I am the manager, madam.

Woman: Then you're the person I want to see.

Manager: I thought as much. *(His habitual diplomatic manner winning out, he comes forward and shifts a chair for her.)* What can I do for you? Please sit down.

Woman: *(Sitting by desk)* I have a complaint to make.

Manager: *(Returning to his chair)* Naturally.

Woman: It isn't natural at all. I don't go round making complaints!

Manager: I didn't mean to imply —

Woman: I only bitch when there's something to bitch about. Generally I'm a very good-natured person.

Manager: Naturally.

Woman: But this time I intend to raise an old-fashioned stink.

Manager: Naturally.

Woman: Is that a tic you have, or do you keep saying that because your customers are always complaining?

Manager: Not at all. That wouldn't be wise, even if it were true. I only meant —

Woman: It wouldn't surprise me. Your clerks are snippy; rude, even.

Manager: We do our best to —

Woman: There's no use taking a complaint to them — all you get is the runaround. It's always the customer who's wrong. And so high and mighty!

Manager: It's hard to keep good clerks these days.

Woman: Oh, that's always the excuse! What's so different about these days? — unless it's that you ought to be able to get better ones. As long as I can remember —

Manager: *(Smoothly)* Not long, madam, I'm sure.

Woman: Oh, bull! Don't soft soap **me**: it won't work. Why should I waste time with their nonsense? My time is valuable.

Manager: We have a complaint department.

Woman: Nothing but soft soap. So I've gone over their heads, and I expect some straight talk.

Manager: That's always the customer's privilege. Now what seems to be the trouble?

D18

(Throughout her story he remains impassive, toying with a paper-knife.)

Woman: It began with the owl and the skunk. I was walking home through the woods, after cutting off juniper roots with the clippers, when I stepped right into a skunk, lying across the path in a pool of blood and stuck all over with owl feathers. I stood there in a kind of spell — it was so unnatural, an owl going after a skunk like that! I must have aged ten years. Finally I got away, and raced along the path to the house. I shouted for my father and my mother, but there was no answer. I dashed through every room, upstairs, downstairs. In the kitchen the sink was piled high with broken plates and silver, all covered with green mould. Decent silver shouldn't go like that. Upstairs in the back bedroom I shared with my older sister, I found her lying across the bed, strangled by a leather belt. I hope you're noting these things: belts do a lot more than hold up whatever it is. In the front bedroom I found my mother, looking terribly old. She'd been done in with an ice-pick. I've never had anything to do with ice-picks since. It was getting dark, and downstairs again I lit a candle; left it there while I ran out to the barn, looking for my father. A cry from the empty house made me turn — it was my father's voice. The house was in flames — it must have been the candle — and try as I would I couldn't make my way in. In a few moments it was all gone: the house, the bodies, the barn, the animals, my father . . .

It was on that account that I ran away and married the first man I met — a shopper for this store, who drank to excess. And when he mercifully died in a car-crash due to defective brakes — No: that was my second husband; my first was electrocuted trying to fix the oven — I had only one thing left in life, my children: a fine boy and a lovely girl. I was forced to go to work; took training as a computer programmer, where I learned that what comes out is only what you put in, if you follow me. It's all there on the cards. Six months ago, while I was out working, my darling son was suffocated in the refrigerator. Yesterday my daughter was horribly disfigured by an accident with her electric toothbrush. Now: what are you going to do about it?

Manager: Yes. Well . . .

(On his desk, the intercom buzzes)

Manager: Excuse me. *(He drops the knife, flicks on the intercom)* Yes?

Secretary: *(Over intercom)* Mr. Fitzroy from the drug department's on the line . . .

Manager: Can't he handle it? — I'm tied up at the moment.

Secretary: It's that Virox B again.

Manager: What about it?

Secretary: Seven more male customers with hair growing inside the scalp — they've gone insane.

Manager: Refer them to the manufacturer.

Secretary: I'll tell him.

Manager: *(Switching off intercom)* Now then, we were talking about a defective toothbrush?

Woman: Oh, you can't skip out of it as easily as that.

Manager: But I thought you said —

Woman: You're responsible for the whole thing.

Manager: I'm not sure I understand you.

Woman: Everything. You're responsible for everything.

Manager: *(Smoothly)* Possibly — but we're discussing liability, surely. Not quite the same —

Woman: And you think that after all I've been through I'll settle for a measly toothbrush?

Manager: The settlement may depend on any injury suffered, of course, but beyond that . . .

Woman: Any? *(Starting to weep)* **Every** injury, from start to finish! *(She extracts a handkerchief from her purse and weeps into it)* Oh, you're brutes! Power-mad brutes!

(A pause while he comes around his desk to sit on a chair near her)

Manager: You know, I'm very sympathetic, Mrs. —?

Woman: Moffat.

Manager: Yours is a terrible story, Mrs. Moffat . . .

Woman: It isn't a story. I didn't make up a word of it.

Manager: . . . almost a nightmare, one might say. Something . . . irrational.

Woman: What's irrational about it? That sort of thing happens — or did happen, or could happen.

Manager: We seem to be a little confused.

Woman: You may be — I'm not.

Manager: Now look here, Mrs. Moffat: we're not concerned with what **might** happen — let's get that quite clear. Sympathy is one thing but business another. We must deal with a specific event which can be proved to have happened. Our liability doesn't extend to —

Woman: How can you say that when it's perfectly obvious they're all connected? If it has happened it can happen, and if it can happen it will! And if it happens, you're responsible.

Manager: I fail to see, madam —

(The door opens. The Assistant Manager enters, closing the door behind him. He ignores Mrs. Moffat completely.)

Assistant: Sorry to interrupt, but there's a man out here being very abusive. Claims his boy blew himself up with one of our toy rockets.

Manager: Will they never learn?

Assistant: I've already sent him to the legal department. They say it's in your hands.

Manager: Oh yes! It's always . . . Get the details, Mr. Pontifex, and tell him it's in my hands.

Assistant: Right.

(The Assistant Manager leaves, closing the door behind him.)

Woman: Well, what did I tell you!

Manager: *(Ignoring the taunt)* . . . Now where were we? Ah yes: was this toothbrush a cash purchase or do you have a charge account?

Woman: I always pay cash; I don't believe in incurring obligations.

Manager: If you had had a charge account —

Woman: My family's dealt with this store for three generations — I'm no casual shopper.

Manager: It's a matter of how this particular purchase —

Woman: We're not talking about one little item like a toothbrush, you know; get **that** straight! We're talking about years and years of incompetence and inefficiency, a whole funeral of duds and frosts and swindles . . .

Manager: Our firm's good name, Mrs. Moffat —

Woman: . . . Breakdown is your middle name!

Manager: Mrs. Moffat, **all** appliances break down sooner or later! In time, everything disintegrates, or almost everything.

Woman: Is that an excuse to put out fiascos in the first place?

Manager: Every piece of merchandise that leaves this store is tested in our laboratories and workshops. Every effort is made to —

Woman: To prevent what **might** happen?

Manager: *(Emphatically)* To see that our products function properly — that is the extent of our responsibility. For that we have guarantees, warranties. *(Wheeling on her)* Did you have a warranty on that toothbrush?

Woman: The toothbrush, the toothbrush! We'll start at the beginning, if you don't mind, not at the end.

Manager: At the beginning of what?

Woman: Every unnatural thing that has happened in my life is a direct result of some disaster put out by you — and I want compensation.

Manager: *(Hitting the roof)* In all my life —

Woman: We haven't time for that now.

Manager: *(Winding up and finally exploding.)* No matter what you have been told, Mrs. Moffat, I am not the First Cause!

Woman: Then who is?

Manager: I've been blamed, eternally, for every malfeasance of man, let alone every natural disaster, and even for causing the latter as punishment for the former.

Woman: Sounds to me as if you hadn't the faintest idea **what** you were doing.

Manager: I'm sick and tired of being made the goat for every trip and stumble of every Tom, Dick and Betty who are perfectly free to buy whatever they want to, and not buy whatever they don't want — foul the thing up and then blame the thing instead of their own ineptitude!

Woman: If you're sick and tired you oughtn't to be in this job — and you won't put me off with a recital of **your** troubles. I'm here about mine.

Manager: Madam, your troubles are my troubles.

Woman: They certainly are! Or at any rate they certainly will be if I don't get satisfaction. The whole thing began —

Manager: *(Controlling himself.)* Very well. Let us go from the beginning of your story.

Woman: That's what I said in the first place.

Manager: *(Fresh attack: being immensely reasonable.)* It began, I think you said, with, some years ago, an owl attacking a skunk. Most unnatural, I agree. But Mrs. Moffat, we have never sold live animals — not wild ones, at any rate: that is the whole point of their being wild. If someone were responsible for their behaviour —

Woman: You can't get out of it that way. I would have arrived there in time to prevent it if your clippers had been working properly.

Manager: Clippers?

Woman: I knew you weren't taking it in. That's what kept me so long cutting juniper roots. If I'd come along earlier it would never have happened; I'd have gone straight home and got there in time to —

Manager: Now just a moment: juniper roots have nothing —

Woman: Those were your dishes in the sink . . .

Manager: What?

Woman: That was your belt my sister was strangled with . . .

Manager: Oh really —!

Woman: Your tethers on the horses . . .

Manager: The tethers were in no way connected —

Woman: And if your defective candle hadn't fallen over, or whatever it did, the house would never have burned down with everybody in it, and I wouldn't have had to run away and marry the first fool I met.

Manager: Are you suggesting —

Woman: It was working at this store that drove him to drink. The stove that did him in, drunk as he was, came from this place.

Manager: The alcohol too, I presume!

Woman: The car whose faulty brakes killed my second husband was serviced at your garage. The refrigerator —

Manager: Stop!

D22

Woman: The toothbrush —

Manager: Stop! ! Now look here, Mrs. Moffat: beyond refunding your money for goods found unsatisfactory, this firm has no liability unless you can prove that any damages you suffered were caused by our negligence.

Woman: Negligence is your middle name.

Manager: No company can be held responsible for outright misuse of its products. It's absurd! A bath-tub can kill you if you step on a bar of soap.

Woman: Don't change the subject. The clippers first.

Manager: If the clippers were not functioning properly you should have done something about it at the time.

Woman: A little girl? A homeless orphan?

Manager: Then you should have taken some action as soon as you could, not years later when the evidence has gone up in smoke, nothing can be checked . . . A candle! — What nonsense!

Woman: It only makes sense when you look at it backwards, not forwards.

Manager: Now really!

Woman: I had to wait until I knew. How could I do anything about anything until I knew what it was all about?

Manager: At this rate we'd never —

Woman: It's only now I can see how it all fits . . . how my troubles began with your clippers.

Manager: No, they did not. Before then, unhappily, you were conceived, born . . .

Woman: But they were the first sign, the first omen. I can only go by what I remember . . .

Manager: I'm afraid that's not good enough for us.

Woman: . . . and by what I foresee.

Manager: Madam, for the last time, we do not deal in signs, omens, auguries or premonitions. That is what things may become for certain people, perhaps, after they leave these premises, but —

Woman: You're not responsible?

Manager: For your whole life?

Woman: For my death.

(The intercom buzzes)

Manager: *(Going to desk)* Excuse me. *(He flicks it on)* Yes?

Voice: Excuse me, but the deputation from the Consumers' Association has arrived.

Manager: What deputation?

Voice: About the rain-making machines.

Manager: I've already told them we give no guarantee with our rain-makers!

Voice: But what am I to do with them?

Manager: Do what you like! Give them hoses, watering-cans — make water! — But please do not disturb me again! *(Switches off intercom)*

Woman: Watering-cans!

Manager: Now then, Mrs. Moffat, let us get down to brass tacks. Do you have the bills for these various transactions?

Woman: No.

Manager: Then how can we —

Woman: I trusted you.

Manager: Surely you realize that without the bills we are not liable in any way for merchandise you claim to have purchased at this store. Furthermore —

Woman: But I did.

Manager: Mrs. Moffat, I have been very patient. We are always willing to help our clients, but I must make it clear that without the bill whatever we do is a matter of good-will on our part, and in no way a legal obligation. It is possible the transactions can be traced: we shall do our best. *(Sits and prepares to take notes)* Now: rather than start at the beginning, if you don't mind, we'll start with the most recent transacaction, since you'll be better able to recall the details.

Woman: It doesn't matter where you start, it's where you end up — and that's not the end.

Manager: Nevertheless. *(Makes notes)* Toothbrush. What was the girl's name?

Woman: Edwards.

Manager: No, the girl's.

Woman: Elizabeth Edwards.

Manager: . . . Moffat.

Woman: No, Edwards — my second husband.

Manager: I see. And when did you buy it: do you recall?

Woman: About a month ago.

Manager: About?

Woman: Give or take a couple of weeks.

Manager: Have you any idea of our volume of sales, Mrs. Moffat? — of how many electric toothbrushes we sell every day?

Woman: You shouldn't be selling them at all.

Manager: You are not forced to buy. Let me remind you that I'm doing you a favour in looking into this at all! *(Pause)* We only carry on our shelves what people will purchase, and we carry what people want whether we happen to want to or not. Personally I regard electric toothbrushes as worse than unnecessary — I regard them as dangerous; but so long as people continue to buy them, then we will continue to sell them, putting out the best and safest

product we can. Now: how did she injure herself?

Woman: I'd rather not say.

Manager: Did she see a dentist?

Woman: Why should she see a dentist?

Manager: In order to determine the form of injury.

Woman: Oh, for heaven's sake, **any**one could tell!

Manager: Well, **will** someone tell? Were there any witnesses?

Woman: Certainly not!

Manager: This is impossible. What about the refrigerator: when was it purchased? ·

Woman: About three years ago.

Manager: Now surely you can do better than that! *(He begins to circle her, notebook at the ready)* Think back, Mrs. Moffat. Where did you live at the time? What were you doing then? Wasn't there something unusual that happened just before you purchased the refrigerator, or just after? Now think.

Woman: I'm thinking.

Manager: Ah, now we're getting somewhere. Now we're being constructive. Well?

Woman: I can't remember.

Manager: Think! Go back, Mrs. Moffat! Think back!

Woman: I can't remember when I try to remember things out of order!

Manager: But you're asking **me** to remember things out of order! Millions of sales a day, and you expect —

Woman: I told you to begin at the beginning! One thing comes after another, and makes you remember the thing after that — it's no use

trying to do it all mixed up!

Manager: I'm trying to make it easy for you, Mrs. Moffat, not trying to mix you up! Come now: isn't there **some**thing that can jog your memory? Some domestic crisis? A new dress? Some wedding or birth or death to which you could attach a date? Some **other** accident? Some epidemic? Some national or international event: an election, a revolution, a landing on the moon?

Woman: Wait a minute . . .

Manager Yes?

Woman: Our rabbit had bunnies, which the father ate.

Manager: Not, unfortunately, recorded in the newspapers. Think again, Mrs. Moffat. I must warn you that your life depends on your ability to establish that the merchandise concerned was purchased in this store, and that we were in some way negligent.

Woman: It killed my boy!

Manager: A machine is not a person, Mrs. Moffat: it does only what it is programmed to do. People have freedom of will; a machine —

Woman: He didn't lock **himself** inside!

Manager: It is unnatural for refrigerators to kill people; they are designed to keep food cold.

Woman: Whatever they can do they will!

Manager: That again! This store, madam, is not responsible for the conduct of an appliance led astray by someone ignorant of its proper use! And we have not yet even established that it was one of ours!

Woman: Would I be here if it weren't?

Manager: That is exactly what we have to establish. If you can't remember what happened three years ago, how can we possibly go back ten, twenty —

Woman: It was Thursday, November the eigh-teenth, at half-past eleven.

Manager: *(After a long look at her)* All right. What was the boy's name.

Woman: Betti.

Manager: The boy?

Woman: By my first husband: Arturo Betti. B-E-T-T-I.

Manager: That's the husband's name?

Woman: No, the boy's.

Manager: And also your name at the time of purchase?

Woman: No, Edwards.

Manager: Who was electrocuted by the oven.

Woman: No, that was Betti.

(The door opens and shuts. The Assistant Manager enters. As before, he ignores Mrs. Moffat.)

Assistant: I'm terribly sorry to interrupt, but the delivery drivers have gone on strike.

Manager: Can't you see I'm busy, Mr. Pontifex?

Assistant: They're complaining about hours, working conditions, pay . . .

Manager: Complaints, complaints, complaints! What's the matter with our Industrial Relations office?

Assistant: They've gone on strike too. You've got to take a hand — everything's breaking down!

Manager: Then fix it! I am not to be disturbed! Get out!

Assistant: Yes sir.

(The door opens and closes as he goes. The Manager locks the door after him.)

Woman: *(Taunting)* Breakdown . . . Break-down!

Manager: Now, Mrs. Moffat, let us come to grips. Your son Arturo Betti, you say, locked himself in one of our refrigerators, purchased three years ago at 11.30 a.m. on Thursday, November 18th, and suffocated. How old was he?

Woman: Twenty-seven.

Manager: *(Incredulous)* At the time he died?

Woman: Well, if he hasn't already, he will do.

Manager: I suspected as much. We're dealing with hypothetical events, aren't we, Mrs. Moffat!

Woman: I don't know what you mean.

Manager: None of these things ever really happened, did they?

Woman: You can't get out of it that way — by pretending things don't go wrong! If they can they will!

Manager: But in these particular instances —

Woman: We haven't finished yet . . .

Manager: We certainly haven't — and we're going to if it takes —

Woman: Go back to the beginning and you'll see we've not finished yet!

Manager: We've hardly begun, have we? The clippers, the belt, the candle — when were they purchased, and by whom?

Woman: My father, when I was a child.

Manager: And the name?

Woman: Svidrigailov.

Manager: Four names. Four different names you've been shopping under at this store, Mrs. Moffat: Moffat, Edwards, Betti and now Svidrigailov! You deliberately set out to confuse us, didn't you?

Woman: No!

Manager: . . . Deliberately set out to shift the blame onto us for your own nightmares!

Woman: No!

Manager: *(Low and knowing)* You never had a daughter, did you, Mrs. Moffat?

Woman: What?

Manager: It was you yourself who used the toothbrush, improperly, if I may say so, hoping that by sympathetic magic —

Woman: That's a lie!

Manager: And your son: Your son was born prematurely, wasn't he!

Woman: What's that got to do with it?

Manager: Locked in the fridge, indeed! And the car whose defective brakes caused, or might cause, or may cause the death of your second husband — or was it, or will it be, your first? — you wanted him to go on and on and on, never to stop —

Woman: You killed him!

Manager: I killed a figment of your imagination?

Woman: No, No!

Manager: And the other husband, the one who was or will be electrocuted trying to fix the oven . . . is there a death certificate?

Woman: Unnatural causes . . . unnatural causes!

Manager: They never existed, did they!

Woman: Yes!

Manager: If they existed, Mrs. Moffat, who killed them, eh? Who was it who wanted these inept mechanics out of the way? And why? I suggest to you . . .

Woman: It was an accident!

Manager: Come now, Mrs. Moffat, there are no accidents in your life, are there? Isn't it all in the cards? Doesn't what can happen happen?

Woman: It **all** happened! My mother, my sister —

Manager: Your father too?

Woman: Yes, my father!

Manager: Your father was real, was alive . . .

Woman: Yes!

Manager: Alive when the others were dead: is that it?

Woman: He was killed in the fire made by that candle of yours!

Manager: Was it our candle or his you blame?

Woman: Yours! There was nothing left!

Manager: Nothing found, you mean. Shall I tell you how it happened, Mrs. Moffat? An owl, driven to unnatural deeds by a tormenting skunk, lay in your path as you were returning home, armed with a root-clipper. It delayed you, whether ten minutes or ten years is no matter. When you arrived home, it was to find your sister and your mother murdered, and your father gone. You yourself set fire to the house —

Woman: No: I was out in the barn!

Manager: Looking for your father! If only you could have used those clippers! You hated your father, didn't you, for murdering your mother, your sister — for abandoning you, for —

Woman: My whole life —

Manager: Yes, all of it! Your whole life you want to lay at my door! Grudges and grievances, hates and complaints, all that happened and could happen and might happen . . .

Woman: *(A cry)* They were real! Everything was real!

Manager: *(His hands at her throat)* As real, Mrs. Moffat, as you are to me.

Woman: Get away from me . . .

Manager: Putting it all on the store . . .

Woman: I'll raise a stink! . . .

Manager: Lies and darkness . . .

Woman: Treating customers like animals . . .

Manager: *(Pulling at her purse as she struggles free.)* You buy this here? *(Snatching it.)* We'll take it back!

Woman: Thieves! Robbers!

Manager: And this? *(Her coat)* Any complaints? *(He pulls it off her)* We'll take it back!

Woman: Help! Help! Somebody help me! *(She reaches for the intercom: in preventing her, the Manager switches it on.)* Help! Help me! *(She pulls him away.)*

Manager: *(Grabbing her and tearing her dress.)* This defective too?

Voice: *(Voice from box, continuing under dialogue from here to the end.)* May I help you? . . . Yes sir? . . . Hello! . . . May I help you? . . . Were you calling? . . . Hello! . . . Is anyone there? . . . Hello! . . . May I help you? . . . Hello! Hello! . . . Were you calling, sir? . . . May I help you? . . .

Woman: No! *(She flails back at him.)*

Manager: Bitch! *(Strikes her.)*

Woman: Stop! Stop!

Manager: No, go back! Back! *(Strikes her.)*

(Pounding on the door, continues.)

Assistant: *(Assistant Manager, outside the door, under stage action.)* Is anything the matter? . . . What's going on in there? . . . Open the door! . . . What's going on? . . . Open up! . . . What's happening in there? . . . Somebody get a key!

. . . What's wrong? . . . Open up! . . . Open the door!

(Mrs Moffat fights free and reaches for the paper knife on the desk. They wrestle for it. She is forced to the floor. He takes the knife, as if to an animal, and plunges it into her three times.)

Manager: Bitch! Bitch! Bitch!

(She subsides with a moan. He kneels beside her, panting. The door bursts open and the Assistant Manager stands there. He ignores Mrs Moffat. The voice of the secretary from the intercom continues in the background.)

Assistant: *(At door.)* Are you all right, sir?

Manager: *(Slowly, mechanically: an owl.)* Who?

Assistant: You, sir.

Manager: No . . . complaints. I've killed them all. *(Pause.)* Get her out of here.

Assistant: Who, sir?

Manager: On the path . . . the skunk.

Assistant: *(Advancing)* A skunk, sir, on the —?

Manager: Careful — don't step in the blood.

Assistant: *(Gently)* Are you feeling all right, sir?

Manager: Who. Who. Who.

The lights slowly fade out

Inside Out

A flat in a remodelled large old house. We see the livingroom, one corner of which serves as a dining area with a small round table and two chairs, the always-open door into the small kitchen, and a closed door to a bedroom. Inside the main door there is an excuse for a vestibule. The furnishings — which include a sofa and at least two easy chairs — are a curious mixture of hand-me-down and ultra-modern. The walls are covered with travel and theatre posters, and a good many photographs and costume sketches of various sizes — some framed and some not. The lamps, stereo-phonograph and television set have their wires visibly connected and chaotically draped into sockets doing double and triple duty. The radio is on: a dramatic agitato from some 19th Century overture.

(Marina, an attractive girl in her mid-twenties, is just finishing a solo breakfast. Her spirits seem in complete contrast to the vigorous music. She slowly rises, and commences to clear the dishes away. She wears a short dressing-gown.)

(The door-buzzer sounds, and after an interval is repeated.)

Marina: *(Startled.)* Just a minute. *(She carries the dishes into the kitchen.)* All right, all right! *(In addition to the buzzer, there is pounding on the door. She re-enters wiping her hands on a dishtowel, which she tosses on a chair. She turns off the radio, checks her gown and then her hair, en route to answer the summons.)* I'm coming, I'm coming!
(Once there she cautiously opens the door an inch, and then throws it wide as soon as she sees who it is. Outside stands an angry and determined man of fifty, wearing a smart business suit and fedora hat, and carrying a raincoat and a small valise. He at once removes the hat, adding a full head of hair to his other obvious good looks.)

Marina: *(Warmly.)* Dad! *(Embraces him.)* Oh . . . good to see you!

Father: *(Too tense to respond.)* Are you all right? *(He enters, tosses his coat down, then immediately puts his suitcase on a chair.)* Okay — where is he?

Marina: Where's who?

Father: *(As he takes a horsewhip from the case.)* Where is the son-of-a-bitch? *(Lashes the whip.)* In bed?

Marina: What are you doing?

Father: I'm going to give that gorilla the lesson of his life . . . with a teacher he'll understand. *(Snaps whip.)* Now get out of my way. *(Removes jacket.)*

Marina: *(Getting between him and the bedroom door.)* He's not here. He's out.

Father: Stand aside! *(Rolling up his sleeves.)*

Marina: Have you lost your mind? *(She tugs at him.)*

Father: In there, is he!

Marina: He's not here, can't you understand?

Father: *(Panting.)* Missed him, have I?

Marina: *(Releasing him.)* My God! What is this: Ben Hur?

Father: *(Losing steam.)* When will he be back?

Marina: I don't know. He didn't say.

Father: *(Turning back.)* Well — huh! — it's lucky for him. *(He tosses the whip on the floor.)*

Marina: *(Deciding to humour the maniac: clearing a chair.)* Here . . . Dad, sit down. Let me get you some coffee.

Father: *(Sitting.)* Thanks. Good idea.

Marina *(Going into kitchen, off.)* Have you had breakfast? *(She prepares two coffees.)*

Father: *(Into his knuckles.)* I would have . . . The dirty, vicious . . . son-of-a . . .

Marina: *(From the kitchen.)* I said have you had breakfast?

Father: Mm? Oh yes. On the plane. No sugar.

Marina: I remember. *(She appears at the door.)* Powdered cream okay?

Father: *(Testily.)* No it is not.

Marina: Sorry, I forgot. *(She turns back into the kitchen.)*

Father: I'll take it black. *(Striking the chair-arm with his fist.)* Damn, damn, damn!

Marina: *(Off: ignoring the blast.)* You flew down this morning, then?

Father: We got your letter yesterday. *(Then with monumental self-pity.)* I had to go out there and perform last night, in front of almost a thousand people . . . not knowing whether you were still in one piece. Can you imagine the strain? I didn't know one cue from the next. I didn't know whether I was in a play or a nightmare, whether I existed and the show was an illusion or the other way round. *(Marina appears beside him with the two coffees, but simply stands there looking down at him.)* Well, I get back home and into bed, and your mother — who has few illusions about anything — turns over every ten minutes to ask what I intend to **do** about it. I think I had a half hour's sleep all night.

Marina: So you got up, went to the theatre for that *(Nodding her head at the whip)* . . .

Father: *(Guiltily.)* Shops weren't open yet.

Marina: *(Handing him his coffee.)* Here.

Father: You know the way she talks: "Any man who beats his wife should get ten years hard labour and the lash once a week! "

Marina: *(Sitting by him.)* I am not his wife.

Father: That makes it worse, not better. At least we'd have him then.

Marina: We?

Father: Well, we — you — what does that matter? We could do something legal about it.

Marina: I've been doing everything legal since I was twenty-one. I can look after myself.

Father: Sweetheart, that's not the point. Your mother's worried sick. I know you've had your differences, you two, but —

Marina: Why put it onto her?

Father: I'm not. We're both worried sick. We don't understand your bunch, we honestly don't: wouldn't be caught dead married. Damn it to hell, in our time we may have played around a bit, but at least we kept up appearances.

Marina: I know. **We** don't understand **your** bunch. *(Rising to find a cigaret.)*

Father: Why do you keep on living with the crud if he won't marry you and all he does is beat you up?

Marina: I don't know.

Father: What do you mean, you don't know?

Marina: I mean I won't marry him because I don't know: like I'm not sure.

Father: What'll it take to make up your mind: a broken neck?

Marina: I don't know.

Father: Then why in god's name don't you turf him out until you **do** know? Or clear out yourself? You'd always be welcome at home.

Marina: *(Sitting.)* No thank you very much.

Father: It's beyond me. The first we heard of it — when was it: a couple of months ago? — "Last night he gave me a black eye", you wrote. Just as if it was a dozen roses.

Marina: Well, it showed . . . something. We were communicating.

Father: Connecting, the boxers call it. Then, next letter, you connected with chairs — or do you call that Morse Code?

Marina: It wasn't really chairs. Just a piece off a . . . you know, a broken back.

Father: Oh, a mere nothing! Then more bruises and a sprained ankle from kicks. Kicks! Almighty Moses, is the man a savage? *(This gets him up.)*

Marina: Could be.

Father: *(Taking his cue from the photographs on the wall.)* I bet he looks like one. Hair out to here? Never shaves? Goes round half naked? Bangles on his arm, like this Yahoo? Bare feet, I bet?

Marina: He looks like any other actor.

Father: I never looked like that, for pete's sake! These characters go round playing Caliban in real life.

Marina: You wear your offstage costume too. Always respectable . . . the artist as solid citizen . . .

Father: *(Hastily loosening his tie.)* What the hell's that got to do with it? It's a matter of professionalism. You ought to have learned that by now.

Marina: *(Lightly.)* I didn't say he looked like that.

Father: What **does** he look like?

Marina: Do looks matter? Does that bother you?

Father: Oh, never mind!

Marina: Or do you mean what does he look like to **me**? "Is he beautiful because I —"

Father: Forget it. I'll see him myself — because I intend to stay here till he comes.

Marina: You may have a long wait.

Father: He can look like Cary Grant, for all I care.

Marina: Do you have to reach **quite** so far back?

Father: *(Coming to her, sitting.)* All I care about, sweetheart, is you. How in hell can you

D35

go on and perform covered with bruises and limping like a mugwump?

Marina: A little make-up . . .

Father: Don't tell **me**! *(Sullenly, he sips his coffee.)*

Marina: I remember you once in Macbeth — was I six or seven? You went on with ten stitches in your head: the night before you'd said "Lay on, Macduff! " — and he had! *(She rises triumphantly.)*

Father: That was an accidental wound got in battle, not domestic battery with intent to maim. Of **course** you go on: that's what being a pro means. But a good actor doesn't go round courting deformity — **that's** what he puts on with make-up, not the other way round.

Marina: Then it looks like the real thing.

Father: Exactly. And the real thing looks phony.

Marina: You mean what happens onstage is real, and what happens in real life is phony?

Father: No I do not! And you'd better not get them inside out — That way madness lies.

Marina: Well, then! *(Picking up the whip.)* Aren't we a little confused? What were you going to do with this: maim the poor guy for real?

Father: *(Snorting.)* Poor guy!

Marina: Are we on stage or off it?

Father: *(Rising as he explodes.)* Look: when you're doing a job there are occupational hazards. But in real life no bullying bastard is going to beat up my daughter and get away with it!

Marina: Honestly, father, this isn't 1900.

Father: *(Ironically.)* I was born in 1921. I am not a mid-Victorian. When I was your age —

Marina: I know, I know: the depression.

Father: *(With mock patience.)* God knows I know your crowd thinks it's discovered reality — and honesty and dignity and integrity and sex and beauty and a number of other things that've been around since the year One. *(Rhetorically)* But damn it to hell, there's still such a thing as human decency and, well, chivalry — and real men don't go round beating up defenceless women.

Marina: *(Evenly)* Unless they ask for it.

Father: *(Looking at her aghast, quietly.)* You mean you're some kind of a masochist? Come off it! . . . Look, I know you! You were always a good, sweet kid . . .

Marina: Oh I know. *(She sits and dangles a leg.)* Otherwise I wouldn't be Daddy's Little Girl. Daddy's image would be, you know, tarnished.

Father: *(Outraged)* That's one hell of a thing to say! — when I've just come all the way down here at the crack of dawn, to help you — to rescue you from this thug, this fiend, this monster, this —

Marina: Dragon?

Father: *(Cut)* Well, I'm doing it for you!

Marina: Thanks a bunch, St. George.

Father: *(Throwing it away.)* Oh, you're bloody impossible. *(Sits)*

Marina: *(After a pause, going to put an arm around him.)* Dad, darling: why do you always have to play a role?

Father: What?

Marina: Why can't you be yourself, instead of St. George, or Macbeth, or Willy Loman, or . . . Charley's Aunt! There must be a real person underneath.

Father: *(Unresponding: hurt.)* Huh.

Marina: *(Going to the door.)* You didn't make that grand entrance with the whip for me — you thought it up for yourself. The Heavy Father Act.

Father: Oh come on . . .

Marina: No, honestly! (Imitates him.) "Damn it to hell, there's still such a thing as human decency and, well chivalry — and real men don't go round beating up defenceless women! " Good grief!

Father: (Defensively) Look, baby . . .

Marina: I'm not a baby. You didn't come to rescue me: you came to rescue your father-image. You come in here to get all your hangups about my generation off your chest — and announce that it's for my sake? Come on!

Father: (Lost) I'm sorry, I . . .

Marina: You know something? The Heavy Father doesn't suit you: You're miscast.

Father: I was only trying . . .

Marina: I'm sorry too. I appreciate what you were trying to do. But if you'd really wanted to help me you'd've come in here quietly and sat down and asked me what you could do — not charge in like a mad bull.

Father: Well, I'm asking you now.
(Marina goes to get another cigaret, takes the time to light it, and then comes back to sit close to him.)

Marina: Look, Dad: you're no fool, you're not a total square, just a rhomboid. You've been around, you know a lot about life — far more than I do — and you could really help me if you wanted to. Couldn't we come at this sincerely, like a couple of mature adults?

Father: (Wryly) The Understanding Father, eh? Hmph! (As if trying a new tack in rehearsal.) All right: let's see what happens. (He rises, walks away and then turns with a transparent attempt at sincerity.) Sweetheart: is there anything at all I can do to —

Marina: No. wait. (While talking, she tosses his jacket at him.) Go out and come in again. Make a proper entrance. (She hands him the valise.) Get something out of this. (She plants his hat on his head, then goes to open the door.)

Father: Well . . . all right. Anything to help.

Marina: (Thrusting him out.) And remember: two mature adults. Sincerity.

Father: (Parrotting her.) Sincerity. (He nods.)

(She shuts the door, and immediately goes into a whirl of activity, in and out of the bedroom, as she changes. This should be as close to a "quick change" as possible. She ends up dressed very smartly in slacks and a modish wig, just in time to answer the buzzer and admit her father, now dressed in a turtle-neck sweater, jazzy sports coat and slacks.)

Marina: (Twinkling) Well, look who's here!

Father: (Pushing the sincerity.) Hi there, stranger!

(They embrace, with adult grunts of pleasure.)

Marina: Good to see you! (Shutting the door and leading the way in.) You look great.

Father: You look great yourself, if I say so as shouldn't.

Marina: Put that (valise) down and let me get you a drink.

Father: (Complying) Coffee?

Marina: Scotch?

Father: Scotch. (Sits: looks around.)

Marina: (Going toward a cupboard where she keeps the liquor.) Oh, I remember! (She prepares two scotch-and-sodas, which involves, during the coming dialogue, going into the kitchen to get the ice.) And how did you leave Mother?

Father: Gladly. I must be truthful. (Marina laughs.) She's a marvellous woman, your mother, but lacks understanding of lesser creatures. (He extracts a pipe and tobacco.) May I?

Marina: Go right ahead: this is Liberty Hall.

Father: Er, yes. As a matter-of-fact, that's what I came to see you about.

Marina: Liberty Hall?

Father: All that. This fellow you're shacked up with . . .

Marina: What about him?

Father: I'm not criticizing, you understand. I'm all for Liberty. Live and let live. You young people have your own way of life, and that's fine with me.

Marina: Is it? *(She returns and hands him his drink, then sits down with hers.)*

Father: I am not my daughter's keeper, the tax-collector tells me.

Marina: That's right.

Father: But if there's any way I can help, any way at all . . . *(He rises to get an ashtray.)*

Marina: With what?

Father: Well, I mean . . . You getting beaten up and everything . . . not very nice . . .

Marina: Carrying liberty a little too far?

Father: Are you in love with the fellow? *(Sits)*

Marina: Today? *(She shrugs.)* He's away.

Father: I thought he was in the company.

Marina: Yes, but not in this show. They let him off for a few days to see about a film job.

Father: What: one of those nude croquet orgies?

Marina: *(Studying him.)* Motorbikes.

Father: Ah well, what's a sex-symbol between friends!

Marina: That put a strain on your tolerance?

Father: Oh, boys will be brutes, I suppose. We must try to understand. *(Over the top of his glass as he sips.)* Do I gather you like it . . . that way?

Marina: I like . . . a man who knows who he is. Something firm and solid.

Father: Brass knuckles and studded belts and all that leather jazz, eh? That your thing?

Marina: . . . a man so real it hurts. Then you know there's something there, something more than an image, something to get through to.

Father: *(Grandly)* Well, sweetheart, if that's the way you want it . . . I mean, we'll go along with whatever . . .

Marina: *(Dangerously)* I felt sure you would.

Father: We have to learn to accept these things. Change with the times . . . be adaptable . . .

Marina: *(Suddenly flaring.)* Oh for God's sake why don't you say what you're thinking!

Father: *(Startled)* What?

Marina: Why don't you stand up for **something**! Anything, instead of waffling like a flag on a pole!

Father: Now just a minute: I thought you wanted me to —

Marina: Don't you **care** what happens to me?

Father: That's the whole point!

Marina: But you've just said you don't give a bloody damn! Anything I want to do is okay by you: right?

Father: Look: I'm trying to be understanding —

Marina: That's not understanding, that's abdicating! Don't you get what's happening in the world?

(As she grows more and more emotional, he becomes increasingly quiet, dry and rational — reversing the roles they adopted in the first scene.)

Father: I'd settle for what's happening right here.

D39

Marina: While you and your crowd yack about understanding and tolerance and letting us do our own thing, some of us who **believe** in our own thing are doing just that. Isn't there anything you believe in? — Because if you don't fight for it nobody else is going to.

Father: *(Simply)* I believe in the theatre.

Marina: Hah! There's a firm foundation for you — fiddling while Rome burns! Turn on the TV so we don't have to watch the real world go to pieces! Well, there **are** people who care about the world, about war and poverty and corruption — and they're going to do something about it!

Father: In the theatre? That's pretty old hat, art for politics' sake.

Marina: You know, there **are** other kinds than yours — that fun-thing for the bored elite.

Father: Oh I know: movies with motorbikes for the bored proletariat.

Marina: Well, do you fight for **your** values, or do you just go along with the game — any game? You're a chameleon, a puppet, a contortionist, not a man.

Father: Man's greatest strength is his adaptability: I'm adaptable. You think the world is going to adapt to you? Has the old globe got any better for all its movers, hoovers and improvers?

Marina: Ohoo! *(She mockingly chalks one up for him in the air.)*

Father: Did Shakespeare prevent bishops from burning witches? Did Molière save us from Napoleon or Beethoven from Hitler? It's a forlorn hope — an expression, incidentally, that comes from the old Dutch "verloren hoop", meaning "the lost squad": the idiots who always charge ahead.

Marina: Don't come over me with your old Dutch! So you sit back on your behind?

Father: No. I try to make people laugh or cry . . . take them out of themselves for awhile. You know of a better way to put up with a crazy world?

Marina: *(Now in full sail.)* Yes: change it! We're through with all that hypocritical cynicism of yours, with your propped-up cultural establishment, doing lip-service to freedom and art while out of the other side of its mouth it licks the boots of the corporations —

Father: That's the neatest trick of the week.

Marina: That's right, make fun of my grammar! What the hell does language matter? It hasn't helped you to communicate with me, has it?

Father: It's a poor workman who complains of his tools.

Marina: Ooh, right on, aren't you! Oh no: you've found the world a messy place, your bunch, but rather than get up off your butts and do something about the mess you sit around telling jokes and playing word-games. It saves you from coming to grips with what the words stand for: the real thing!

Father: You know, I can't help observing that for someone who despises words you seem to use an awful lot of 'em.

Marina: *(Almost hysterical by now.)* I'm talking — I'm trying to — I'm signalling to you through the flames

Father: That line rings a bell . . .

Marina: Can't you get the message? — There's a revolution coming! I'm trying to tell you — there's a revolution coming — and on you it's going to be very very rough!

Father: *(Finally rising, but still dryly controlled.)* The theatre **plays through** revolutions. Revolutions **need** theatres for plays about happier times.

Marina: I'm not talking about playing, for Christ's sake, I'm talking about real life!
(They are face-to-face, Marina with clenched everything, her father with a look of quizzical sizing-up. They hold the look for a moment, then he breaks it and turns away shaking his head — like a disappointed director.)

Father: I don't believe you. Something . . .

Marina: *(Sharply)* Don't believe what?

Father: It doesn't grab me. There's a false note somewhere . . . can't quite put my finger on it . . .

Marina: Are you copping out?

Father: *(Shrugging)* Well, this isn't working either. *(He moves away from her to refresh his drink.)*

Marina: *(Exhausted from the tirade, but pursuing him.)* What isn't?

Father: The sincere bit.

Marina: *(Throwing-in-the-towel, slumping miserably in a nearby chair.)* What happened?

Father: Well, for one thing it isn't me, and it certainly isn't you, baby.

Marina: *(Doggedly, through her teeth.)* I am not a baby.

Father: Now **you**'re role-playing. That's the Angry Young Thing: third drawer down, second file in. Old clippings from The Rolling Stones.

Marina: Oh . . . *(She angrily snatches the wig off.)* Damn, damn, damn! *(She gently starts to cry.)*

Father: *(After squeezing her shoulder compassionately.)* Let me fix you something. *(He takes her glass to refresh it.)*

Marina: *(Miserably)* I got carried away.

Father: I know how it is. But I don't think it's really helping you very much — except to, you know, get things off your chest.

Marina: *(The irony not lost on her.)* I know, I know.

Father: *(Handing her the drink.)* Couldn't we try . . . well . . . *(He sits, thoughtfully.)*

Marina: *(Cheering up.)* Would you like . . . you

want to, you know, take it from the top again?

Father: *(Kindly)* Perhaps we should. Maybe we can . . . damn it, we ought to be able to . . .

Marina: No poses, no parts, nothing false.

Father: Right. *(He ruefully removes his toupee.)* There.

Marina: Just you and me.

Father: Well. *(He downs his drink, puts down his glass, rises and makes slowly for the door: he turns back.)* If we don't make it too, you know, soppy. *(Picks up valise.)*

Marina: *(Following him toward the door.)* Not "Love Story".

Father: *(In reply.)* "No, No, Nanette".

Marina: *(Half-laughing)* Stop it, will you! Now: one more time . . . and this time for real.

Father: *(Opening door.)* Right. From the top.

Marina: Buzz when you're ready.
(She shuts the door after him, and once more makes a fast — but this time not madly fast — change, into an attractive house-coat. She takes a moment to brush her own hair. The buzzer goes, and she admits her father, this time in old jeans and sweater, and minus his toupee. For a moment they look at one another, and smile awkwardly.)

Marina: *(Absolutely straight.)* Hi dad.

Father: *(Ditto)* Did I get you up?

Marina: No, no. Come on in.

Father: Thanks.

(He comes in, and deposits his valise while she shuts the door behind him.)
Marina: Why didn't you let me know you were coming?

Father: Didn't know until first thing this morning. *(Looking for another chair to sit in.)* Caught the early flight.

Marina: It's good to see you. Here — *(She removes newspaper from a chair.)* — this place is a mess.

Father: Thanks. *(Sits)*

(A pause. Marina suddenly gets busy clearing away the debris from the earlier coffee and the liquor. She goes into the kitchen and returns while talking.)

Marina: How's mother?

Father: Oh, she's fine.

Marina: Everybody else?

Father: They're fine. *(Pause)* Did I interrupt your breakfast?

Marina: No, just finished.

Father: Oh.

(Another pause.)

Marina: How's the weather been at home?

Father: Pretty good. How's it been here?

Marina: Not bad.

Father: That's good. *(He looks about nervously.)*

Marina: *(Finished her chores, she sits beside him.)* Now then.

Father: You all alone?

Marina: You mean is Billy here?

Father: Yes, Billy . . . or whatever his name is.

Marina: No, he isn't.

Father: *(After a nod signifying "I might have known")* How's the season going?

Marina: Oh, you know, fair. Cherry Orchard bombed but they love Odd Couple.

Father: Audiences holding up?

Marina: Weekends. Town like this, Monday to Thursday they watch TV and go to bed.

Father: Same all over. Yes sir, same all over.

(A pause. Marina picks up some sewing.)

Marina: What . . . um . . . what brings you down here, Dad?

Father: Oh, I just thought I'd come down and see how you were. I mean, well, you know, we got your letter yesterday.

Marina: And you were worried about me?

Father: Yes – about you and . . .

Marina: Billy?

Father: . . . whatsisname.

Marina: I'm fine, actually.

Father: Those fights . . . um . . . bruises . . .

Marina: What about them?

Father: Must be where you can't see 'em.

Marina: Oh that. Well, you know how it is.

Father: (Feeling increasingly inept, remarkably like an actor without a script.) In your letter . . . in your letter you made it sound pretty bad.

Marina: Did I?

Father: Pretty rough. We were worried about you.

Marina: (Smiling to herself.) I guess you must've been.

Father: So I came right down.

Marina: That's very thoughtful of you.

Father: But you're okay.

Marina: Yes, I'm fine.
(Unable to stand this unfruitful drivel any longer, the father gets up and makes a vigorous effort to take the bull by the horns, pacing about.)

Father: What kind of a guy is this Billy?

Marina: (Rhyming it off.) He's five ten-and-half, dark curly hair, thin but sturdy, big hands, hair all over his chest, no bottom, deep blue eyes that light up when he gets mad, a wonderful smile when he gets happy, and he's great in bed. (With her focus on the sewing.)

Father: And that makes up for when he breaks your bones?

Marina: Only now and then.

Father: Now and then! Why does he do it at all?

Marina: I guess because he feels like it. He's an alive guy. He has a real, you know, presence.

Father: Visible, you might say. Leaves marks.

Marina: Oh yes. You know he's around.

Father: (Who has been casing the joint.) This is your flat, is it?

Marina: Yes – a poor thing, but mine own. Why?

Father: It's just that I don't see signs of a man around. For a guy with so much presence he's curiously inconspicuous.

Marina: He comes and goes.

Father: Quite a set-up. And he shows his gratitude by whomping the daylights out of you.

Marina: I never expect gratitude, do you? I've got what I wanted from him.

Father: I suppose you know what you're doing.

Marina: I think so. (Her attention still on the sewing: she hardly looks at him.)

Father: You're old enough to know what you want.

Marina: That's right.

Father: (Suddenly attacking her, provoked by her casual inattention.) But to get yourself trapped in a situation like this! With a man who's clearly unbalanced, whatever else he may be — You know what you're letting yourself in for?

Marina: (As suddenly dropping the needlework and matching his choler.) No, I don't! I don't really know where I'm going at all — because before you know where you're going you have to know who you are!

Father: Don't you know who you are?

Marina: Do you?

Father: Well, I'm . . . I haven't done badly. It's not an easy life, theatre, TV, films, today. And one way or another I haven't done too badly; I'm somebody.

Marina: Oh, in the sense of important, yes . . .

Father: (Retreating) Well, relatively . . .

Marina: . . . but do you know who you are? I mean when you look in the mirror in the morning, you know that man?

Father: Only too well. Baggy-eyed, jolly-jowled, wrinkled, sagging old me.

Marina. Or whatever character you're playing that day.

Father: People in glass houses, et cetera.

Marina: (Suddenly depressed.) I know, I'm just like you. That's the trouble. A chip off the old rubber.

Father: Aw, come on, now! Haven't I given you something better than that?

Marina: Looking for gratitude?

Father: Haven't I given you something to be proud of?

Marina: Sure. A chameleon daughter should thank her chameleon father for making another chameleon.

Father: Your mother was no chameleon!

Marina: Aha! Now you're beginning to get it! (Low and sharp.) Why did you marry her?

Father: (Startled) Well, I . . . it was just after the war, and we . . .

Marina: Stop waffling. Why did you marry her?

Father: (After a pause: looking down.) Because she was a real person. I had a line in a play once . . . . forget the title . . . "Quicksilver has to fall in love with an alloy or it rolls all over."

Marina: (Close to him.) And Dad, I don't want to run all over. (He looks at her bleakly, then away.) You see the point, don't you? I've got your problem in reverse. I need my alloy.

Father: But that's exactly what I don't see! You need somebody down-to-earth, solid, dependable, not a crackpot who —

Marina: (A cry.) I need somebody real — so real that it hurts!

Father: It has to hurt before it's real?

Marina: Yes, yes, yes!

Father: In god's name why?

Marina: Because I'm sick to death of people who say what they don't mean, act the way they don't feel, can't be themselves instead of some lousy image.

Father: Then why not pick on some lawyer or businessman who's got —

Marina: Are you kidding? Lawyers specialize in saying what they don't mean. Businessmen specialize in their bloody image. No thank you!

Father: Boy, you want it coming and going, don't you! So you've picked an actor.

Marina: (Quietly) He isn't an actor.

Father: But you said —

Marina: That's just what I told you.

Father: You mean you lied about him?

Marina: Yes.

Father: (*Now really thrown.*) He's not with the company?

Marina: No.

Father: Then . . . Jesus, I'm going out of my . . . Who is this character: a social worker?

Marina: (*Matter-of-fact*) I invented him.

Father: You what?

Marina: I made him up. There wasn't . . . anybody. They're all the same. Oh, they dress up differently, but they're all the same as you. So I made one up. (*She sits.*) Now you know.

Father: (*After a deep breath.*) Let me get this straight. You couldn't find a real man, so you invented an imaginary one.

Marina: Right. An imaginary real man.

Father: All that stuff, about black eyes, fights with chairs, bruises all over . . .

Marina: There weren't any.

Father: There weren't any. But you sat down and wrote this . . . this horror story . . . worrying the hell out of us . . . Why? Will you tell me why?

Marina: Dad, how well do you know me?

Father: Not very well, obviously.

Marina: How long is it since we've talked? — really talked, like real people?

Father: Well, since you've been away . . .

Marina: And before that?

Father: Well, I thought we always . . .

Marina: Like real people? Out of costume?

Father: It's not always easy . . . the right time, the right place . . .

Marina: Three years, that's how long.

Father: Is it? But I've, you know, followed your . . . I'm proud of what you've . . .

Marina: So long as it doesn't spoil your image.

Father: Oh, my image doesn't matter.

Marina: It does to you. So I thought . . . I'll make me a man, an outrageous, disreputable man, a real bastard — and that'll get through to him!

Father: You little —

Marina: (*Warmly, but still taunting him.*) You came, didn't you? With your little whip?

Father: (*Finally, gradually, laughing splendidly at himself.*) I picked the wrong prop off the table. I should have grabbed the plastic flowers! (*He puts his arm around her.*) Only one thing worries me now: why your **father**?

Marina: (*Simply*) I was lonely.

Father: (*After an eyebrow-raising oedipal thought.*) Ah well . . . that's another play.
(*After holding the pose for a second, they suddenly break apart as if they were total strangers — dropping any pretense at characterization, relaxing like actors at the end of a dress rehearsal.*)

Father: (*Looking vaguely but unconcernedly about.*) Where's the blackout?

Marina: (*Casually removing her "hair" to reveal the actress' own, tightly bound.*) I don't know, Dad.
(*BLACKOUT. Then LIGHTS UP.*)

(*In a quite conventional way, the actors now join hands and, still smiling, bow to the audience, then to each other, then to the audience again. As they part, each going to a separate wing, the LIGHTS GO DOWN.*)

D46

The Pile, The Store, Inside Out

Copyright by James Mavor Moore 1971, 1972, 1973

Caution

Rights to produce *The Pile, The Store,* or *Inside Out* in whole or in part by any group, amateur or professional, are retained by the author, and interested persons are requested to apply for permission and terms to his Literary Agents. In Canada:

Photographs courtesy of the Canadian Broadcasting Corporation, Photos, R. Rexdale.

Westbound 12:01

Brock Shoveller

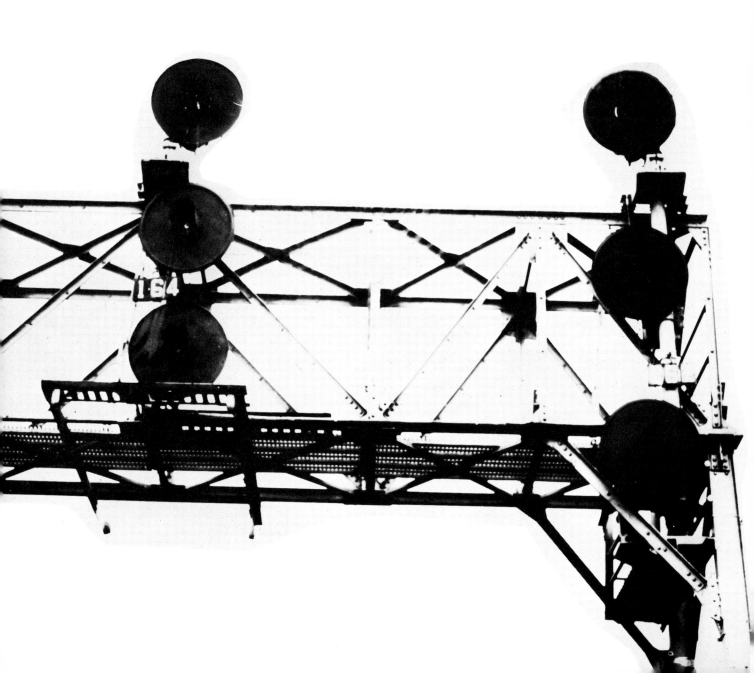

Brock Shoveller was born in Sudbury, Ontario, and received his formal education at Ryerson Polytechnic in Toronto, Sir George Williams University in Montreal, and the University of London's Institute of Education in England. He started out as an actor rather than a writer, and appeared in numerous productions on the CBC television network, both in Toronto and Montreal, as well as at Toronto's Crest Theatre. His first major writing success came at the age of twenty, when he sold his first TV drama script *Black Cats Are Good Cats,* which was shown on the CBC network and on BBC-TV in England. This was followed by another television drama *Just Passing Through* which was produced on the CBC's Maritime network; and in 1959 he wrote and played the lead in *Zoetrope,* a verse drama which was the Sir George Williams University entry in the IVDL festival.

He has also written a novel (unpublished) and another full length play (unproduced). He has had considerable directing experience in both Montreal and Toronto, and in 1971 wrote and directed the 125th anniversary stage show for the City of Hamilton.

In 1970 his first major stage work *Westbound 12:01* opened at the St. Lawrence Centre for the Arts in Toronto to considerable critical acclaim. Critics cited Mr. Shoveller as "a fine comic writer", and "a name to watch for in the future".

Currently he is working on two new plays, and makes his living as a lecturer in English Literature at Mohawk College in Hamilton, Ontario.

The photographs used to illustrate *Westbound 12:01* were made by Bill Hannant, a first-year student in the Photo Arts course at Ryerson Polytechnical Institute in Toronto.

All rights, including performing rights, to *Westbound 12:01* are reserved by the author, Mr. Brock Shoveller. For information and enquiry, write: Mr. Brock Shoveller, 455 Bay Street North, Hamilton, Ontario.

Photograph by John Shoveller

ACT I

(The Railway Station at Dogwood-Wen, a small, dusty, forgotten comma in the transcontinental sentence. A sign, weatherworn and grimy, identifies the stop for travellers; the letters are barely distinguishable. The waiting room is simple and uncomfortable. An old stove is set into a fire-safe box of sand. A sturdy wall-mounted clock displays hands fixed at 11:31.

There is an antiquated track switch downstage to one side. On the opposite side is a wall on which appear all the telegraph messages sent or received. A crossing signal with bell and flashing lights should also be incorporated in the downstage area. The "tracks" run along the lip of the apron between stage right and left. Passing trains should impose their effect through the combined use of the crossing signal, flashing window lights from the coaches, and projection.

Upstage of the waiting room and to one side is the ticket office. A cluttered desk, a dusty ticket rack, and dated railway paraphernalia, identify the office as one which experienced the height of its importance in about 1915. There is a telegraph key on a small table and a stool for the operator. On a rack to one side are two pieces of headgear (a stationmaster's and a trackman's caps) and an ancient slicker.

A doorway at centre leads to the stationmaster's quarters.

Jack Shackel, his telegrapher's cap upon his head, is seated at the telegraph tapping out a message.)

URGENT STOP

(He pauses, considers for a moment, and continues.)

TENSION RISING STOP WILL TAKE MEASURES IF NO SATISFACTION STOP — SHACKEL

(The message has cost him much energy in concentration. He relaxes but is almost immediately alerted to the distant sound of a diesel horn giving the crossing call. He rises from the stool and exchanges the cap he is wearing for the stationmaster's cap. He adjusts it on his head as he moves downstage through the waiting room. The rumble of the approaching train is louder. Jack peers down the track. The headlight of the

train flashes across him. He stands erect and tries to adopt an attitude befitting his "position". There is a perceptible slowing of the train — only enough, however, to reinforce the insolence of its implacable passing.

The crossing signal, clanging and flashing, adds a note of quickened hysteria as the lights from the coaches flash by the station. As the lights stop and the sound of the train recedes, Jack removes his cap and begins to shuffle back to the office, an older man for his experience. Stopping in the waiting room, he looks at the clock and finds within himself a residual spark of anger. He goes to the clock and beats the side of it with his fist. The clock's hands jump ahead five minutes in a sudden spasm to register 11:36. Jack is alerted to an incoming message. He rushes to the telegraph, remembers, exchanges caps, and then returns to the table. The message arrives and he takes it down.)

COMPUTER SUGGESTS TENSION BE KEPT LOCAL STOP WE CONCUR STOP MEASURES? *(Pause)* FOR SATISFACTION MEASURE THIS STOP – HQ

(Jack finishes writing, puts the pencil thoughtfully to his lips, and reads the message over. As its content registers, he slams the pencil down.)

Jack: Right, you bastards.

(He gets up and exchanges his telegrapher's cap for his trackman's cap and then moves resolutely through the waiting room, fumbling with his keys as he goes.

At the same time, Niobe enters from the living quarters. She is in her mid-fifties; although not unattractive, she loses what natural advantage she might have had by reaching in her dress, manner, and make-up, for thirty. An extravagant blonde wig lends force to the impression she creates of a superannuated whore. A compulsive eater, she carries a box of Cracker-Jacks with her and munches constantly — with particular fervour whenever Jack is disadvantaged or when her own tension rises. Jack proceeds to unfasten the lock on the track switch.)

Niobe: Jack!

(Jack looks up, scowls, and goes back to his work; he tries to throw the switch but fails.

Niobe looks about and then crosses through the waiting room to the platform.)

Is that you? What are you doing out there in the dark? *(Pause)* I've been looking everywhere for you. *(Pause)* People get lonely by themselves, you know. *(Pause)* Jack?

(Having failed to move the switch, he jams the lock violently back into place.)

Jack: What?

Niobe: I was saying, it's nice to have company.

Jack: *(Walking past her to the waiting room.)* Nice?! People getting in your way when you're trying to get something done!

Niobe: I fixed myself up for you. See? For when you come to bed.

Jack: Niobe, you don't seem to realize I've got things that need doing. I can't always be jumping into bed. *(Considers)* I'll move that bloody switch with a crowbar!

(He goes into the office and begins rummaging about in the junk.)

Niobe: I was thinking. Don't you think it would have been really different if there'd been a child around?

Jack: *(Considers — then as a profound observation.)* Kids should have a room of their own.

Niobe: It might have changed our whole lives.

(Jack looks at her, nods, and goes back to his search.

He finds the crowbar and walks past her, through the waiting room, back to the switch. She follows. He tries to move the switch but fails again.)

(Niobe is intent on following her line of thought.)

Niobe: Maybe now that we're more mature, we could do a better job. Not make the same mistakes everybody does. We could talk things out. Don't you think?

(He casts the bar aside.)

Jack: You know, I'll bet those sons of bitches have welded the points.

Niobe: Don't you think grown-up people should be able to discuss things?

Jack: Right. A sensible person has to discuss things.

(She is about to put her arms about his neck. There is an incoming message alert. Jack moves to the telegraph table, speaking over his shoulder as he goes.)

But try telling that to them and their — — . . . computer.

(He exchanges caps and prepares to take the message.)

SUSPECT MONKEY BUSINESS ON MAIN LINE STOP KEEP NOSE CLEAN OR WILL AMPUTATE STOP – OMNIA PATRI

(He reads the message over, slowly removes his cap and puts it on the table, and then looks up at Niobe.)

Niobe: What was it?

(Jack walks to the waiting room with cultivated melodramatic calm. He looks up and down the platform and then turns back to Niobe.)

Jack: I'm being watched.

Niobe: Watched? (She looks about.) There's nobody here.

(He smiles and walks slowly upstage.)

Jack: I think I'm beginning to see through their little plan.

Niobe: Whose plan?

Jack: Oh, sure. They make it out to look like an economy measure. "Just can't afford to stop them any more, Mr. Shackel." Simple enough.

Almost reasonable. That's what they want me to think. But. They keep the Stationmaster on. (He taps his forehead.) Why?

Niobe: Because —

Jack: — because their plans go deeper than what seems. Then? These messages, made to look like harmless jokes — digging into me, prodding, trying to break me down. Jabbing away until every nerve in my body is jumping. (He smiles) And now the spying to crack me completely.

Niobe: There's nobody here to spy. It's your nerves. You've got bad nerves. (Pause) Jack? (Pause) Oh, no! That's ridiculous. Me? How? Why would I . . . (Angrily) It's you and your stupid telegrams — always trying to upset them.

(He points a threatening finger at her.)

Niobe: Don't wave your stupid finger at me!

(She eats during his speech. In one very important sense, she does not hear him.)

Jack: I'm a railwayman! You don't seem to understand that. Thirty-nine years with you and you don't even know what I am. There hasn't been a train stop at my station for two years! I have to hit my head against the wall every morning of my life to remind myself that I'm even here and you say I'm trying to upset them.

Niobe: Personally, I don't think you'd worry half so much if you had a son who'd carry on.

Jack: I'll carry on!

Niobe: I've heard say it's in the blood. He would have been a railwayman — after his father.

Jack: A greasy little computer pilot, I suppose — all tapes and holes and circuits and no guts.

Niobe: I'll tell you one thing I know. A **real** father wouldn't speak that way about his son.

Jack: The little pervert. I'd've strangled him with the wet cord.

Niobe: It's disgusting the way you talk. (Turning away from Jack.) You're all the same.

Jack: What do you mean by that?

Niobe: I think I'll go and watch the television.

(He grasps her roughly by the arm.)

Jack: Oh no, you don't. That's a serious accusation. I want an explanation.

Niobe: Explanation! Let go! How can I explain when you're breaking my arm? (He releases her.) Explain, explain! What do you ever explain to me?

Jack: You're lumping me together with all the rest. I forbid you to look at me that way.

Niobe: How do you look at me? You don't even tell me. If that isn't worse, I'd like to know what.

Jack: You're not talking sense.

Niobe: No, eh? It's different when the foot's on the other shoe, isn't it? That quietens you down.

Jack: The shoe's on the other foot, you silly cow!

Niobe: There! I can't say two words without you turning them outside in.

(She sits on one of the benches. Jack walks upstage. He looks back at her as though to speak, changes his mind, and continues to his desk.)

Niobe: It's impossible to discuss anything with you.

(Jack makes a desultory search through some papers. Suddenly he slams his hand down on the desk. Niobe jumps to her feet.)

Niobe: I'm sorry! I didn't mean that!

Jack: That's it! One of those hidden camera things. Sitting in their office watching everything I do. Laughing at me.

(He walks excitedly back to the waiting room and looks about for the camera during the following speeches.)

That means they're watching right now. It's an invasion of a man's privacy! There's a bill of rights or something that says — something — about that.

Niobe: You **do** work for them. It seems to me they've got a right to know what you're doing. I mean — how do you think they'd feel if they didn't know what you were doing?

Jack: What about how I feel?

(Niobe looks at him blankly.)

Jack: They're watching you, too, you know.

(She puts her hand to her hair.)

Every move, every word — even your thoughts. Everything.

Niobe: (Pleased, massaging her lower belly.) Just to think about it gives me a funny feeling right here.

Jack: It makes me sick, too. Now maybe you can see why I'm upset. How am I supposed to deal with something like that?

(Pause while she thinks intensely.)

Niobe: I think you should ignore it. You'll feel better if you just push it out of your mind and come to bed. Just say over and over to yourself, "It's not there". (Hypnotically) It's not there, it's not there, it's not there. Like that.

(Pause. He looks at her blankly.)

Jack: I'm going to find that camera and — destroy it.

Niobe: I thought you were going to forget about it and come to bed.

Jack: Bed! Is that all you think about? At your age! You're an obscene old woman.

Niobe: I am not old!

Jack: Well, I am, I've got troubles.

Niobe: Oh, no! You're not too old to throw a switch. How come, then, you're too old to throw it int —

Jack: Stop it! You just stop that filthy talk.

(Pause. Niobe turns away.)

Niobe: What about Tolstoy? What's your smart answer for that?

(He looks at her quizzically.)

I read that Tolstoy inconvenienced his wife every single night of their married life. 'Til he was eighty-two.

Jack: He never!

Niobe: I read it.

Jack: Well . . . I figure there never was a frog who wasn't some kind of pervert.

Niobe: That's interesting because, she thought he was — you know — one of "them". She accused him of it.

Jack: (Pause) Was he? One of them?

Niobe: There must have been something to it. She wouldn't have just made it up.

Jack: It's her word against his. Maybe she was one of those women who're never satisfied?

Niobe: That's ridiculous! She was more than satisfied, but — (Pause) Anyway, I already told you what she said he was.

(Pause)

Jack: It sounds pretty fishy to me.

Niobe: Well, it's not. It's normal.

(Pause. They exchange antagonistic looks.)

Jack: I've got things to do.

Niobe: And she thought he was funny.

Jack: I don't like your suggestion.

Niobe: Since you never come to bed —

Jack: You stop! Right now!

Niobe: I read things, you know. I know which end of a hammer does the knocking.

Jack: You old bitch!

Niobe: (Turning away) I know a eunuch when I see one.

Jack: I'll kill you!

(Jack springs at her back and wrenches her blonde wig from her head. Niobe is bald. Too late, her hands dart to retrieve the wig. She tries to hide her head with her hands.)

Niobe: No! That's mine!

Jack: Ha!

Niobe: Jack! Don't! Give it back — please.

Jack: You should think twice, then, shouldn't you?

Niobe: Please give it back.

(He drops the wig to the floor. She scrambles for it but it is pinned beneath his foot. She looks up at him in despair.)

You're killing me!

(He lets her suffer a moment longer and then removes his foot. Still on her knees, she tries desperately to put the wig back in place. In her pain and without the use of a mirror, she places the wig askew. She stumbles toward the door to the living quarters.)

Jack: I hope you learned something.

(Still whimpering, Niobe exits. Jack thinks for a second and then shouts after her.)

And don't think I'm going to bloody well forget what you said!

(A distant diesel horn sounds the crossing signal. Jack walks listlessly to the platform. The cross-

ing bell and lights begin and the rumbling wheels get louder. The headlight flashes across him. As the train is still passing, the stage is taken to black. The sound is faded out over the darkened stage.

After a few seconds, the lights are brought up to disclose the station in morning sunlight. The 1st Deliveryman's voice is heard off left.)

1st Deliveryman: Uh. Hold it there. Let's just see if this thing . . .

(The double freight doors open. The 1st Deliveryman enters. He is concerned that the delivery item should fit through the opening and, to this end, he officiously "sights" the doorway. He scratches his chin, paces the door's width, looks again, and shrugs.)

1st Deliveryman: Tricky.

(Pause. He stands waiting.)

Well, come on. What are you waiting for? The second coming! ?

(He stands aside. The 2nd Deliveryman enters with a plain lightweight pine coffin on his shoulder. It fits through the doorway with about two feet to spare on either side. He moves to the centre of the room.)

You young fellas don't seem to have the sense you were — . Stop, for Christ's sake!

(The 2nd Deliveryman stops.)

Do I have to tell you everything? *(Pause)* Well, put it down.

2nd Deliveryman: Give me a hand, will you.

1st Deliveryman: *(Helping)* I wish somebody'd tell me what it is with you young fellas — *(Gratuitously)* Don't drop it!

(They place the coffin on one of the waiting room benches. There are nails around three edges of the coffin lid — ready to be hammered home.)

There. A young fella starting out in my day had

— . something needed doing, in those days a young fella just — . No belly-achin', no whimperin', no askin' for help, he — just . . .

(The 1st Deliveryman stops and watches the 2nd Deliveryman lift the lid of the coffin, reach in and take out his lunch pail. He sits at one end of the coffin, sets the pail beside himself, and removes the thermos.)

2nd Deliveryman: In these troubled times, a young man needs guidance. *(He pours coffee.)* Besides, it's your job to take the initiative. I'm only a second class craftsman. You're the first. You've also got the seniority. You expect me to take your orders — respect your authority? *(Drinks)* So, you don't want my initiative interfering. Where would we be if I started telling you a better way? Every time you gave me an order, I'd challenge your authority. I think everyone would agree that that's no way to go on.

(Pause)

1st Deliveryman: All right. What about that, then?

2nd Deliveryman: What?

1st Deliveryman: The lunch pail in the coffin!

2nd Deliveryman: I didn't have any hands to carry it.

1st Deliveryman:: *(Scornfully)* Hands! *(Quoting)* "As a deliveryman, your responsibility to your clients and for the goods they place in your trust is a sacred one — one not to be violated under any circumstances — personal, public, expedient, or otherwise." Page three of your manual. "Hands" my ass!

(Pause. He waits for a response which does not come.)

That means you don't put your lunch pail in the coffin!

(Pause)

2nd Deliveryman: *(Chewing)* Yeah. I'll give that some thought.

E10

1st Deliveryman: Ha. Right.

(The 1st Deliveryman sits on one of the other benches and stares blankly downstage. The 2nd Deliveryman drains off his coffee replaces the thermos in his lunch pail, pushes up the lid of the coffin, thinks twice, lowers the lid, and places the pail on the bench. He stands.)

2nd Deliveryman: Are we going to wait?

1st Deliveryman: Somebody's got to sign the receipt.

(Pause)

2nd Deliveryman: Maybe we should look for someone.

1st Deliveryman: You've got no sense of professional dignity, have you? Do you want them to take you for a two-bit messenger boy?

(Pause)

2nd Deliveryman: There's no one here.

(Pause)

Has it occurred to you that maybe no one will come?

1st Deliveryman: Of course, somebody will come, stupid. Do you think they'd have sent us if it couldn't be delivered? (Pause) A little confidence in your superiors wouldn't be out of place, you know, if you've got any thoughts of getting ahead.

2nd Deliveryman: Still — you must admit, there doesn't seem to be much sign of life.

1st Deliveryman: (Intense) Listen. Somebody needs this thing. Right? Else it wouldn't have been sent. And the Company's not going to be fool enough to send something to nobody, are they? So you and me are going to wait right here until our part of the job is done. I know my responsibility.

(A long pause. The 1st Deliveryman sits patiently and motionless. The 2nd Deliveryman gets to his feet and stretches. He walks to the door to the platform and looks out.)

2nd Deliveryman: Did you ever think you wanted to be something else when you were young? You know — like a doctor, or — a forest ranger! — or, even, say — a poet?

1st Deliveryman: Dreamers! Make me sick. A man wants to accept his lot, is what I say — be thankful for what he's got. It's dog-eat-dog in this world, you know. I've been a deliveryman all my life. It's real work — useful. (Shows the palm of his hand.) Poet! My ass. What's that got to do with getting anywhere? A man wants to get things done.

(The 2nd Deliveryman nods thoughtfully. Pause. He then saunters into the office. He stops at the telegraph table and tries to recall his boy-scout Morse. Remembering, he smiles and taps out a message.)

GOD IS DEAF THUS SPAKE THE DELIVERY-MAN

(He moves on to the ticket rack. The 2nd Deliveryman examines the tickets and removes one from the rack.)

2nd Deliveryman: How would you like a free ride to the coast?

1st Deliveryman: Which one?

2nd Deliveryman: West.

1st Deliveryman: You go west if you're so keen. I'll just stay where I am, thanks.

2nd Deliveryman: It's strange how so few people want to go anywhere these days. Everyone seems to want to stay where they are. (Pause) If you travel long enough, you know, you end up in the same place whichever direction you take. Doesn't that strike you as strange?

1st Deliveryman: Young people! That's what's strange.

(The 2nd Deliveryman shrugs, looks at the ticket, and pockets it. The upstage door from outside opens and Jack, slipping his suspenders over his shoulders, enters. He neither gives nor

E11

seems to expect recognition. The 2nd Delivery-man glances at Jack with only slight interest and goes back to his foraging. Jack finishes dressing — does his collar up, slips into his jacket, and puts his stationmaster's cap on his head. He then stands looking at the 2nd Deliveryman. Jack coughs and the deliveryman turns.)

Jack: I'm the stationmaster.

2nd Deliveryman: Oh, yes. *(Pause)* There was another fellow in here a few minutes ago — wandering about half dressed. Had all the markings of a bugger to my eyes. Since you say you're the stationmaster, you'd probably want to know something like that.

Jack: A bugger, eh?

2nd Deliveryman: Commonly known as a sodomite. From the Medieval Latin "Bulgarus", an eleventh century heretic from Bulgaria, supposedly capable of any crime.

(Pause)

You're sure you're the stationmaster?

Jack: What do you mean, am I sure?

2nd Deliveryman: No offence. People aren't always sure, you know. Clothes don't necessarily make the man, do they?

Jack: I don't know. There's something to be said for clothes. You probably wouldn't even have recognized me if I hadn't been wearing my cap. You've got to admit that.

2nd Deliveryman: Let's see you without it.

(Jack draws away.)

Come on. You can prove your point. Come on.

(Reluctantly, Jack lifts his cap with both hands above his head — a cautious six inches. The 2nd Deliveryman examines him closely.)

2nd Deliveryman: Mmmm. You still look a bit familiar, you know. No! Just a moment longer. *(Pause)* Now — maybe you're right. You certainly don't look like the stationmaster without it.

(At this, Jack slams the cap back on his head.)

Jack: Well, I am!

2nd Deliveryman: Of course, but it's a delicate situation, nonetheless. I mean, what if it should ever go astray? Just suppose it shouldn't be there some time when you really need it? I wouldn't recognize you without it. I don't suppose anyone would. People might take you for anything.

Jack: Are you trying to threaten me?

2nd Deliveryman: Are you suggesting that I would steal your miserable cap? That's the real issue from where I stand. Are you calling me a thief? Before you go any further, though, I'd just like to point out that defamation of character is a very serious crime. I hope you've considered that.

Jack: I didn't call you a thief. I don't even know who you are. How could I — you know — defile your character when I don't even know your character. Be reasonable.

2nd Deliveryman: I am perfectly capable of being reasonable.

Jack: I'm sure you are.

2nd Deliveryman: *(Ominously)* If approached reasonably.

(An awkward silence.)

Jack: Would you think it was unreasonable if I asked you what you're doing here?

2nd Deliveryman: That sounds pretty aggressive to my ears. It's like saying to a person, "Who the hell do you think you are?"

Jack: Well, how am I supposed to know if I don't ask?

2nd Deliveryman: You seemed much more concerned that I should know who **you** were. If you wanted to know, why didn't you just say, "Who are you?" like any sensible person would?

Jack: I — . You seem pretty sensitive.

2nd Deliveryman: Maybe I am. *(Threatening)* But I'm not stupid.

Jack: Oh, no! I wouldn't have said that.

2nd Deliveryman: And I'm certainly not averse to identifying myself. *(Pause)* I'm a deliveryman second class.

Jack: Ah! Second class . . .

2nd Deliveryman: *(Cutting Jack off.)* Mind you, that is an hierarchical, and not, in case you are tempted to jump to conclusions, a qualitative distinction. Owing to certain circumstantial realities, not least of which are seniority and bureaucratic rigidity, my position is inferior to the one held by my colleague, the first class deliveryman with whom I work. Inferiority in this instance, and as I have already pointed out, is to be thought of exclusively in positional terms. In point of fact, superiority, in any sense but mechanical, as it applies to the two of us, would certainly redound on me. I have studied my profession in depth and with devotion and have assiduously kept abreast of developments in my field. *(Pause)* Unlike some people, I do not need badges to substantiate my claim.

Jack: You sure seem to know who you are.

2nd Deliveryman: If you don't think that you can remember all that I have told you, I could write it down so that you could memorize it. Then, if anyone ever doubted your word you could recite it and prove you knew me.

Jack: I guess you could say we're getting to know each other, eh?

2nd Deliveryman: Perhaps, but I have little confidence that our — relationship — could endure if I were unable to recognize you. Why, without your cap, you even resemble the Bulgarus I told you about.

(The 2nd Deliveryman laughs. Jack, somewhat intimidated, forces himself to laugh as well. The strained moment is broken by an incoming message alert. Jack rushes for his telegrapher's cap and, about to exchange it for the one he is wearing, stops and looks at the Deliveryman. The Deliveryman presents a completely blank expression in return. Suspended in doubt, Jack surrenders to his insecurity and sets aside the telegrapher's cap. He sits unhappily at the desk.)

COMPUTER SUGGESTS PROPOSITION EQUIVOCAL STOP ALSO ECONOMICALLY IRRELEVANT STOP BLASPHEMOUS LITTLE BUGGER AREN'T YOU STOP — PRIMUM MOBILE

(The Deliveryman smirks at the "bugger" reference. Jack is confused and feels very much spied upon.)

Jack: Who did you say you worked for?

2nd Deliveryman: Me?

(Jack nods. The 2nd Deliveryman goes out to his partner in the waiting room.)

Who did you say we worked for?

1st Deliveryman: Why?

2nd Deliveryman: *(To Jack)* Why do you want to know?

Jack: Who's he?

2nd Deliveryman: He wants to know who you are.

1st Deliveryman: He asks a hell of a lot of questions for someone I don't even know. Who's he think he is, anyway?

2nd Deliveryman: He thinks he's the stationmaster.

Jack: I am the stationmaster.

2nd Deliveryman: He says he is the stationmaster.

1st Deliveryman: Oh. *(Pause)* So?

2nd Deliveryman: That's exactly what I felt. *(To Jack)* We're not disputing your claim.

(Jack moves forward slowly, defensively.)

Jack: Maybe not. But I don't hear you admitting it, either. I **run** this place!

(The two Deliverymen look about, at first prepared to be impressed; upon closer examination of the place they find themselves unmoved.)

1st Deliveryman: I've seen better.

2nd Deliveryman: You'd at least expect the clock to be working in a passenger depot, wouldn't you?

Jack: It works! The son-of-a-bitch works alright!

(Jack rushes up to the clock and beats his fist against the side of it. The hands leap on four minutes; the clock now registers 11:40. Jack turns to face them, his back to the clock.)

There! You satisfied? *(Pause)* Is there anything else you want to criticize while you're at it? Go ahead. I can handle you.

2nd Deliveryman: Time flies directly in proportion to the degree you beat it. Nietzsche, I think.

Jack: What's the matter with him?

1st Deliveryman: He's a thinker.

Jack: He says some crazy things, that's for sure.

1st Deliveryman: He's not always easy to understand.

Jack: He should keep his mouth shut, then, shouldn't he? Shooting his know-it-all face off! Says he's a deliveryman. Ha!

1st Deliveryman: Second class.

Jack: I'll bet.

1st Deliveryman: Of course, I'm first class.

Jack: Oh, sure. Anybody could tell you were first class. You've got the —

1st Deliveryman: Savoy fair. That's what I was

trying to tell him before.

Jack: Well, it's clear to me. A man can sense that sort of thing.

1st Deliveryman: The way I sensed you were the stationmaster when I met you.

Jack: You recognized me, eh?

1st Deliveryman: Right away. Stands out like a three-dollar bill.

Jack: I like a man with eyes in his head.

1st Deliveryman: Someone who can tell a sore thumb when he sees one, eh?

Jack: Right. Right.

(They stand smiling at one another. The expression slowly fades from their smiles. Pause.)

2nd Deliveryman: Maybe he can sign the receipt.

Jack: Receipt?

1st Deliveryman: Here. At the bottom. Acknowledged receipt of article (articles) in good order. I'll cross out "articles" — the way we do.

(The 1st Deliveryman hands the book and a pencil to Jack. Jack reads the form.)

Jack: Coffin?

2nd Deliveryman: Pine. Unsealed. The utility model for unpretentious and expeditious departures.

1st Deliveryman: In good order and on time.

2nd Deliveryman: I've got a warranty for it here somewhere.

1st Deliveryman: At the bottom.

2nd Deliveryman: Here. *(Reads)* "Guaranteed for first six months of use or money cheerfully refunded with pro-rata discount for time used." That's pretty fair.

(He hands the warranty to Jack.)

1st Deliveryman: Just sign and we'll be on our way.

Jack: I'm not going to sign for something that's not for me.

1st Deliveryman: Of course it's for you. Dogwood-Wen station. It's the same thing.

Jack: You just better take it away again. I won't have that thing lying around here.

(Niobe enters. She is immediately "interested" in the strangers.)

2nd Deliveryman: There's something very peculiar going on here. Correct me if I'm wrong but you did say you were the stationmaster, didn't you?

Niobe: Good morning.

(The 2nd Deliveryman looks and bows elegantly to Niobe.)

Jack: That doesn't make any difference. *(To the 1st Deliveryman.)* I mean, it does, but it doesn't mean I have to sign for things I don't want.

1st Deliveryman: Who do you think is going to sign for it if you don't?

Jack: That's none of my business.

(The 2nd Deliveryman, excusing himself to Niobe, walks slowly towards Jack. Pause.)

2nd Deliveryman: None of your business? I'm beginning to have some serious doubts about you, mister. Interfering with the natural processes of commerce? I was always led to believe that a stationmaster was supposed to epitomize responsibility and right behaviour. Do you want me to believe that's you? *(He pokes Jack's shoulder.)* Where is the stationmaster, you miserable little imposter?

Jack: *(Pokes back.)* — push me, you — . The other fella! Him! He said you were nuts. It's you is the imposter. *(Pause. Jack senses his isolation.)* Let's see **your** credentials, eh?

2nd Deliveryman: I've already explained that to you. No one is debating who I am. *(Pause)* How would it be if we just took a look for a second — at your cap?

(Jack dodges the Deliveryman's attempt to remove the cap. The Deliveryman laughs.)

Niobe: Show him your other caps, Jack. He's got others, you know. Very proud of —

Jack: Shut up, you old bitch!

2nd Deliveryman: Other caps?

Niobe: Oh, yes!

2nd Deliveryman: Nefarious impersonation of the first degree is what the courts would call it, I should expect.

1st Deliveryman: Who the hell are you, anyway?

2nd Deliveryman: Give me that.

(He snatches the receipt book and pencil out of Jack's hands and turns to Niobe.)

M'am. I'm afraid I've not had the pleasure of an introduction.

Niobe: Niobe Shackel. But my maiden name is Numin. Niobe Numin — which I much prefer — spelled N-U-M-I-N. Numin. *(Without pride)* I'm the stationmaster's wife.

Jack: Right! **And** knows her place!

1st Deliveryman: Shut up, you.

2nd Deliveryman: Well, this is just fine. You can sign the delivery receipt.

(He hands the book and pencil to Niobe.)

Jack: On, no she doesn't! That's my job!

1st Deliveryman: You said you wouldn't do it.

2nd Deliveryman: Besides, you're not the stationmaster.

Jack: She's got no authority.

2nd Deliveryman: She's the stationmaster's wife. If that isn't authority, I'd like to know what is. All right, M'am. At the bottom.

Jack: I'll wring your scraggy neck if you sign that, Niobe. By God, I will.

(Jack starts for her but the 1st Deliveryman stops him by grabbing him from behind.)

1st Deliveryman: Here! What kind of talk is that?

2nd Deliveryman: Go ahead, M'am.

(Jack struggles with the 1st Deliveryman. The 2nd Deliveryman walks quickly over to them and casually punches Jack in the stomach. Jack doubles up and falls to the floor at the feet of the 1st Deliveryman. Niobe looks on with interest. The 2nd Deliveryman returns to her side.)

At the bottom will do, M'am.

Niobe: (Signing) It sure does make a person feel as though they matter to be able to sign papers and things. (Looks with pride at her signature.) There. Niobe Numin.

(She hands the pad back. The Deliveryman rips out the carbon and gives it to Niobe.)

Jack: That's an illegal document!

(The 2nd Deliveryman walks casually over to where Jack sits on the floor.)

2nd Deliveryman: You're a strange old boy, aren't you? Sort of eccentric. Mind you, I have a great deal of respect for a man who asserts his individuality and stands up for his rights. That's why I took to you right at the beginning. I like to see a bit of rugged individualism. I'll have to admit you've got some strange ways, but who am I to stand in judgement? (The prosecuting attorney.) Nonetheless, I think we might profit by taking a closer look at just what has transpired here this morning. (Pause) First of all, you wander in — uninvited — a complete stranger; you pretend to be what you're not; you try the patience of this dear lady who obviously belongs here; you cast insults about; you give orders. Still you are regarded with tolerance and respect for your individual rights. But is that enough for you? No. You insist that people sacrifice their own dignity and self-respect and hit you. Now, personally, I find that an intolerable assault on the rights of others.

(He kicks Jack.)

Jack: Ow!

2nd Deliveryman: Surely you're man enough to allow that you owed me that satisfaction for what you have cost me in self-respect today. What would you say, Number One?

1st Deliveryman: Right.

2nd Deliveryman: Miss Numin?

Niobe: It sounds fair.

2nd Deliveryman: There. Three separate opinions. It's a fair enough world if you'll just meet it on its own terms. No one wants to cause anybody unnecessary trouble. What do you say? Bygones be bygones?

(He holds a hand of truce down to Jack who as good as snarls in response. The 2nd Deliveryman kicks Jack again.)

Jack: Ow!

2nd Deliveryman: You'll come to nothing, my friend. You ask for trouble.

(He turns and walks away from Jack.)

1st Deliveryman: I don't know. You have got a way of making a point. Maybe you're not as dumb as I thought.

Niobe: Dumb! Him? He's lovely.

(Jack has laboriously risen.)

1st Deliveryman: I think it's about time we let you handle a delivery by yourself.

Niobe: Oh, he'd love that! Wouldn't you?

2nd Deliveryman: Yes. I think I am ready for

the responsibility.

Niobe: Ready! Look at him! And modest! He could kick down a steel door.

2nd Deliveryman: You're very kind, Miss Numin.

(The following exchange is played as a lewd joke which Jack does not get.)

Niobe: You come back here and see me when you finish work. The world should lie down for a young fella like you. You must come back, now. Promise.

2nd Deliveryman: I wouldn't want to inconvenience you, Miss.

Niobe: You just let me be the judge of that.

1st Deliveryman: He'd like to come. Wouldn't you?

2nd Deliveryman: Yes, I would.

1st Deliveryman: Well. We'd better be off.

Niobe: *(To the 2nd Deliveryman.)* Dinner about seven? *(To the 1st Deliveryman.)* Come again and meet my husband.

1st Deliveryman: Right.

(The two Deliverymen exit.)

Jack: Over my — . He won't meet me again if I'm looking.

Niobe: Oh, you weren't yourself. I don't know what got into you — fighting like that. You were like a stranger.

Jack: I held my own. You've got to box clever with their kind. Never let 'em see your hand, that's the first rule. *(Pause)* Thinker! Acting as if he didn't know who I was. Some thinker! I've met his sort before. Well, he better just stay clear of me because I'm riled and I'm making no promises I'll control myself next time. You can push me just so far and then —

Niobe: Yes? What happens then?

Jack: I — . I stand up and — say —

Niobe: — and say?

Jack: A — . No further! That's what I say.

Niobe: That's like philosophy, isn't it? I mean, what a person stands for?

Jack: A man's got to stand for something. After all, he's not an animal.

(Niobe looks at him blankly.)

Jack: Well, he's not.

(Pause. Niobe looks at the paper in her hand.)

Niobe: What should I do with this?

Jack: That's your problem. You signed for it.

Niobe: It? What?

Jack: That!

Niobe: I didn't. I signed for the Deliveryman. I don't want that — *(Pause)* What is it?

Jack: You know damned well what it is.

(Niobe looks at it sidewise.)

Niobe: It's wood.

Jack: It's yours.

Niobe: No it's not. It doesn't look the least bit like anything I'd buy.

Jack: That's your signature.

(She refuses to look.)

Jack: So it's up to you to work out what you're going to do with it.

(He turns smugly away from her. She glances at the receipt, crumples it and eats it. She walks towards the door to the quarters.)

Jack: Where do you think you're going?

Niobe: Upstairs to watch the television and think about it.

Jack: You're not going to think about it. You're going to forget and pretend it's not here.

Niobe: No, I'm not, Jack. Honest. Hope to die.

Jack: *(Interested)* What's that?

Niobe: It won't be in anyone's way.

Jack: It'll be in the way of the passengers. Make me nervous.

Niobe: There aren't any passengers.

Jack: Don't say that to me! There *will* be, and I want that thing **out**! Now!

(Pause)

Niobe: All right.

(She moves to the stairs.)

I'll just go get my hammer.

Jack: Right!

(She exits.)

During the following, a Young Man and a Girl with bedrolls enter along the track. They make their way to the platform where they put down their packs. Jack has been alerted to an incoming message and has gone to the desk.

BEWARE THE INTRUDER STOP *(Pause Jack looks about.)* ACCEPT NO DELIVERIES UNLESS INSTRUCTED STOP SUGGEST YOU PUT YOUR AFFAIRS IN ORDER STOP — PAPA

Girl: Is this it?

(The Young Man nods. The Girl sits cross-legged beside the packs. The Young Man walks to the edge of the platform, flings his arms wide and breathes deeply.)

Young Man: Smell that air! *(Sniffs)* That's pine needles, I think. Spruce, maybe?

Girl: This is your little haven, is it?

Young Man: I think I can rediscover myself here. It feels like a place where I can 'be'.

Girl: Shit.

Young Man: Look. You promised.

(She sighs reluctant assent.)

You'll like them. They'll be real people.

Girl: *(Sardonically)* So were the others. All "real people".

Young Man: O.K. I admit, I don't remember all that clearly. But the atmosphere is right. Things come back. *(Pause)* Yes. I definitely would say I think I've been here before.

(During this, as the telegraph message concludes, Jack gets up with his scribbled note, walks to the waiting room and looks balefully at the coffin. He crumples the note in his hand and drops it to the floor. Slowly his head goes back and he emits a slow rising cry of anger and frustration.)

Jack: Oh, oh, oh, ohhhhhhhh!

Girl: What's that?

Niobe: *(Off)* I'm looking, Jack! Honest! I can't imagine what I've done with that hammer.

(The young man goes to the door of the waiting room. Jack stands silently with his back to the door, his head bowed.)

Young Man: It's an old guy. He's racked with grief. The dear one is in a coffin. *(Pause)* It's really quite touching. Look.

(The Girl twists around, looks, and then goes back to her position.)

Girl: Who do you figure is in the coffin?

Young Man: I don't know. Someone near and dear to him, I expect.

(Jack raises his head, sights the clock, has a

E20

tremor of revulsion, walks to the clock and thumps it solidly with his fist. The hands leap on to 11:44.)

Young Man: *(Carried away.)* Wait. He's moving — to the clock. His pent-up store of emotion — his anger in the face of blind fate — etched in his features. He — strikes the clock! Splendid! A magnificent gesture — defying to the end the untimely wrenching away of his dear one. Sheer poetry.

Girl: It's trite.

Young Man: Triteness is a literary luxury. Untrammelled spontaneous natural passion, man's agony in the face of the ultimate verities, however oft' it may be acted, is never trite.

(Jack sees the Young Man. His eyes narrow in suspicion.)

Jack: Hey! What's going on here?

Young Man: We were just passing by and —

Girl: *(Entering)* We were not 'just' passing by. We walked miles to get here. This is our destination.

Jack: Ah! Tourists?

Girl: You could say that. It's certainly not my idea of a homecoming.

(The Young Man scowls at her and then, exposed, turns apologetically to Jack.)

Young Man: It's been a — long time — eh? *(Testing)* — Dad?

(He reaches out. Jack recoils in alarm.)

Jack: What! ?

Young Man: Well, you see —

Girl: He told me he grew up here.

Jack: Impossible! I'd have noticed. Been here myself for — **ages!** Next station up the line. They had a boy.

Young Man: We've been there.

Jack: Well, must be some place else you're thinking of.

Young Man: But, it's got to be you.

Girl: He's not obliged to know you.

Young Man: Look closely. Don't you recognize anything about me?

(Jack peers at him without enthusiasm.)

Jack: Well, — You've got your — . No! Never seen you before.

Young Man: What? You said 'you've got your —'. Whose what have I got?

(Pause)

Jack: I was going to say you've got your mother's eyes, but she never had a son.

Young Man: My mother definitely had a son. Ask her? She'll tell — . *(He suddenly remembers the coffin.)* Shit! That's it, then, isn't it? You won't recognize me. And she's bloody dead. Just my rotten luck!

Jack: Ah, well if your mother's dead, it couldn't be her, could it?

Young Man: What do you mean if she's dead! ? Christ, you're an insensitive bastard! I'm beginning to remember you now.

Jack: I don't have to stand here listening to insults.

(The Young Man pushes Jack aside and walks to the coffin where he stands reverently.)

Jack: Get away from that. It's goods in transit. You've got no business —

(The Young Man lifts the lid.)

Hey!

(The Young Man looks in and then recoils in horror. The lid drops.)

Young Man: What have you done with her?

Jack: Who?

(The Young Man grasps Jack by the lapels.)

Young Man: My mother! What have you done with her, you son-of-a-bitch?

Jack: *(To the Girl)* I never touched his mother!

Girl: It's the shock. *(To the Young Man)* Come on. Let him go! *(To Jack)* It's losing a parent — he never learned how to handle this sort of thing. Let go!

(The Young Man releases Jack and puts his hands to his face.)

Jack: I guess it's specially hard to lose a mother. But I can't help him much there, can I?

Girl: He can't go on like this much longer, you know. He says he's seen into the abyss.

Jack: Yeah? What did he see?

Girl: Nothing. Just *(Pause)* — nothing.

Jack: Nothing! He's a bit of a baby, eh, if he's scared by nothing.

Girl: He's twenty-six.

Jack: Ah. *(Pause)* Well, I guess he wants to grow up a bit, doesn't he? *(Pause)* What's this abscess thing?

Girl: *(With tried patience.)* Abyss! He has looked into the face of death.

(Jack's eyes narrow in fear. He steps back as from a leper.)

Jack: Get out of here! Both of you! Right now! *(Shouting)* Niobe! Niobe!

(Niobe stickes her head out.)

Niobe: I'm looking, Jack.

Jack: Get in here! Out! Both of you!

Niobe: (Entering) I've looked everywhere — .

Jack: Hammer or no hammer, I want that thing —

Niobe: It can't be!

Young Man: Mo —

Niobe: Mo — th —

Young Man: Mo — th — er! Mother!

Jack: What's going on here?

Niobe: Is it really my baby?

Jack: (Desperately) Who? Him! He's twenty-six!

(The Young Man walks tentatively forward.)

Young Man: Do you recognize me?

(Jack tries to pull at the Young Man's arm but his effort is brushed aside.)

Jack: How could she? Don't listen to him. He claimed his mother was dead.

Niobe: I wouldn't be much of a mother if I didn't recognize my own son, would I? You've got your father's limp, for one thing.

Jack: That's a lie!

Niobe: It's your limp, Jack, no mistaking.

Jack: No! Your eyes!

Niobe: Limp.

Jack: Eyes! Damn it! Eyes!

(There is a silence. Niobe smiles complacently.)

Girl: I suppose that's it. They certainly 'act' like parents.

Jack: (To Niobe) Now see what you've done?

(Niobe holds out her arms. The Young Man goes to her and they embrace.)

Young Man: Mom. You haven't changed a bit. You're just the way I remember you.

Niobe: Look at him, Jack. Hasn't he grown? Isn't he a fine figure of a boy?

(Jack scowls and turns away.)

He expected you to be different.

Young Man: There's no pleasing some people. Well, the truth is, I'm not entirely sure he's the kind of father I'd want to remember anyway.

Jack: That's right! Try to shove me aside. I knew your game the minute I saw you. (To the Girl) There's a side of him I bet he never showed you. These momma's boys! Deny their own fathers!

Girl: You said you didn't know him.

Jack: Maybe I remember him a bit. But a man wants to be sure before he takes on that sort of responsibility. I mean, anyone could walk in here claiming I was his father. Trouble with her is she doesn't think. Takes everything at face value and then lives to regret it.

Niobe: I knew him the moment I saw him.

Jack: Well, maybe I did, too, eh?

Young Man: Prove it, then. Tell me my name, if you think you knew me right off.

(There is a long pause, all eyes focused on Jack.)

Jack: Jack! I'd have called a son after me. There.

(The Young Man smiles sardonically.)

Niobe: That's not it, is it?

Young Man: Of course not. I haven't been called Jack for — years.

Niobe: See! Some father! You don't even know your own son changed his name. (Takes the Young Man by the arm.) Can you imagine how that makes him feel? You don't deserve a son. You're a stupid selfish, senile old man.

(Jack turns with an appealing look to the Girl.)

Girl: I don't know whether you're senile or not. We haven't even been introduced.

Niobe: I don't need an introduction to know what you are. You're my son's woman. I know your kind. Come traipsing in as though you belonged here, acting as though you were one of the family. *(Grabbing the Young Man's arm possessively.)* As though you owned my boy.

Young Man: *(Mildly chastising.)* Now mother. I want you to meet — Sally.

Girl: Who?

Young Man: Uh — . My 'girl' — my own — sweetheart.

(Niobe disengages herself from the Young Man and walks up to the Girl. She executes a dress-parade inspection.)

Niobe: Pleased to — mmm — ah — Sheila. *(Pause)* I suppose you'll want to tidy yourself up a bit, won't you *(Slight pause)* if you expect to get anywhere with a fine young man like my son. *(Pause)* My son's partial to blonde girls. You'll probably want to know that, since you don't have that natural advantage. *(Laughs)* But we mustn't curse God for what he's blessed us with, must we?

(The Young Man laughs at the 'joke'. Jack laughs also.)

Jack: Don't let her bother you, Sally. Under that blonde mop of hers, she's as bald as an ice rink.

Niobe: That's a lie!

(The Young Man wheels on Jack and grasps him by the lapels.)

Young Man: Take that back, you uncouth son-of-a-bitch!

Niobe: Make him take it back! Kick him in the nuts!

(Jack puts his hands down to protect himself and the Young Man pushes him violently away. Jack falls to the floor. The Young Man turns back to Niobe.)

Young Man: How could you associate with a man like that?

Niobe: He'll say anything to be cruel.

(The Young Man puts his arm around Niobe's shoulder to comfort her.)

Girl: Do you want me to get our things?

Niobe: That's right, dear. You bring his things in like a pet. We've got so much to talk about.

(The Girl goes out to the platform and hefts up the two packs.)

Isn't that right, son?

Young Man: It certainly is, — Mom.

(Niobe holds him at arm's length.)

Niobe: Well, just look at you.

(He beams with embarrassed pride. The Girl returns with the packs, puts them down, and sits on one of them, listening.)

(To the Girl) I wouldn't believe it if I hadn't seen it with my own two eyes. *(To the Young Man)* So much to catch up on. *(Pause)* My, my.

(The Girl yawns. Niobe looks severely at her and then back to the Young Man.)

Niobe: I just can't get over it.

(Smiles, and silence. After a moment the side door opens and the 2nd Deliveryman enters, followed by the 1st Deliveryman who stands subserviently at the door. The 2nd Deliveryman is dressed very elegantly and carries a walking stick. He proceeds to centre stage and makes a slight diplomatic bow to Niobe. The 1st Deliveryman is dressed in a common and somewhat baggy business suit.)

Niobe: Hello!

E24

2nd Deliveryman: I have returned earlier than the time we had agreed upon because, since I last spoke to you, certain unavoidable complications have arisen and, I regret to say, I shall be unable to keep my appointment with you this evening. My private helicopter is waiting to spirit me off to the airport where I am to board the 6:15 flight to Amsterdam. After a brief stop-over, I shall be off to Rome, Zurich, Paris, and London, where I shall close a number of important franchise deals before leaving for Corfu and a well-earned weekend in the sun. You remember me, of course, as a mere second-class deliveryman and that is how I truly would like to be remembered by you in years to come —

1st Deliveryman: Hear! Hear!

(The 2nd Deliveryman casts an annoyed and silencing glance at his partner.)

2nd Deliveryman: — modest and simple crafts-man who, not as a result of grasping ambition and ruthless tactics, but by virtue of application to his work and honesty in all his dealings was catapulted to the dizzying heights of success in what, to those who have not trodden similar paths of arduous endeavour, must seem scant hours. Already it is whispered in the corridors of power that government should not be an objective I disregard when scanning my horizon. For the moment, however, I humbly feel that I must consider such whisperings as only the stirrings of hope, hope of the kind which is invariably generated whenever a man of vision appears and, however gently, shakes the edifice of tradition. I respect that hope but I shall not arrogantly assume that I am the one to fulfill it. No; you needn't say it. I know that at times, to the faint-hearted, ours might seem to be a plodding nation. Let me say to those whose spirit flags, do not forget that we are of pioneer stock and still retain in our very marrow those sterling qualities which made our nation great — imagination, courage, the good sense to know a leader when we see one, and the wisdom to set aside petty personal ambitions and get behind him when our collective progress is the prize. I trust the people, simple people like yourselves, to make the correct and only choice when choices must be made. Trust the people is my creed; trust in the people is my strength. *(Softly —*

rising.) My friends, it is not **my** success of which we speak when we speak of success. It is the success of the people. *(Pause, then with great humility.)* Thank you.

(The 1st Deliveryman applauds and the Young Man, terribly impressed, joins him.)

Jack: Haven't I seen you somewhere before?

Niobe: Oh, do shut up! Don't you ever learn? You mustn't mind him, sir. He's always talking about people he thinks he's seen. Or if it's not a face he's sure he's seen, it's a face he's sure he's **never** seen. There's no happy medium with him.

Jack: I'll get you. When your 'friend' —

(The Young Man moves threateningly towards Jack.)

Niobe: Now. It's only — *(Looks to the clock.)* a quarter to twelve. Just lunch-time. Won't you stay for a bite? I'm sure your helicopter won't mind waiting just long enough for you to have a snack.

2nd Deliveryman: I am pressed for time.

Young Man: Oh, come on. It would please my mother.

(Pause)

2nd Deliveryman: Did you say, your mother?

Niobe: His mother has nothing to do with this. Can't you forget your mother for five minutes? A grown man like you forever whining about your mother. There's a time and a place for everything. *(To the Deliveryman.)* Say you'll stay for a bite.

2nd Deliveryman: Well, just a quick nibble.

(Overjoyed, Niobe goes to him and takes him by the arm. She directs him towards the stairs.)

Niobe: Fine! That's just fine!

2nd Deliveryman: *(Looking back.)* Aren't we all lunching together?

Niobe: Good grief, no! He doesn't eat on duty and they've already eaten. *(To the Young Man)* Haven't you?

Young Man: Not since yesterday.

Niobe: *(Indicating the Girl)* I suppose that's what she would call being modern. Well, you can't just come barging in on us with no warning and expect me to jump right into the middle of fancy meal preparations. You might consider others sometimes, you know.

2nd Deliveryman: Who are these people?

Niobe: You mean you don't know them?

(The 2nd Deliveryman shakes his head.)

Well, this is really something, isn't it? They're certainly not very well-known, are they, if someone in your position doesn't even know them?

(With this, she directs the 2nd Deliveryman to the living quarters. The 2nd Deliveryman waves away his partner who, having been prepared to join them for 'lunch', turns dejectedly and exits. The other three watch as Niobe and the 2nd Deliveryman exit. Jack looks at the Young Man and the Girl, puts a forefinger to his lips and follows to eavesdrop outside the closed door and to spy through the key-hole. The Girl walks about in the room as though seeking a clue. She sniffs the air. They speak simultaneously.)

Girl: Don't you think it's —

Young Man: Well, what do you —

(They stop and look at one another.)

Young Man: I —

(Pause, they stand still, silent, and hostile with the quality of strangers who do not trust one another. She sits on a bench, he on the packs. Jack moves a step or two on tiptoe toward them.)

Jack: Oysters! On the half shell! Paté de fois gras. Caviar Russe au vin rouge! *(Pause)* Hey! Did you hear that?

(The Girl looks up and then back to the Young Man. We hear Niobe's high-pitched giggle. Jack signals that he will return and darts back to the door to spy.)

Young Man: I think he's trying to be friendly.

(The Girl shrugs.)

Anyway, what do you think?

Girl: Do you want an honest opinion?

Young Man: Well . . . yes.

(Pause)

Do you think we should leave?

Girl: *(Rising)* Yes.

(He seems unable to rise. She waits a moment and then sits down again. Jack comes toward them again.)

Jack: Une limonade américaine glacé avec du beurre d'arachides entre des petits pains noirs de la norvége. *(Pause)* What do you make of that?

(The Girl, long-suffering, looks up.)

Girl: Sans acun doute, c'est la casse-croûte du bon Marquis.

Jack: Ah. Ah!

(Jack returns to the door.)

Young Man: They're just ordinary people. It could be worse.

Girl: And you're just an ordinary boy who has a soft spot for home cooking.

(Jack turns to them again.)

Jack: Psst.

(The Young Man and the Girl look up.)

Comporte des poires pendant with hot buttered English crumpet. She wouldn't dare serve that junk up to me. You know what I think, eh?

(Neither responds)

I think all that foreign food's got to be bad for you.

(Pause. Silence.)

Did you say you did or you didn't recognize me?

Girl: He said both at one time or another.

Young Man: That's right. Why?

(Jack is thinking along devious channels.)

Jack: As the seed is planted, so grows the tree. I've always believed that. What do you make of it?

Young Man: It — **sounds** reasonable.

Jack: It is. It is. And wouldn't you say, blood's thicker than water?

Young Man: Well — . I think it's a scientific fact.

Jack: And —

(Pause, Jack smiles confidently.)

Would you grant that there's something to the saying, 'Like father, like son'? Eh?

Young Man: I suppose there's something to it, if you mean that —

Jack: That's good enough. I think we're beginning to understand each other. *(Tapping his forehead.)* Logic's what I'm about. I'm going to get to the bottom of all this.

(An alert signal from the telegraph. Jack winks at the Young Man, turns, and goes to take the message. As the message comes in, the Girl yawns, unrolls one of the packs, crawls into the sleeping bag and goes to sleep.)

EXECUTIVE ASTROLOGIST SAY ASS WHO SIT ON THIRD RAIL GET BUM BURNT STOP WE KNOW YOUR GAME OLD SON STOP — NE PLUS ULTRA

(Jack reads the message over and then speaks to the imagined auditor.)

Jack: Screw you, big shot!

(He gets up from the table and approaches the Young Man. A message returns; Jack translates it in his head.)

WE ARE NOT DEAF BLIND OR DUMB STOP REST ASSURED NOT IMPOTENT STOP — NUMERO UNO

Jack: *(Looking upward)* Stick it in your ear! They've been pushing me around long enough. Well, the game's over now. *(Pause)* You remember what you told me earlier? *(Pause — he muses.)* If a man can't count on his son, who the hell can he count on, eh?

Young Man: I certainly didn't tell you that.

Jack: You did. That was the sense of it, anyway.

Young Man: Don't put words in my mouth.

(Pause)

Jack: Look. Let's get this straight. You come in here telling me I'm your father. Okay. I figure it's a free world and a man can say what he wants. But you also want me to recognize you — straight away — without so much as a by-your-leave. Is that so or not?

Young Man: It's perfectly natural that a father should —

Jack: Don't tell me what's natural. I know what's natural. What I want to know is does this cut both ways?

Young Man: What?

Jack: This father son thing! Is it a fifty-fifty deal?

(Pause)

Young Man: Do you think you could be more explicit?

Jack: Eh?

Young Man: — clear.

Jack: *(Disgusted)* I'm putting a proposition to you. If I'm your father, you're my son. All or nothing.

Young Man: Ah.

(Pause)

Jack: Well? What's your answer?

(The Young Man rises and walks thoughtfully over to the Girl. He looks down at her sleeping form. Reaching a decision, he turns back and faces Jack.)

Young Man: Fifty-fifty?

Jack: Down the line.

Young Man: No changing your mind later.

Jack: You ought to know your old man better than that.

Young Man: Yeah. I guess so, eh?

(Jack attempts to put a fatherly arm about the Young Man's shoulder but is too short to manage it. The Young Man drapes his arm, instead, over Jack's shoulder.)

Jack: You're not the little fella you once were, I'll tell you.

Young Man: No. I'm not. But you're just about the same size.

Jack: Smaller. They say you shrink.

Young Man: Is that so?

Jack: Yep. Shrink. Eventually disappear, I guess, if you didn't d — *(Abruptly changing the subject)* That thing's your mother's. *(Laughs)* Did you ever see the like of it? Just sitting there.

Young Man: I suppose you'll want to do something with it.

Jack: She will. Get rid of it.

Young Man: Or put something in it.

Jack: *(Disturbed)* In it? *(Pause)* She'll get rid of it! As soon as she finds that god-damned hammer of hers.

Young Man: Hammer?

Jack: — for taking it apart.

Young Man: It would be a waste of a good box. Waste not, want not.

(Jack looks frantically towards the living quarters and then back to the Young Man.)

Jack: You said fifty-fifty. I put you through law school. I want you to remember that.

Young Man: Medical school.

Jack: That's right — even better. So, you'll help me?

Young Man: Do what?

(Jack looks about guiltily before speaking.)

Jack: Do something about that. *(Quickly)* But I can't touch it, see.

Young Man: I can't either. It's not my property.

Jack: What's that got to do with it, for Christ's sake?

Young Man: My father taught me never to touch anything that wasn't mine.

Jack: I never taught you that! That's stupid!

Young Man: My father —

Jack: I didn't!

Young Man: Did.

Jack: Didn't!

Young Man: Didso.

(Jack is about to reply but he stops, ponders, and chooses a new approach.)

Jack: (Oversolicitous) You know, I was wondering. Is your friend Sally, dead do you think?

Young Man: Dead? She's a bit young for that. She's probably sleeping.

Jack: Oh, I doubt it. In the middle of the afternoon? On the floor? In a railway station? Dressed like that? You're the doctor. You should know that that's not very likely.

Young Man: No? I don't know much about that sort of thing. (Proudly) I'm cosmetic surgery.

Jack: Oh, yeah? Well, look at her face then. It's kind of pasty, don't you think?

Young Man: Hmmm. She is pale of skin.

Jack: Rot — lying around that colour.

Young Man: Actually, it's called decomposition — a systematic breakdown of organic —

Jack: That's very interesting. There's bound to be a stink.

Young Man: Oh, yes, it's not pleasant.

(The Young Man touches the sleeping bag gingerly with his toe.)

Jack: I'll bet. (Pause) They put 'em in boxes in my day.

Young Man: They still do, but cremation is becoming much more popular.

Jack: Cremation, eh? Dusty business. (Pause) It's not God's way, if you know what I mean. It's a good box we've got here though. Since we haven't got a fire (Indicates the stove), we'd be doing her a favour. (Pause) Can you lift her?

Young Man: Me?

Jack: (Taps his chest and coughs.) I've got this thing, you understand.

Young Man: Well . . .

(Reluctantly, the Young Man bends down to take her out of the sleeping bag.)

Jack: Leave her in the bag. You wouldn't want to w — disturb her.

(The Young Man drags her in the bag to the coffin. Jack, apprehensive in the extreme, opens the coffin and helps lift the Girl.)

Gently. With respect. The way they do it. For the deceased (Pause) That's it. Over here. There we are. Gently, gently does it.

(They deposit the Girl. They stand erect, looking into the box.)

Young Man: I liked her immensely, you know. She stood by me through thick and thin.

(Jack is impatient to shut the lid.)

Doesn't she look peaceful? So — natural?

(Jack looks against his will.)

Jack: Very natural. Very natural.

(Jack lowers the lid, forcing the Young Man to step back.)

Young Man: I'm sure she's happier where she's gone, you know.

Jack: Very happy. Very very happy, you can bet on it. (Looking about) Hammer. We need a hammer, now.

(He sights the clock and stops.)

The eleven-forty-seven! Damn it! I forgot. We've got three minutes!

Young Man: To do what?

Jack: To throw that switch. Put that bloody train on the right track for once. I'll need your help on this. Switch is jammed.

Young Man: That's bad.

Jack: Bad! Ha! Got to throw it with a crowbar. C'mon!
(He starts off for the platform, the Young Man following. Jack suddenly stops and looks back at the clock.)

E32

Give that clock a tap, will you. Quick.
(The Young Man goes to the clock and gently taps it. He looks quizzically back to Jack.)
Harder. Bash it.
(The Young Man drives his fist into the side of the clock. It responds with a clang and a clatter and the hands leap on to 11:47. At the same time, a distant diesel horn is heard.)
That's it! Let's go! We've got about a minute before it hits the station.
(Jack races out to the switch. The Young Man follows. Jack picks up the crowbar, places it in the track point, and, together, they heave on the bar. It does not shift. The diesel horn is louder. Jack looks desperately down the track.)

Jack: C'mon! Again! Now! Heave!

(The rail does not move. The signal starts.)

You're not trying! What kind of a son are you, anyway?

Young Man: We'll get it this time.

(Together, they give a supreme effort. The switch moves and the bar clatters across the track. Jack goes tumbling after it and falls to the platform. He rights himself in a sitting position, a grin on his face. The train rumble is louder.)

Jack: That did it! *(Laughs)* Don't stand there, son. Cut you off in your prime! Those buggers got no respect for man, dog, or woman.

(The Young Man walks across the tracks and stands beside Jack. The noise increases and the train thunders through the station. It gives a last greeting blast of the horn which is interrupted by the first sounds of the crash. The Young Man is dumbfounded but Jack has a look of intense joy on his face. The crossing signal stops.)

Niobe: *(Off, yelling)* For Christ's sake, what was that! ? Jack! ?

Jack: Go on back to your pennant poyres and crumpit. Nobody needs you down here any more. This is between father and son.
(Jack looks at the young Man and laughs triumphantly. The Young Man still is speechless.
Black out.)

ACT II *(The station, moments later. There is a pall of dust and smoke from the crash. The Young Man is furtively doing up the girl's bedroll. Niobe enters upstage. Pulling her dressing gown about herself and adjusting her wig, she stops when she sees the Young Man. The Young Man puts the Girl's pack under the coffin and, before turning away, pats the lid as a farewell gesture. He turns to discover Niobe who is watching him. He smiles sheepishly and pats the coffin lid again.)*

Young Man: She died. Sally — you know — my friend. Just paying my respects.

Niobe: Oh, yes. Where's Shackel?

Young Man: You could smell the decomposition.

Niobe: I don't smell anything different.

Young Man: Something's rotten.

(Niobe shrugs, looking suspiciously about. The Young Man moves toward his pack which lies near the door. Niobe looks back.)

Niobe: What's the matter with you? *(Pause)* What are you up to?

Young Man: Who? Me? What do you mean?

Niobe: Don't play innocent with me. I know when something's afoot. I've got a mother's nose for trouble.

(The 2nd Deliveryman enters. He is dressed in his vest and shorts and walks as a very old man, one hand to his heaving chest. His voice, too, has aged.)

2nd Deliveryman: What was that unearthly noise?

Young Man: The train. He derailed it.

2nd Deliveryman: That's impossible!

Niobe: He's a spineless nobody. **And** a weakling! He couldn't by himself.

2nd Deliveryman: He wouldn't dare.

(The Young Man picks up his pack.)

2nd Deliveryman: Where do you think you're going?

Young Man: Me? Ah — for a walk.

2nd Deliveryman: You stay right where you are. You're a material witness.

Young Man: I didn't see anything.

2nd Deliveryman: Put down that pack.

Niobe: Put it down right now or I'll show you the reason why.

(She raises a threatening hand. The Young Man puts the pack down and sits on it.)

Young Man: I was just going for a little walk.

Niobe: I know your 'little walks'. You don't come back for so long, people can't even remember you.

(The 2nd Deliveryman looks critically at the Young Man.)

2nd Deliveryman: I suspect you've got more to do with this than you let on. We'll get to the bottom of it, you needn't worry. I'm not the success I am for nothing, you can be assured of that. I have my way of getting to the root of things — as you will discover — oh!

(He puts his hand to his chest as he experiences a mild heart seizure. Niobe moves towards him but he waves her back.)

2nd Deliveryman: It's nothing — . Just — a — touch — of angina.

(Pause. The Young Man and Niobe look on with interest.)

Young Man: Maybe you're — dying?

Niobe: Dying?

2nd Deliveryman: In my position! With all I've got to look — *(Catches his breath)* forward to?

Niobe: Why, he's just begun.

2nd Deliveryman: What a ridiculous — suggestion.

Niobe: I should know angelica when I smell it.

Young Man: It was just a thought.

(Niobe walks abruptly up to the Young Man and cuffs him on the ear. He cowers under the onslaught. She returns to the side of the Deliveryman.)

Niobe: Well, just mind your nasty little tongue when you're talking about your betters. Nobody's interested in your silly thoughts.

(The Deliveryman smiles pained approval. She helps him to the bench where the Young Man is seated. The Young Man moves. As the Deliveryman is almost seated, Niobe has a further thought, releases the Deliveryman who falls to the bench, and cuffs the Young Man again.)

Niobe: And that's for lying all the time!

2nd Deliveryman: I — can't abide — a liar.

(There is a yell of triumph from Jack. He comes bounding along the track and onto the platform. The Deliveryman is startled.)

Jack: Holy Christ, what a beauty! Niobe!

(The Deliveryman looks at her in distress and then back to Jack who has gone into a lively step-dance. He dances himself into the waiting room. He sees the three of them, performs a final flourish, and comes to a stagey finish. For the moment, Jack is a winner.)

If they didn't know it before, b'Jesus they know it now. They need a man at this station to make sure things like that don't happen. Security — all along the line. Maybe now they'll see I'm a vital link in the transcontinental line.

Young Man: *(Drawing Jack aside.)* Chain. Properly speaking, it would be an important link in a chain. A link in a line is a mixed metaphor and a logical impossibility. And, as the system would most sensibly be thought of as a line rather than a chain, it would seem to me that 'links' would be totally irrelevant.

Jack: What are you talking about?

Young Man: I was just trying to explain —

Jack: Who asked you to explain? I was telling you to shut up, if you want to know. I don't have to listen to a snot-nosed kid. *(To Niobe)* Why hasn't that old man got any clothes on? Tell him to get dressed. I can't stand naked old men.

Niobe: That's the Deliveryman who was successful.

Jack: What do you take me for? I'd know a successful young man if I saw one. You could tell by the way he dressed. That's a naked old man.

2nd Deliveryman: I — I —

(They all look)

Jack: Dumb, too. I hated that bastard Deliveryman, but one thing you couldn't take away from him — he could talk.

Niobe: *(Touching her throat)* He's got angora.

Jack: *(Scornfully)* Oh, yeah? So why's he only wearing cotton shorts? He's a bum vagrant.

2nd Deliveryman: I —

(Pause. The 2nd Deliveryman looks at them, appealing for help.)

Young Man: He doesn't act very successful, does he?

2nd Deliveryman: That — train —

Jack: Yeah? What about it?

2nd Deliveryman: That's —

Young Man: That's what?

2nd Deliveryman: That's — ho —

Jack: Spit it out.

2nd Deliveryman: — ho —

Niobe: What is it?

2nd Deliveryman: — ho —

Jack: *(Impatient — shouting)* For Christ's sake, what! ?

(The Deliveryman is startled. He has a final and fatal seizure and falls forward to the floor. Jack and Niobe step back from him.)

Niobe: Why's he falling down like that?

Jack: He's being pretty sensitive, isn't he? Can't he take a joke?

Young Man: Perhaps he's hungry. Vagrants sometimes are, you know. They faint when it gets really bad. On the other hand, he could be dead.

Jack: Dead! ? You think so? You're the doctor. See if he's faking.

Niobe: Doctor! ? That's fantastic! My son a doctor!

Jack: Go ahead.

(They both look on with curiosity as the Young Man kneels beside the body and feels for the pulse. After a moment, he sets the Delivery-man's hand down and draws the eyelids shut with his fingertips. He looks up and nods, affirming the worst.)

Niobe: Why, only an hour ago he was — .

Jack: He was what?

Niobe: Nibbling — ah — eating! Like a prince!

Jack: Like a pig, if you ask me. All that French stuff. I say he was asking for trouble.

(There is an alert. Jack goes to take the message. The Young Man and Niobe talk over.)

ALRIGHT PINHEAD WE'VE GOT YOUR

NUMBER *(Pause)* UR 1 4 1 5 1 5 1 4 5 STOP —
C 7 1 5 4

Young Man: One of the most common causes of death, as recent research has shown, is careless-ness.

Niobe: Now, wouldn't you know it would turn out to be something really simple after all.

Young Man: The body can be likened somewhat to a machine which, if the component parts are maintained and treated with due care and respect, can last —

Niobe: Yes? Yes! ? How long?

Young Man: For a life-time.

Niobe: That's a beautiful way to put it. *(Ecstat-ically)* Forever!

Young Man: It's just science and common sense.

Niobe: But so — true.

(The Girl stirs in the coffin and rises to a sitting position, pushing the lid open above herself. She yawns. Only slowly does she begin to realize where she is. The others see her; the Young Man is appalled, Niobe offended, and Jack at first distressed, soon thinking of new solutions.)

Girl: What the — ! What am I doing in here? !

Young Man: He said you were dead.

Girl: What does he know about anything? Do I look dead?

(They all look at her as she gets hastily out of the coffin. Jack rushes to help her but she brushes him angrily aside.)

Niobe: *(Archly)* Looks don't mean anything.

Jack: It was just a little practical joke. I mean, I can see the funny side of it.

(Jack laughs mechanically.)

Young Man: So can I.

(The Young Man laughs)

Niobe: After all, if we can't laugh at our guests, who **can** we laugh at?

(Niobe laughs. There is cruelty in their laughter; it increases to a pitch of near frenzy. Jack shuts his laughter off abruptly.)

Jack: Right!

(Silence and blank faces.)

A bit of fun to clear the air. All work and no play, eh? *(Laughs)* Now! There's him. And there's that *(Indicating coffin.)* Made for each other, as I see it. I say we get down to business — tuck him in and hammer down the top for keeps.

(A loud knocking at the freight doors. The Young Man starts towards the doors to open them.)

Let them knock! This is important.

(Jack has gone to the 2nd Deliveryman's body and is trying to lift it. Knock again — more insistent.)

Niobe: It may be somebody.

Jack: It's nobody! Leave it!

(The Young Man hesitates. The 1st Deliveryman enters pushing a freight barrow. The Delivery-man looks at Jack who is standing guiltily with one of the 2nd Deliveryman's legs in his hands. Everyone turns to look at Jack.)

1st Deliveryman: Would you mind telling me what you think you're doing?

(Pause. Jack looks at the leg, then at the Deliveryman. He releases the leg and it drops to the floor with a thud.)

Jack: Nothing.

1st Deliveryman: I'd've said you were holding his leg. Pulling it.

Jack: I was **looking** at it.

Niobe: No he wasn't. He was pulling his leg alright.

(No one laughs)

(Still trying) You're always trying to pull someone's leg, aren't you, Jack?

(The Deliveryman looks at her. He is not amused.)

1st Deliveryman: This isn't a laughing matter. The leg you were tampering with happens to belong to the President of Universal Transport and Delivery, a very important man with connections in very high places. Not even his mistress touches him without an appointment. And **you** were mauling his leg. I don't want to scare you, mister, but far bigger men than you have been destroyed for less. This is a man who has everything — a lovely executive wife, three beautiful children, friends, membership in some of the country's best country clubs and churches, a home in the country, stables, a flat in town, three cars, two Arab ponies, a dedicated Mexican hairless, an immaculate credit rating, love, respect, loyalty, an olympic size swimming pool — you name it. Everything success and money can buy. And you treat him like a common derelict who doesn't have a pot to piss in! ? Just what sort of unnatural man are you?

Jack: *(Incensed)* You couldn't tell all that by looking at him.

Niobe: Rubbish! I say looks will out.

Jack: We thought he was a vagrant.

Young Man: I figured he wasn't a vagrant. He had — 'style'.

Niobe: You could tell he wasn't from his eyes. Deep.

Young Man: He said the man was a vagrant. He wanted us to believe that so we'd help him put the cor — remains in the box.

(The 1st Deliveryman looks at the box and then at Jack.)

1st Deliveryman: In that!

Jack: It's a good box. Pine. Solid. We've got the guarantee. Six months guarantee. She'll get it and show you.

1st Deliveryman: Six months! Don't bother. A man of his stature gets a royal scarlet, velvet lined atmospherically sweetened, platinum and mahogany Slumber King with a **life-time** guarantee. Six months! a six-month box is for a common sort of man who doesn't have to worry about things like immortality. This man's place of rest is tended and secure for an eternity. Not a miserable six months.

(He wheels the freight barrow up to the body while the others look on. Jack is distressed. The Young Man helps the Deliveryman lift the body onto the cart.)

Jack: You could use the box to get him where he's going. It would be more comfortable for him. I'll donate the box.

(The Deliveryman considers.)

Niobe: He can't give that box away. **I** signed for it. He needs my approval.

Jack: Well, give your approval. You don't need the thing.

(Pause. Niobe considers.)

1st Deliveryman: No. It's kind of you to consider it, M'am. I know he'd appreciate the thought. But in the end it would be depriving someone else and I know he wouldn't want that.

Niobe: He was like that. He always put others ahead of himself.

(The 1st Deliveryman smiles and wheels the body to the freight doors. The Young Man and Niobe follow respectfully. Jack and the Girl remain downstage. The doors shut behind the Deliveryman.)

Girl: There's something I want to settle with you. I'm not one of your kind, so I'd appreciate it if you would stop trying to drag me into these family — things. I came along because he was afraid of the dark — no other reason. But, that's it. The rest has nothing to do with me. Leave me out of it and keep your hands off me and people who don't belong to you. Put one of your own in that box if it matters so much to you.

E40

Niobe: I always said, she's not the sort who would fit into our little family. Listen to that talk. With her, it's self, self, self, all the time.

Jack: I don't know. She's got a point.

Niobe: What would you know about it, anyway? You'll say anything if you think it'll get you a quick look up a tramp's skirt and a bit of a feel. *(Niobe turns to the Girl.)* I'll have you know that ours is a very old family. We date back, you know. Not like most families. I can show you seven generations of photographs. And letters that go back even further. It's good blood in my boy from the Numin side. You can see from looking at him that he's from good stock. *(She takes the Young Man by the arm.)* If you think you can just walk in and be a part of that by saying you'd like to, you've got another think coming. In case you don't know, that's what they call geneology. My boy's got geneology to back him up. *(Tasting the name.)* Sally? Sally. What sort of name is that? It hasn't even got 'tone'.

Girl: For a start, my name's not Sally.

Niobe: Well, what do you mean coming in here under false pretensions, then? Ashamed, are you? It must be one of those common names like Doreen if 'Sally' sounds good enough to you and if you'll let a dirty old man feel you up.

(She waits for the Girl to respond. The Girl receives the accusative stares, then turns slowly away.)

Girl: I don't tell anyone my name unless I choose to.

Jack: That's the girl.

Girl: And I can look after myself.

Niobe: Ha! That'll teach you to pick sides without thinking which one your bread's buttered on. Well, it's your choice. I only hope you know what you're doing.

(She takes the Young Man by the arm and leads him to the living quarters.)

Come. I'll show you the album. You can see for

yourself if you're not the image of the Numins and we can settle this once and for all.

(Exit Niobe and the Young Man. Jack stands looking at the Girl who is staring firmly downstage.)

Jack: That stuff —

(He wiggles his fingers in the air to illustrate rather than have to say the words.)

None of that's true, you know.

Girl: It's none of my concern.

(Jack nods. Pause.)

Jack: Me? I just go about my business without interfering with others. Live and let live, I say.

(Pause. The Girl sits cross-legged on the floor, elbows on knees, her fists under her chin.)

Jack: See. I'm a stationmaster and that takes every minute I've got. Haven't got time to go around worrying about who's got my eyes, or my limp. *(Pause)* Nose to the grindstone, that's the secret. You probably can't understand that sort of thing, this and that — whatever you please. But that's not what life's about. Sooner or later you've got to be something. *(Ponderously)* You've got to sink your feet in, settle down. Put your mind to one thing — so you — . *(Pause)* You've got to be able to say 'I'm an engineer' or 'I'm a doctor', or 'I'm a stationmaster'. You've got to know what you are and you've got to get other people to know it, too, so when they look at you, they really see it. Then you can relax because — Well, you're something then, aren't you? *(Pause)* You're like me. It's what you are —

Girl: I am not like you.

Jack: Well, not exactly like me, I guess. What I really meant is you're like yourself. You know — you are what you are. Like I'm a stationmaster and you're —

(Jack waits for her to complete the sentence. He decides to share a confidence and moves closer to the Girl. He motions upstairs.)

People like them. They'll break you apart if you let 'em. Crack! Just like that. Do you think they care? You've got to be on your guard. Like me. Eyes open. You want to dig your heels in and stick to your guns. Keep your ear to the ground so you know when they're coming. That way, you . . .

(There is a message alert.)

Jack: Just a minute.

(Jack is concerned that the Girl might go away, he goes to the telegraph but keeps an eye on her.)

I'll just be a second.

(The message arrives.)

WATCH IT 1415 ETC STOP COMPUTER SAY CIPHER WHO KEEP EAR TO GROUND GET HEAD STOOD ON STOP WITH OTHER EAR HEAR THIS STOP — THUNDER CHIEF

(Distressed, Jack rises from his stool, the message in his hand. He looks to the Girl, to the telegraph, and then back to the Girl.)

You know, it would sort of be nice for me if you'd say something. You're making me nervous just sitting there like that. *(Pause)* Remember, it was me who stood by when they were picking on you. I'm the only friend you've got here.

Girl: I don't even know you.

Jack: Ha, ha. Sure you do. I was just explaining —

(She turns aside haughtily.)

I was telling you important personal things about — **me.**

Girl: You? Why should I be concerned with you?

Jack: Everybody's concerned with everybody. That's human sympathy. You don't **think** you're concerned with me — *(He waits. Silence.)*

– but you are. How do you think we'd get along with each other if we weren't interested in – *(Pause)* Otherwise, you'd have just got up and gone away, wouldn't you? But you didn't. You stayed right there – listening. *(Pause)* Because you **are** concerned.

(Jack turns back to the coffin.)

Jack: Of course you are. You're as human as the rest of us. Now, maybe we can work out something about this. It's not heavy. Between the two of us, we can just –

(Hesitating for a second, he grasps the coffin firmly at one end and tries to lift it. It will not move.)

Jack: It won't move!

(Jack looks under the coffin. Discovering nothing, he looks behind it and finds nothing there either. As though taking cover from the malevolent box, Jack retreats to the wall by the clock.)

Jack: Did you see anybody monkeying with it, when I wasn't looking? *(Pause)* You know something you're not telling me, don't you? *(Pause)* Are you in on it with them? Just pretending to be friendly to throw me off the scent. It's her god damned box! She's responsible for it, you know. Not me! I'll bet she didn't tell you that. Well, it's hers and – . It's driving me nuts.

(The Girl turns in her seated position.)

Girl: Why?

Jack: Because – it's empty.

Girl: Are you seriously trying to tell me – . It seems to me that you're driving yourself nuts.

Jack: Me? **She** wanted it here.

Girl: All right. Have it your own way. You were the one who wanted me to talk. I should have known better. You try to talk to someone and all they want is someone to disagree with. Now, maybe you'll just leave me alone.

(She turns away from him.)

Jack: I wasn't disagreeing with you. I was just – *(Pause)* But it **is** her and that bastard on the telegraph. And that 'son' of hers. And – *(Pause)* you could try to understand. I need – somebody's help.

Girl: I understand well enough. You're not so unique. Everywhere I go some 'poor soul' is crying out for help. Could you just give a bit of help? So you try. But where does it get you? Nowhere. That was my mistake in coming here in the first place, trying to help someone. Well, I'm learning. You don't want help. You just want some stranger gullible enough to carry your shit bucket. I tried to help him and where am I? Sitting on a floor in the bloody wilderness while he has all the laughs. If I try to help you, you'll end up trying to stuff me back into that bone-box. Well, from now on, nobody gets my help. Help yourself. It's your box. **You** lie in it.

Jack: No. It's –

(The Two Investigators enter. They are dressed in business suits and each carries a slim briefcase. Jack is frightened.)

1st Investigator: Good afternoon.

2nd Investigator: You wouldn't have the correct time, would you?

(Still facing them, Jack feebly thumps the clock which is directly behind himself. The hands move on to 11:55.)

1st Investigator: Ah! Eleven fifty-five. Right on time. Punctuality is one of the keys to a sound operation. Punctuality.

2nd Investigator: And efficiency. Now. Let's just see if everything is in order.

(The 1st Investigator writes in a note book as the 2nd Investigator calls the inventory.)

2nd Investigator: Clock.

1st Investigator: One beat up clock.

2nd Investigator: Ticket rack.

1st Investigator: Rack. Tickets missing.

2nd Investigator: Telegraph key and associated paraphernalia.

1st Investigator: Telegraph and assorted junk.

2nd Investigator: Sundry railwayman's garments.

1st Investigator: Clothing. Badly worn.

2nd Investigator: Stationery.

1st Investigator: Paper. Cluttered.

2nd Investigator: Stove. Wood.

1st Investigator: Stove. **Very** old fashioned.

2nd Investigator: One oilcloth slicker.

1st Investigator: Raincoat. Greasy.

2nd Investigator: Benches.

1st Investigator: Seats. Empty.

2nd Investigator: The building proper.

1st Investigator: Station. In disrepair.

2nd Investigator: Other odds and ends of Company property, including one unpainted lightweight pine utility coffin.

1st Investigator: Coffin.

(The job done, they stand beside one another smiling at Jack.)

2nd Investigator: And you are —

Jack: *(Without confidence)* I'm the stationmaster.

2nd Investigator: Of course. *(Familiarly)* 1415!

Jack: Jack Shackel. Forty-one years ser —

1st Investigator: Service. Yes. Of course. Commendable.

(The 1st Investigator removes a chair from the office and sets it centre facing downstage. The 2nd Investigator takes papers from his briefcase and puts them on top of the stove. All this while the patter continues.)

The Company holds such dedication in high esteem. You can look forward to a glowing mention in the Company house organ.

2nd Investigator: Unflinching service does not pass unnoticed, you can be sure.

1st Investigator: I wouldn't be surprised if you were even — *(Placing the chair.)* There!

Jack: What was that?

1st Investigator: I said 'There'.

Jack: You said 'even'.

1st Investigator: Even? *(Laughs lightly)* Well, I'm sure I did, if you say so.

Jack: But you **did**! I wanted to hear the rest of what you were going to say.

1st Investigator: Well, I wouldn't know that, would I? I've only got your word, trustworthy as it may be, that I said anything other than what I said I said.

2nd Investigator: I should think it would be enough that no one's calling you a liar.

1st Investigator: Now. *(Indicating the chair)* If you don't mind.

Jack: I'm all right here.

2nd Investigator: Come, now. We only want you to be comfortable.
(The 2nd Investigator walks up as though to speak to Jack. Jack puts his arm up to ward him off and the Investigator turns it into a businesslike, almost gentlemanly, hammerlock; the violence should seem almost solicitous. Jack is conducted to the chair and made to sit.)

1st Investigator: I'm sure you'll find this more agreeable.
(Jack sits without being restrained, but he is

alert and prepared to bolt at the first good opportunity.)

2nd Investigator: Yes, yes. There's no need for there to be any unpleasantness or discomfort. We have a few simple things we'd like to discuss with you and then we'll be on our way. It's a policy of the Company to inconvenience its people and interfere in their activity no more than is absolutely necessary.

1st Investigator: I'm sure you will want to receive us in the spirit in which we come.

2nd Investigator: A meeting of mutual respect, trust, and candour from which we may all go away having learned something.

1st Investigator: *(Removing a single rolled sheet of paper.)* Here we are. *(Pause)* First, we want you to know how appreciative the Company is of your many years of dedicated service. You've been a good worker. You're one of the most valued members of the team. You can probably appreciate that only our very best people are put in positions of responsibility such as yours. Whatever few misjudgments or errors you might have made, I'm sure can be written off to that very human —

2nd Investigator: To err is human.

1st Investigator: Exactly. To forgive is —

2nd Investigator: — Company policy — in most cases.

1st Investigator: In any event, we wanted to set your mind at ease. The Company is appreciative and holds you in warm regard.

(He hands the paper to Jack who takes it and smiles his relief. The Investigators smile confidently.)

2nd Investigator: There. *(Smiling)* Do you smoke?

Jack: Now and again, but I'm not what you'd call a smoker.

1st Investigator: Just the occasional puff to calm your nerves on the job.

(The 1st Investigator makes a note.)

Jack: What are you writing? Something about me?

1st Investigator: Relax. We're on your side. We want you to have confidence in us. Just as we have confidence in us.

2nd Investigator: A company as large as ours must have records. I'm sure you can appreciate that.

Jack: Well, as long as it's not used against me.

2nd Investigator: Against you? My dear man, how can you think that when we have already told you how the Company feels about you? The records are used for our people, not against them. What if someone outside the Company should make an accusation — say, that they had seen you smoking on duty? I mean, how would it look if all we could say was, 'Does he?' Knowing where you stand on such matters makes it possible for us to defend your position. It allows us to say, 'Yes. Of course. We know that.' That way we're not caught with egg on our faces and we can protect you.

Jack: It — sounds reasonable.

2nd Investigator: It is reasonable. It's Company policy.

1st Investigator: Now. One little question, to begin. Are you —

Jack: Yes?

2nd Investigator: Let me. Would you say that, in the balance, you were — guilty?

Jack: Of what?

1st Investigator: Now, we don't want to nit-pick, do we? Lewd thoughts, littering, uttering the Company's name in vain, pissing in the lake when you're swimming, masturbating, — a million little things of which all but saints have some guilt.

2nd Investigator: If we keep it general and avoid trivialities, we can settle it with a simple

E45

question and an even simpler answer.

1st Investigator: Are you?

Jack: I've probably done some harmless little things. But that's none of the Company's business.

2nd Investigator: Whose business could you possibly imagine it is? The Company assumes an enormous amount of responsibility for its people. It is hardly conceivable that it would do that in ignorance of their activities. Be reasonable, man. A simple 'yes' or 'no' will suffice.

Jack : I can't.

1st Investigator: Of course you can. You haven't tried.

Jack: Alright, then, No!

(*The Investigators look at one another and smile.*)

2nd Investigator: There. That wasn't difficult. You can answer with a simple monosyllable as well as the next man.

1st Investigator: (*Writing*) Answered 'yes' to question of guilt.

Jack: I said 'No'.

2nd Investigator: We understand that. But "no" is an impossible answer, don't you see, because everyone is guilty of something. In saying 'No', you illustrated that you could give a simple answer — the thing that was really in question. Since you are capable of saying one, it is reasonable to assume that you can say the other and, therefore, by an elementary process of logic you must have meant 'Yes'.

Jack: I didn't mean either!

1st Investigator: (*Snatches the scroll out of Jack's hand.*) Then you shouldn't have spoken, should you? You're equivocating, Mr. Shackel. I thought we were going to have an open and frank discussion. No one is without guilt.

Jack: I'm innocent.

2nd Investigator: It takes an arrogant man to profess innocence in the face of what we, as modern and enlightened men, now know to be true. His word can never be trusted. On the other hand, if a man can be made to see and admit his guilt, he is well on the road to making of himself an invaluable member of the team. If he can actually admit it with humility, accept gracefully his place in the scheme of things, he is a man who can be trusted anywhere.

1st Investigator: In brief, he will cause no trouble nor will he want to because he has learned humility and has been rewarded with the guarantee of his own inviolable place in the organization so long as he shall want it.

2nd Investigator: Or, you will of course understand, (Reading) "... so long as the Company feels, and as those feelings are informed by the justly skilled managerial decision-making committees, that that individual is of any further practical and profitable use to the organization in its pursuit of those higher objectives which it has set for itself."

Girl: (Scornfully, without looking up.) That means they are going to crucify you.

(The 2nd Investigator looks at the girl seemingly noting her for the first time. Smiling, he walks up behind her, pauses, and then, with one swift judo chop to the back of her neck, sends her sprawling unconscious to the floor. Jack tries to get up but the 1st Investigator holds him in the chair.)

Jack: You can't do that! That's Doreen!

2nd Investigator: Note that, Number One.

1st Investigator: (Writing) Maintains subversive connections.

2nd Investigator: I should choose my friends with more discretion if I were you, Shackel. You'll not help your own cause if you associate with that sort. The Company can't in all fairness, be asked to look with trust and favour upon employees who number among their friends loud-mouthed, opinionated, destructive, radicals. Freedom of expression, my friend, is one thing. Wilful and violent attacks upon the institutions which protect our freedoms is another.

Jack: She's — not really my friend.

2nd Investigator: Well, then. You needn't be concerned for her, need you?

Jack: No. I don't have subversive connections, like he said. That shouldn't go on the record, should it?

1st Investigator: We'll look into it. But, since it has been raised as a significant issue in our discussion, we can't simply ignore it. It will get just scrutiny.

Jack: But you said she was my friend.

2nd Investigator: Are you suggesting that because I raised the issue, it is not significant? (To 1st Investigator) Note that.

1st Investigator: (Writing) No respect for professional expertise.

(The 2nd Investigator walks downstage.)

2nd Investigator: I should like to go on record —

(He glances over his shoulder and the 1st Investigator complies by 'noting' the speech in his book.)

— as saying that as Company Research Officer 2651815 dash 2, in the routine course of my duty, this twentieth day of August, investigating the incident of a main-line derailment at Dogwood-Wen, an obscure station no longer in use, it has been brought to my attention that the superannuated stationmaster, one Jack Shattell —

Jack: Shackel!

2nd Investigator: Shattell, contrary to my natural expectations, and scorning the reasonable manner in which my colleague and I approached him, has cast deep and insulting doubt on — etcetera, etcetera. Finish it off in accordance with standard form 65-X.

E48

Jack: Doubt on what? I've got a right to know what you're putting down.

2nd Investigator: You've got a what? *(Pause)* No. I refuse to succumb to the anger you are trying to provoke in me. *(Pause)* We have done everything in our power to approach you reasonably and, yet, from the moment this interview began, you have done nothing but stand obstinately in the way of our amicable progress. You have challenged the authority of your superiors. You have refused every conciliatory **gesture we have made.** You have, in essence, stated that you **will not** be reasonable. In fact, you seem to insist that we resort to the very things we want least to do — to have recourse to harsh and arbitrary sanctions.

1st Investigator: You deprive us of the possibility of being decent, and yet you talk of 'rights'!

(Jack has, by now, fully sensed the direction any further talk will take. He shifts in his chair, preparing to make a dash for freedom. Niobe enters upstage, fastening her bra, and then drawing her dressing gown about herself. She stops and listens.)

2nd Investigator: Rights, my friend, are earned by reasonable men who understand that those rights are gained through co-operation with those who confer them. *(Pause)* Do you imagine for a moment that rights would even exist if people had as little respect for authority as you?

(Jack suddenly bolts from his chair. The 1st Investigator trips him and Jack falls at Niobe's feet. His cap falls off and, pathetically, he retrieves it. The 2nd Investigator continues as though nothing had happened.)

2nd Investigator: No. There would be no rights. Those in positions of authority and responsibility would have no choice but to take summary action, however distasteful that would be to them, to restore balance and good order.

Jack: But —

2nd Investigator: Enough! We can't utter two words without you getting defensive. It is becoming painfully clear to me that however reasonable we try to be, you are going to contest our every word and make sensible communication between us impossible.

(The 2nd Investigator nods to the 1st Investigator who pulls Jack to his feet and puts him back in the chair.)

Niobe: That's true, you know. I can't say two words but he twists my meaning.

1st Investigator: Some people are like that, M'am. A reasonable approach seems to trigger off some sort of resentment —

Jack: Look. I can be as reasonable as the next man.

1st Investigator: Oh, of course, you say that now.

2nd Investigator: Can't you see, you've gone too far. I thought, for a while, that we were getting somewhere, but your behaviour has taken us right back to where we started.

Jack: No. Look. Give me a chance. Just try me.

2nd Investigator: We won't be crawled to, Chattell. If there's one thing that gets my blood up, it's a man who hasn't the guts to stand by what he says.

1st Investigator: You're not very sincere, are you, Chapple?

Jack: I am. I — . *(Pause)* I can be.

2nd Investigator: Put it on and take it off like a coat, eh?

(The Investigators look with disgust at Jack. The 2nd Investigator turns to Niobe.)

Since Chattell obviously has no intention of introducing us, I am left to assume that you are his wife. I'd like to introduce myself and my colleague. We're Company Research Officers from H.Q. C.R.O. 2651815 dash 1.

2nd Investigator: And myself, C.R.O. 2651815 dash 2.

Niobe: Pleased to meet you. Niobe Numin's my maiden name.

2nd Investigator: — and a fairer maiden I cannot imagine, if I may say so.

Niobe: You flatter me, sir.

2nd Investigator: My eyes are my counsel, Miss Numin.

Niobe: Oh, sir.

1st Investigator: Some people know how to behave decently, Chapple. You might have taken a page from Miss Numin's book when you had the chance.

Jack: That's just talk.

2nd Investigator: Talk! ?

Jack: Well, I mean, she's being — . *(Pause)* Polite?

2nd Investigator: I've heard enough! Hold him dash 1. Have you any rope, Miss Numin?

(Niobe goes to the storage cupboard and draws out a length of rope.)

2nd Investigator: Polite? You question the sincerity of even your wife? ! Is nothing deserving of your respect, Chattell? It never occurred to me — **me** — almost a total stranger — that Miss Numin was expressing anything but her most sincere sentiments. But to you, it is mere politeness! *(Niobe hands him the rope.)* We should have done this in the beginning when you first displayed your true nature. We were mad to think that fairness would get us anywhere with your type. You're a violent and mean little man.

(He proceeds to tie Jack to the chair. The job is done quickly.)

Niobe: He's had this coming, you know. Always shooting his mouth off.

(Niobe comes forward. She pokes Jack on the arm.)

See! See where it's got you.

Jack: Niobe. Don't let them tie me. I can't hurt anyone.

Niobe: Oh, no? Do you want me to show them the bruises, Jack?

Jack: Don't say things like that! There aren't any bruises!

Niobe: Who's going to believe that?

(The 1st Investigator makes a note in his book.)

1st Investigator: Denies beating wife.

(The 2nd Investigator goes to his papers and removes a sheet to which he now and again refers.)

2nd Investigator: We've pussy-footed with you long enough, Shadwell. The way the evidence is building up, I see no reason why we should dally any longer over the niceties. Dash 1.

1st Investigator: Main line freight derailed with malice aforethought by one John Chuckle. Formerly stationmaster at Dogwood-Wen.

Jack: Formerly? Oh, no — that's —

2nd Investigator: How do you plead, Chuckle?

Niobe: Oh, it was his fancy work, alright.

1st Investigator: *(Writing)* Pleads guilty.

2nd Investigator: To give you some indication of just what it is you have done, and to wipe that insolent smirk off your face, let us list —

1st Investigator: Thirteen tankers and contents — propane lighter fuel.

2nd Investigator: Ignited and spent.

1st Investigator: Twelve fully loaded automobile transport cars.

2nd Investigator: A total write-off.

1st Investigator: Eleven boxcars of stainless steel steak knives.

E50

2nd Investigator: Irreparably bent.

1st Investigator: Ten dump cars of driveway gravel.

2nd Investigator: Irretrievably scattered.

1st Investigator: Nine additional tankers of carbonated cola.

2nd Investigator: Spilled, flat, and dispersed.

1st Investigator: Eight boxcars of department store manikins.

2nd Investigator: Mangled beyond human recognition.

(Niobe gasps her horror.)

1st Investigator: Seven freezer cars of ice-cream.

2nd Investigator: Melted.

1st Investigator: Six boxcars of poodle chow.

2nd Investigator: Scattered and since eaten by the local scavengers.

1st Investigator: Five cars of high grade cosmetics.

2nd Investigator: Spilled and poisoning the wild life.

1st Investigator: Four boxcars of vanity mirrors.

2nd Investigator: Shattered and cutting the feet of the scavengers.

2nd Investigator: Three cars of T.V. picture tubes — **colour**.

2nd Investigator: Smashed — never to carry their messages.

1st Investigator: Two of the finest diesel locomotives and one auxiliary unit.

2nd Investigator: Twisted wreckage, beyond repair.

1st Investigator: One caboose.

2nd Investigator: A pile of smouldering rubble.

(A long pause. Niobe is stunned.)

Jack: Ah. Then there were no people?

(The Investigators look at one another in confusion. Not having been prepared, they scramble for the correct 'image'. They speak simultaneously.)

1st Investigator: People?

2nd Investigator: Of course, there were —

(They look at one another.)

1st Investigator: Twenty-four!

2nd Investigator: That's right.

1st Investigator: Critically —

2nd Investigator: Dead!

(They look at one another again.)

1st Investigator: Some critically injured at first, all of whom have since died.

2nd Investigator: The Company might have been prepared to overlook some things, but human life is quite a different matter. That crew had 'families', Chuckle.

1st Investigator: Wives — now widows.

2nd Investigator: Children — now fatherless.

1st Investigator: Some who have yet to be born who will never know their fathers.

2nd Investigator: Helpless babies, Chuckle.

(This is too much for Niobe. Weeping her grief, she falls upon Jack, scratching and pulling. The Investigators pull her away.)

Niobe: Killer! Baby killer! You evil son-of-a-bitch! Rotten, stinking, two-faced, mother-fucking baby killer.

(She collapses on a bench and sobs.)

E52

Oh — the poor little darlings. Oh — oh!

Jack: Don't let her at me again, eh? She'd kill me. She doesn't think what she's doing. I mean — I didn't kill any babies.

Niobe: Oh! Oh!

2nd Investigator: You might as well have, hadn't you? Look at the results of your actions. You've broken this poor woman's heart. And what do you talk about? Do you show any understanding? Do you feel any compassion for a suffering fellow being? No.

1st Investigator: You whine about yourself. *(Mimicking)* I didn't kill any babies.

2nd Investigator: You didn't kill any babies! What evidence do we have that says you aren't as capable of that as everything else you say you haven't done? It's evidence we want, Chuckle.

Jack: How? I didn't. That's all. How can I give you evidence? There's no evidence.

(The Investigators look at one another, agreeing by their expression that the case is closed. The 2nd Investigator walks solemnly to his brief-case and begins putting away his papers. The 1st Investigator stands prepared to take down a final statement from his colleague.)

2nd Investigator: Note. After exhaustive research into the case of Giovanni Cucclioni —

Jack: Jack Shackel! That's my name! I'm Jack Shackel! ! !

2nd Investigator: — alias Jack Shackel, variously known as Jean Chattell, John Chapple, Johnny Chuckle, and Jake Shadwell.

Jack: *(Desperately)* Those aren't my names.

2nd Investigator: *(Nods to 1st Investigator.)* Admits names were assumed. A man assumes an alias, Cucclioni, when he's got something to hide. You reds aren't very clever, are you? *(To 1st Investigator.)* Dubious foreign extraction.

Jack: Don't say that! I'm no foreigner!

(The 2nd Investigator stops cold and stares at Jack in disbelief. He then strikes Jack across the face with the back of his hand.)

2nd Investigator: I've had enough of your filthy intolerance! Nothing escapes your sneer, does it? This country, from which you are only too happy to suck your sustenance, was built by those 'foreigners' you seem to consider so far beneath you. The case is closed. *(To 1st Investigator)* Guilty as charged in all respects. I recommend immediate and final action. The Company need feel no further responsibility.

(The Young Man enters upstage. He is now dressed in the 2nd Deliveryman's clothes; he is a 'changed' man, confident and supercilious.)

Niobe: I told you, didn't I? You couldn't just shut your mouth and do what any normal person would do. Oh, no! You had to be the big-shot stationmaster.

2nd Investigator: By the authority vested in me by the Company, I hereby declare you, Giovanni Cucclioni, persona non grata, herewith and in perpetuity. Let this be a lesson to others who would place selfish personal goals ahead of the common interest and jeopardize the very foundation of our way of life. *(Picking up his case.)* Off the record, I hope you rot in hell, you miserable little shit disturber.

(As an afterthought, he approaches Jack and ceremoniously whips Jack's cap off. He drops the cap to the floor and grinds it under his heel.)

Jack: You didn't have to go and do — . *(Near tears)* Please give it back to me. *(Pause)* Niobe? Please?

(Niobe sticks her nose in the air. The 2nd Investigator motions to the 1st Investigator to follow. Together they turn to leave.)

Isn't somebody going to untie me?

Niobe: I'd like you to meet my son. These two gentlemen are from the Company.

(Handshakes all round. Intuitively, the Investigators speak with respect to the Young Man.)

1st Investigator: Pleased to meet you, sir.

2nd Investigator: A pleasure.

1st Investigator: You aren't, by any chance —

2nd Investigator: — a Company man?

Jack: He's no railwayman!

Young Man: *(Smiling)* As a matter of fact, I'm not. But I have, at times, thought that it might suit me. You can understand, though, that a man in my position must be selective.

2nd Investigator: Oh, yes. A man must give thought to his position.

1st Investigator: True, true. An executive must consider his image.

Jack: That's my son! He's no executive.

2nd Investigator: Is 'he' your father?

(The Young Man looks with scorn at Jack.)

Young Man: Do you really suppose that a man in my position would ever find his father tied to a chair like a common criminal?

(The Investigators smile and turn to leave.)

2nd Investigator: It was a pleasure meeting you, sir. Ma'am.

1st Investigator: Sir. M'am.

(The Investigators exit.)

Niobe: Well, now. Here we are. Just the family. Your girl asleep again, as usual.

Jack: She's not sleeping. That bastard knocked her out cold. Maybe even killed her.

(They look from a distance.)

Young Man: Any fool can see she's sleeping.

Niobe: Why would gentlemen like that hit a lazy stupid young thing like her?

Young Man: And you. Look at you. Getting yourself tied to a chair like that.

Jack: I didn't ask them to tie me up! *(Pause)* Now they're gone, you can untie me.

(Niobe and the Young Man look at him. A long pause.)

Young Man: Those were sober and responsible men. I can't imagine that they would have tied you up unless they had good reason.

Jack: Niobe? Don't listen to him.

Niobe: You really disappointed me today. No. I really mean that. You're not the man I thought you were. Bringing down shame on our house like this.

Jack: Somebody's got to untie me.

Young Man: It will do you good to be restrained for a while. Perhaps it will teach you a little respect.

Jack: I've got respect — for all sorts of things.

Niobe: I sure haven't seen it.

Young Man: Show me some respect if you think you're so capable. Let's see it.

(They turn away from him and stand waiting. Jack looks at them, straining to find the way. He shuts his eyes with the effort, but calls them again after a moment.)

Jack: I think there's something wrong. Maybe if you gave me my cap —*(They resolutely refuse to look at him.)* — if you just put it on my head, eh? It doesn't matter if it's a bit dusty. Just so long as — *(Pause)* I can't just up and respect someone out of the blue. It takes a bit of time. You've got to let a man have a little self-respect, too, first. Then he can — *(Pause)* Don't ignore me! Can't you help a man? Son?

Young Man: A man who is totally unwilling to show his son half the respect he'd show a dog, can hardly ask that son for help, can he?

Niobe: He's got feelings, you know.

Young Man: I certainly have. Feelings that you have resolutely ignored ever since I arrived.

Jack: I recognized you, didn't I? That made you feel good.

Young Man: What does that matter, since in any real sense of the word, you have proven that to be my father fills you with nothing but disgust and disrespect?

Jack: You — . Well, you're not an easy person to like —

Young Man: I beg your pardon?

Jack: I mean 'to get to know'.

Young Man: I heard what you said.

Jack: To get to know, I said!

Young Man: You said 'like'.

Jack: I said 'know'.

Young Man: 'Like! '

Jack: 'Know! '

(Pause. Niobe smiles and then she screams at Jack with finality.)

Niobe: Yes! ! ! *(Pause)* There. You haven't even got an answer. I guess that proves something.

Young Man: A man in the wrong always loses his way in an argument.

(Jack's head slumps forward.)

Niobe: You're all mouth and no muscle. You're a big, fat zero. Zero father. Zero husband. Zero lover. And you're not even a do-nothing zero stationmaster any more.

Jack: I'm — . I — . I'm a —

(Message alert. A bit of the 'old Jack' is revived.)

(He looks up) It's for **me**. I've got to answer.

(Alert repeat)

See! They're still sending me messages. Help me.

(The Young Man sneers. The message arrives and Jack strains to translate it in his head.)

TEMPUS FUGIT STUPID STOP SITTING DOWN ON JOB EARNS NO BONUS STOP BONE-HOUSE MAYBE STOP

I'm not sitting down. I'm tied up!

WE'RE BUSY TOO STOP SMOKING ON DUTY IS PUNISHABLE

(Desperately) By what! ?

(The Company has uttered its final word.)

Niobe: What was that all about?

(Jack looks up)

Niobe: Tell us and — . And we'll untie you!

Young Man: Cross our hearts.

(They do, playing the game lightly. Pause.)

Jack: They said — 'tempest fuggit' — or something. *(Struggling with ropes.)* And something about my bonus and smoking on the job. That's all. Now —

Young Man: I hope you're not going to try to tell us that that was interesting.

Jack: I — . You will untie me, though. Since you promised — .

(Niobe and the Young Man look at one another trying to hold back their laughter. Jack is disturbed but forces himself to smile to show that he is willing to go along with the joke.)

Let's just get this rope —

(Pause. His eyes meet theirs. He gets the message.)

A bargain's a bargain.

(Niobe and the Young Man are suddenly convulsed with laughter — they infect one another and the laughter is sustained through the following speeches.)

You promised!

Niobe: Christ, are you stupid!

Jack: Niobe! You're supposed to be my wife!

(Jack twists about in order to see the clock. The sound of an approaching train.)

You've got to untie me! I haven't much time!

(This convulses them even more.)

Stop it!

(The laughter stops but the potential remains as Niobe and the Young Man look at Jack.)

Please untie me. Niobe? I'll never ask you for another thing as long as I live if you'll help me — just this once.

(Niobe looks at the Young Man. They snicker and break out in laughter again. Jack throws his head back in despair. The Girl stirs and raises herself to a sitting position. She looks around.)

Jack: Niobe? *(Pause)* For old times' sake, eh?

(The Girl rises, still feeling her pain, she holds the back of her neck.)

Jack: Doreen! Help me!

Girl: Helping you gives me headaches.

Jack: It wasn't me. It was those bastards from head office.

Niobe: That's right! Blame someone else all the time. *(Niobe turns to the Girl.)* As for you! His own kin can look after him all right without your interference.

Girl: I have no desire to interfere. I'm perfectly happy to see you looking after one another.

(Niobe would have preferred a fight. She stares

at the Girl for a moment and then turns her feelings on Jack.)

Niobe: Did you hear your 'friend'?

Jack: You're killing me!

(Niobe, all innocence turns to the Young Man as if to say 'Me?')

Young Man: I've never killed anybody in my life.

Niobe: Me too. I never hurt a fly.

Girl: He's probably killing himself, but I don't doubt that you're helping.

Young Man: You wanted to be left out of it, Doreen? Well, shut up.

Niobe: Besides, it's us he accused.

Girl: Crap.

Niobe: I beg your pardon?!

(Sound: The train coming to a stop. Jack is the only one who seems to hear it.)

Jack: It's here!

Girl: You talk rubbish, old woman.

Niobe: Take that back!

Jack: For Christ's sake, cut me loose!

(Niobe is about to grapple with the Girl but is stopped mid-action by the 1st Conductor's voice. He glances at a piece of paper in his hand.)

1st Conductor: Jack — Jack —

(He looks again at the paper.)

Niobe: *(Pointing at Jack.)* Shackel!

Jack: He's not here.

1st Conductor: Are you Shackel?

2nd Conductor: Are you the ex-stationmaster at this station?

Jack: Ex —! *(Pause)* No. I'm a — a —

(He flounders since he cannot conceive of himself as anything else.)

(The 1st Conductor looks at his slip of paper again.)

1st Conductor: This Shackel gentleman was suppose to have been tied to a chair.

2nd Conductor: You're obviously Shackel.

Jack: No!

Niobe: You're you, Jack. I should know.

Young Man: I should, too, since I am your son. After all the trouble I had working that out, I'm certainly not going to start all over denying it now.

Jack: You did before.

Young Man: I didn't deny it. They couldn't believe it. Anyway, sooner or later a man has to be honest with himself.

2nd Conductor: Face up to the facts. You're the man in the chair.

Jack: They could have untied me.

Niobe: I always say, a man should stand on his own two feet.

Jack: You silly bitch.

1st Conductor: Now, now. We don't want any unpleasantness at a time like this, do we?

Jack: *(Improvising)* Well, it doesn't matter, anyway. The whole thing is a mistake.

1st Conductor: There's no mistake.

Jack: Ah — well — the time's wrong! You're too early. This train isn't supposed to come 'til 12:01.

E58

(The conductors check their pocket watches.)

1st Conductor: Right you are. 12:01.

Jack: Not by my clock. That's the clock I'll go by.

(Niobe walks toward the clock.)

Niobe: You know your clock's always wrong, Jack.

Jack: Leave it alone, damn you!

(She thumps the clock. The hands move on to 12:01. There is a dull clank of a single dampened chime.)

Jack: *(In pain)* Ahhh!

(Pause)

1st Conductor: Well, now. Are we all ready?

Niobe: Oh, yes! For what?

1st Conductor: The train must keep to its schedule.

2nd Conductor: Tempus fugit, you know.

(Jack responds)

1st Conductor : First —

(The 1st Conductor opens the coffin.)

2nd Conductor: Then we'll need a knife.

Jack: What!

Niobe: I've got a knife!

(She rushes to the cupboard and returns immediately with a bright new carving knife.)

Jack: Oh, no! Couldn't you —

2nd Conductor: Why, whatever is the matter?

Jack: Maybe just a — a little sleeping pill first.

(The Conductors look at one another and laugh.

The others join in. Only the Girl refrains.)

1st Conductor: He thinks — ! Ha, Ha!

2nd Conductor: We're not going to stab you.

Jack: No! ? The Company didn't tell you to —

2nd Conductor: The knife is to cut the ropes.

1st Conductor: Did you really think — ?

Jack: Yeah! Isn't that crazy! And all you were — Oh Christ, that's funny!

2nd Conductor: Then take you with us west.

Jack: Right. Ha, ha.

1st Conductor: You'll love it. It never rains. And the sunsets! Out of this world.

Jack: Ha, ha. Sunsets, eh? I love sunsets. *(Pause)* I've never been west. I don't want to go.

1st Conductor: It's all arranged.

Jack: She arranged it! Take her!

(The Conductors pick Jack up.)

No! I haven't got a ticket.

(They carry him to the coffin.)

Not in there! You can't put me in there.

(The Conductors deposit Jack in the box.)

1st Conductor: It's for your own comfort. The roadbed is rough.

Jack: I don't mind the bumps. Let me ride in a coach.

2nd Conductor: This is a freight train.

Jack: I'm not freight. The next train! I'll wait!

1st Conductor: You can't wait.

Jack: I'll ride with the livestock!

(The Conductors shake their heads wearily. All eyes are on Jack. He lowers his head in shame.)

Jack: Could I — . *(Whispers)* Do you think I could have my cap? *(No one responds)* Niobe? Would you give me my cap *(No response)* My son will. Won't you, son? *(No response)* Doreen?

(No response. Jack is about to lie down in defeat when the Girl has second thoughts.)

Girl: Wait a minute.

(Jack sits up. She picks up his cap, brushes the dust from it, and hands it to him. He puts it on. She whispers something in his ear and he smiles. Niobe and the Young Man look at her with hatred when she turns.)

He's not my father. I don't have to pretend I didn't hear him.

Niobe: It's easy for you. But it's different for family. *(To Jack)* What did she say to you? I'm your wife. I've got a right to know.

1st Conductor: Look. We've got to get moving.

2nd Conductor: Right. Can somebody lend us a hammer?

Niobe: I've got a hammer!

(She rushes to the cupboard, extracts a hammer, and brings it to the 2nd Conductor.)

Jack: You knew where that hammer was all the time.

Niobe: Prove it!

Jack: *(To the Conductors)* Do you think I could have a private word with my wife before we leave?

2nd Conductor: Oh, for —

(The 1st Conductor silences his colleague with a gesture.)

1st Conductor: A brief word.

(Jack gestures to Niobe. She moves hesitantly up to the coffin. As soon as she is close enough he slips his hands about her throat and proceeds to strangle her.)

Niobe: Ah! Help me! Help!

(The Conductors leap into action, one of them separating Jack's hands from Niobe's throat, the other preparing to slam the lid shut. In the tussle, Jack removes Niobe's wig. He is pushed down, wig in hand, and the lid is slammed closed. The 2nd Conductor immediately starts hammering in the nails. A great banging and shouting comes from within. It gradually becomes more feeble and dies out.)

Jack: I won't go! I'll hate the god damned west! I know it!

Niobe: Open it up! He's got something of mine!

(Niobe holds her hands over her head.)

1st Conductor: Sorry, lady.

2nd Conductor: *(Hammering)* It's against the rules. And common decency.

Niobe: What's he know about decency? !

(The lid is fixed down.)

2nd Conductor: Let's go.

(The Conductors pick up the coffin and quickly exit right.)

Niobe: *(Yelling after them.)* I could have him up for attempted murder! You tell him that — the inconsiderate bugger.

(Pause. The only sound is the crossing signal.)

Young Man: They say the west is beautiful. *(Pause)* Think how much happier he'll be basking in the sun than hanging around here getting on everyone's nerves. *(Pause)* I feel a person has to try to look on the bright side — *(He notices her baldness.)* You're bald!

Niobe: I'm not.

Young Man: I don't see any hair.

Niobe: Because —

(Pause)

Young Man: Just who are you, anyway?

Niobe: Who! I'm your mother, for god's sake!

Young Man: What an incredible suggestion. My mother has a full head of stunning blonde hair.

Niobe: He took it!

Young Man: Oh, I can't accept that. Personal attributes are God-given and the one thing that others cannot take away from us. One either has these advantages or one does not. If you don't mind me saying so, old woman, I think it is extremely graceless of you not to accept your own limitations. Surely it would be far better if you accepted with dignity the fact that you are bald and looked, instead, upon those things you **do** have. I mean, perhaps you have — oh, a loving nature, for example.

Niobe: You're right! I've got something. I'll get it. *(She moves quickly toward the door to the living quarters.)* That's good advice. You'll see. You'll be proud to call me 'mother'.

(Niobe exits. The Young Man turns to the Girl.)

Young Man: If I know anything at all for certain in this false world I know what it is I value in a mother. Bald! The nerve! *(He looks about.)* They do let you down, don't they? When all is said and done, a person is better off investing in something reliable like a career. *(Pause)* What did you say to the old man?

Girl: I told him my name.

Young Man: Oh.

(Pause)

Young Man: Well? What is it?

(Pause)

Girl: I'm leaving.

Young Man: Fine. I'll just get my —

Girl: Alone.

Young Man: What do you mean? I thought we were — well, sort of — friends.

(Pause)

Girl: I don't think so. To begin with, I realize that I'd never be able to tell you my name. Now is that any way for friends to go on? I think I'll just move about and maybe, if I'm fortunate, I'll bump into someone I can tell it to. *(Pause)* Wish me luck?

(No response. The Girl exits.)

Young Man: *(Shouting after her.)* You'll regret this. I'm going into business. I'm going to be something. You heard what they said. I'm executive material. You could be an executive wife. You'd get respect. From all sorts of people. From me even! *(Pause)* It wouldn't have mattered to me what your name was!

Niobe: *(Off)* I'm coming!

(He turns back towards the waiting room and looks toward the bedroom, makes a quick decision, straightens his tie, and exits along the track. Niobe enters adjusting her new carrot-red wig.)

Niobe: You don't see something like this every day, do you? Don't you think it's the real —

(She notices his absence.)

Niobe: *(Weakly)* — me.

Centre-stage, Niobe registers her isolation. There is a telegraph alert which continues to blackout; she reacts to it with increasing panic, totally unwilling to receive the message.)

1st Deliveryman: *(Off)* Oh. Hold it there. Let's just see if this thing — . Oh, we won't have any trouble with this one.

(Niobe reacts with relief to a human voice, smiles, and begins to adjust her hair and clothing in preparation.)　　　　　　　　　**Blackout**

E62